MAKE IT LAST

Make It Last

Project Editor Mary Flanagan
Cover Photography Tom Fenenga
Cover Art Direction Mariah Cates
Page Layout Diana Boger

Text, photography and illustrations for *Make It Last* are based on articles previously published in *The Family Handyman* magazine (2915 Commers Dr., Suite 700, Eagan, MN 55121, familyhandyman.com). For information on advertising in *The Family Handyman* magazine, call (646) 518-4215.

Make It Last is published by Home Service Publications, Inc., a subsidiary of Trusted Media Brands, Inc. ©2018 All rights reserved. This volume may not be reproduced in whole or in part without written permission from the publisher. The Family Handyman is a registered trademark of Trusted Media Brands, Inc.

Hardcover: 978-1-62145-418-2

Paperback: 978-1-62145-419-9

The Family Handyman

Editor-in-Chief Gary Wentz
Senior Editors Mary Flanagan, Travis Larson, Mark Petersen
Associate and Contributing Editors Jeff Gorton, Brad Holden, Rick Muscoplat, David Radtke, Josh Risberg, Jason White
Associate Creative Director Vern Johnson
Design and Production Mariah Cates, Marcia Roepke, Mary Schwender
Illustrations Steve Björkman, Rob Chamberlain, Ken Clubb, Jeff Gorton, John Hartman, Trevor Johnston, Christopher Mills, Frank Rohrbach III
Photography Tom Fenenga
Managing Editor Donna Bierbach
Editorial Services Associate Peggy McDermott
Senior Production Manager Leslie Kogan

Trusted Media Brands, Inc.

President & Chief Executive Officer
Bonnie Kintzer

PRINTED IN THE UNITED STATES

1 2 3 4 5 6 7 8 9 10

Contents

1 PREVENT WATER DAMAGE

2 AVOID APPLIANCES BREAKDOWNS

SPECIAL SECTION: Plumbing Fixes

3 INTERIOR MAINTENANCE & REPAIR

SPECIAL SECTION: Maintain Your HVAC System

4 DOOR AND WINDOW R_x

5 EXTERIOR MAINTENANCE & REPAIR

SPECIAL SECTION: Tools & Equipment

Chapter One

PREVENT WATER DAMAGE

2009FOTOFRIENDS/SHUTTERSTOCK

Stop water damage before it costs $1,000s

Find your shutoff valves

They're the difference between a small puddle and a huge flood!

Your home's water supply system is dangerous. In just minutes, a cracked pipe, burst hose or leaking icemaker line can do thousands of dollars in damage. But if you know the basics about shutoff valves, you can stop the flow instantly and limit the harm.

Find them, test them

Shutoff valves are located near any device that uses water. Most of them are easy to find; they're typically under sinks and toilets, behind the washing machine and above the water heater. Shutoffs for tubs or showers are often hidden behind a wood or plastic "access panel," though some tubs and showers don't have shutoffs. Your main valve—which shuts off water to your entire house—may be indoors or out. Usually, there are actually two valves flanking the water meter and you can turn off either one.

ICEMAKER SHUTOFFS CAN BE ANYWHERE
Valves for icemakers may be under the kitchen sink, in a utility closet or in a basement or crawl space.

VALVE

ICEMAKER SUPPLY TUBE

Shutoff valves go unused for years, and mineral deposits can make them impossible to close. So it's a good idea to make sure yours work. If you have standard valves, just turn the handle clockwise. If you have ball-type valves, crank the lever one-quarter turn. Ball valves rarely fail, but it's good to check them anyway.

The main house shutoff

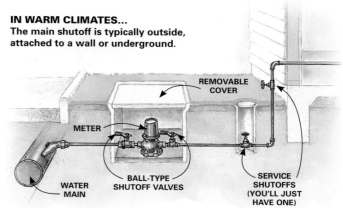

IN WARM CLIMATES...
The main shutoff is typically outside, attached to a wall or underground.

REMOVABLE COVER

METER

WATER MAIN

BALL-TYPE SHUTOFF VALVES

SERVICE SHUTOFFS (YOU'LL JUST HAVE ONE)

IN COLDER CLIMATES...
The main shutoff is typically in the basement. There is also a "curb stop" shutoff that requires a special tool to operate.

SPIGOT SUPPLY SHUTOFF

BALL-TYPE SHUTOFF VALVES

CURB STOP

METER

WATER MAIN

The cost of not knowing

A few weeks after moving into my first home, a washing machine hose burst, releasing a geyser in my laundry room. I knew enough to try the valve behind the washer, but it was ancient. And stuck. What I didn't know about was the main valve, which could have shut off the water to the whole house. So I just stood there like a dummy, waiting for a plumber to show up while water flowed from the laundry room into adjoining rooms. Insurance covered most of the damage, but I paid the deductible, plus higher insurance premiums for years afterward.

—Andy Carson, reader

MAIN SHUTOFF

The smartest move you can make before a vacation

Every insurance adjuster has a hundred stories like this one: The homeowners left town Friday and returned Sunday evening to find thousands of dollars in water damage. The moral of these stories is simple: Before going on vacation, turn off the main valve. In less than a minute, you can eliminate the most common cause of home damage.

Solution for stubborn valves

When a valve won't budge, sometimes it helps to loosen the packing nut just a little. Turn it counter-clockwise while holding the handle steady with your hand or pliers. If you ever notice a leak around a valve stem, tighten the packing nut.

STEM

PACKING NUT

Insist on ball valves

If you have any plumbing work done that requires replacing valves, ask for ball valves. That may add ten bucks to the cost of the project, but it's a bargain. Unlike other valves, which rely on screw mechanisms and rubber seals, ball valves have a simple ball inside, which rotates to open or close. That simplicity means reliability; ball valves almost always work when you need them.

BALL

GOOD: STANDARD VALVE

BETTER: BALL VALVE

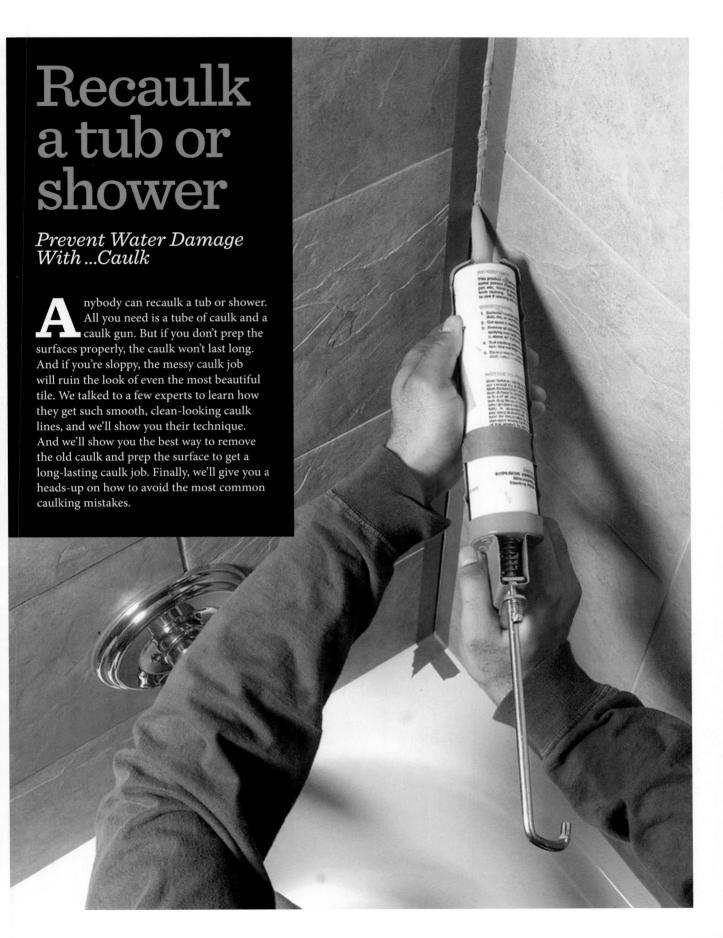

Recaulk a tub or shower

Prevent Water Damage With ...Caulk

Anybody can recaulk a tub or shower. All you need is a tube of caulk and a caulk gun. But if you don't prep the surfaces properly, the caulk won't last long. And if you're sloppy, the messy caulk job will ruin the look of even the most beautiful tile. We talked to a few experts to learn how they get such smooth, clean-looking caulk lines, and we'll show you their technique. And we'll show you the best way to remove the old caulk and prep the surface to get a long-lasting caulk job. Finally, we'll give you a heads-up on how to avoid the most common caulking mistakes.

You can remove the old caulk, prep the surface, and recaulk a tub or shower in about four hours (including drying time). You'll need a razor scraper and single-edge razor blades, caulk remover, mineral spirits, paper towels, a utility knife, a caulk gun, and kitchen and bath caulk. An oscillating tool with a flexible scraper blade really speeds up the job of removing old caulk, but you can do the job without it. Here's how to start.

Buy the right caulk and a quality caulk gun

Tubs and showers require a special caulk that contains mold and mildew prevention additives. The tubes are usually labeled "for kitchen and bath use." Most are 100-percent silicone, but you can also find some latex versions. Latex caulk is easier to tool and cleans up with soap and water. If this is your first time applying caulk, latex may be your best option. Silicone is more challenging to tool and requires mineral spirits for cleanup. However, silicone lasts longer than latex and stays flexible over its life. But it's harder to remove when it's time to recaulk. Both types can develop mold and mildew once the additives wear out.

Most home centers and hardware stores stock only three kitchen and bath caulk colors: white, almond and clear. However, ask a sales associate whether you can special-order a custom color. And check out a paint or hardware store. Some can custom-mix colors right in the store.

A high-quality caulk gun can make a difference in your caulk job. It has a sturdier plunger mechanism to provide a smooth, even flow and a pressure release to stop the flow quickly. High-quality caulk guns cost a bit more, but they're worth it. Economy guns usually have a ratchet action or a sloppy friction mechanism that pushes the caulk out in bursts, so you apply too much in some areas and too little in others.

Remove the old caulk

You can't apply new caulk on top of the old and expect it to last. So the old caulk has to go. If the old caulk was silicone, you have to devote extra effort to remove all traces of it before applying new caulk. Start by

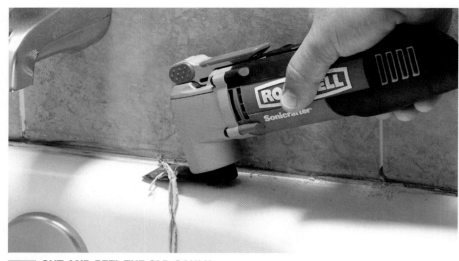

1 **CUT AND PEEL THE OLD CAULK.**
Slice through the caulk along the walls with a utility knife or with an oscillating tool equipped with a flexible scraper blade. Then use your knife or tool to scrape along the tub or shower floor.

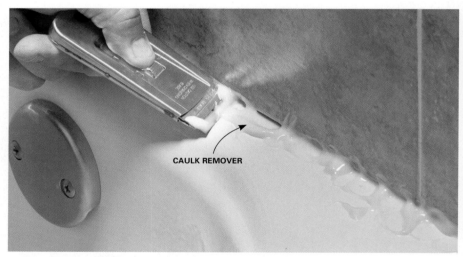

CAULK REMOVER

2 **LOOSEN AND REMOVE THE REMAINING CAULK.**
Squirt caulk remover on all the remaining caulk and let it do the hard work. Then scrape off all the old caulk with a razor scraper. Wipe with a rag.

slicing through the old caulk with a utility knife or an oscillating tool (Photo 1). Then scrape off as much old caulk as possible. Next, apply caulk remover (3M, Goof Off, Goo Gone, DAP and Motsenbocker all make caulk remover products) to break the adhesive bond and make it easier to scrape off (Photo 2).

Once the old caulk is gone, remove any loose grout between the walls and the tub or shower floor. Treat any mold in the grout along the wall/tub gap with a mold-killing product (one choice is ZEP Mold Stain & Mildew Stain Remover). Scrub the grout and then rinse off the mold killer with water and let it dry (use a hair dryer to speed the drying). Clean the surfaces one last time with mineral spirits. Let dry.

Mask the gap

Some pros scoff at the idea of using masking tape. But they caulk every day and can lay down a caulk bead with their eyes closed. For DIYers, we recommend masking the gap. It takes a bit more time, but you'll get much better results than caulking freehand. Start by finding the largest gap between the tub/shower and the walls. That gap dictates how far apart you must space the two rows of tape. Then apply the masking tape (Photo 3). If you have a fiberglass or composite tub, you should fill it before you caulk.

Apply the caulk bead

There are two schools of thought when it comes to tip angle and whether to pull or push the caulk. Our experts prefer cutting the caulk tube nozzle at a blunt 20-degree angle, instead of 45 degrees. And they hold the gun at a 90-degree angle to the gap while pushing a small bead ahead of the tip (Photo 4). That way, they can complete the entire bead in one pass. Plus, the gun pressure forces the caulk deeper into the gap for better holding power and sealing.

If you cut the tip at a 45-degree angle and pull the gun away from the starting corner, your gun will always run into the opposite corner, forcing you to flip it 180 degrees and start the bead again. That creates a blob where the two beads meet, making tooling more difficult. Plus, pulling the gun tends to apply a surface bead that doesn't penetrate as far into the gap.

Whichever tip angle you choose, always cut the tip with a sharp utility knife rather than the cheesy guillotine mechanism built into some caulk guns. Remove any burrs with a utility knife or sandpaper before caulking—the burrs will create grooves in the caulk lines.

Shape the bead and remove the tape

You can find all kinds of caulk-shaping tools at home centers. But if you take our advice and tape off the wall, you won't need any shaping tools. Just use your index finger to tool the caulk (Photo 5). After tooling, remove the masking tape while the caulk is still wet (Photo 6, p.12). Let the caulk cure for the recommended time before using the tub or shower.

3 **MASK THE GAP.**
Mask the wall corner gaps first. Then apply tape to the walls above the tub or shower floor. Finish by applying tape to the tub or shower floor.

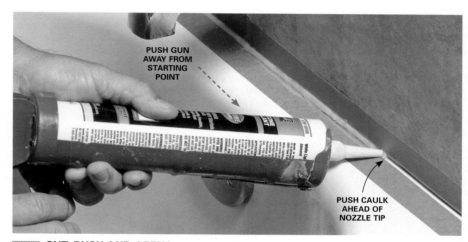

PUSH GUN AWAY FROM STARTING POINT

PUSH CAULK AHEAD OF NOZZLE TIP

4 **CUT, PUSH AND APPLY.**
Cut the nozzle tip to match the gap width. Hold the gun at a 90-degree angle to the gap and push a bead of caulk slightly ahead of the nozzle as you push the gun forward and continue applying pressure. Apply only enough caulk to fill the gap.

5 **TOOL WITH YOUR FINGER.**
Wet your finger with water and start at an outer corner. Wipe your finger across the caulk to create a rounded bead and remove excess caulk from the gap.

6 **PEEL OFF THE TAPE.**
Lift a corner of the tape along the tub and pull it off at a steep angle while the caulk is still wet. Then remove the tape along the wall. Remove the tape from the wall corners last.

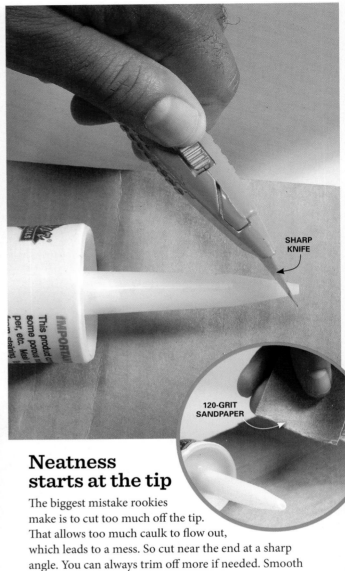

SHARP KNIFE

120-GRIT SANDPAPER

Neatness starts at the tip

The biggest mistake rookies make is to cut too much off the tip. That allows too much caulk to flow out, which leads to a mess. So cut near the end at a sharp angle. You can always trim off more if needed. Smooth and round the cut tip with sandpaper.

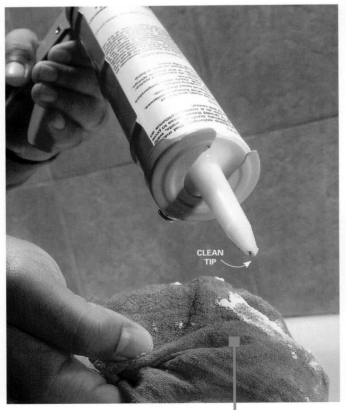

CLEAN TIP

Clean the tip

Start every bead with a clean tip. Plan to muck up two or three rags over the course of a caulking project.

Avoid these caulking mistakes

► **Buying the wrong caulk.** Always use kitchen and bath caulk in a tub or shower. It contains mold and mildew inhibitors that are not present in other types of caulk.
► **Caulking on top of old caulk.** New caulk doesn't bond well to old caulk, especially if the old caulk contains silicone. Just like with painting, better surface prep provides longer lasting results.
► **Not removing mold on grout near the caulk areas.** Grout is porous, and any mold present in the grout above the caulk line will eventually spread down into the new caulk area and destroy the bond.
► **Cutting the nozzle larger than the gap you're filling.** A larger opening applies too much caulk, making it harder to tool and clean up.

Regrout a shower

Prevent water damage with ...grout

By itself, the tile in a shower enclosure is almost maintenance free. With an occasional wipe-down, it can look good for years. Grout, however, is a different story—eventually it's going to break down. Large cracks and crumbly chunks are alarming, but smaller fractures can be trouble too. Fractures and stains that won't wash out, may indicate spots where water is wicking in and working its way behind the tiles. Sooner or later, that water will weaken the adhesive that's holding the tile or cause rot in the walls. When that happens, the only solution is to tear out the tile and start from scratch.

The good news is that if you catch it in time, you can quickly and easily give tiled surfaces a new lease on life—and a fresh look—by applying a new layer of grout. You don't need previous tile experience; regrouting is mostly grunt work.

In some cases, you can finish the job in a few hours, but to be safe, give yourself a weekend. If you start on Saturday morning, you should be able to take a shower on Monday.

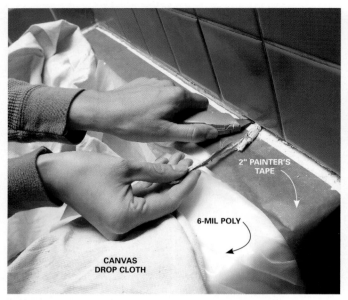

2" PAINTER'S TAPE

6-MIL POLY

CANVAS DROP CLOTH

1 Slice along each edge of the caulk/wall joint with a sharp utility knife. Pull out the old caulk.

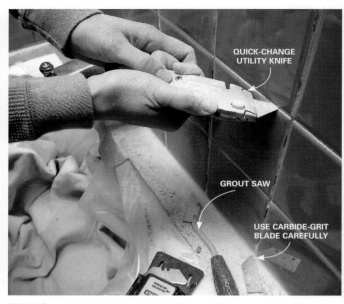

QUICK-CHANGE UTILITY KNIFE

GROUT SAW

USE CARBIDE-GRIT BLADE CAREFULLY

2 Scratch out at least 1/8 in. of grout from all the horizontal and vertical lines with a utility knife or grout saw. Change blades often.

Choosing the right tools and grout

Before you begin digging into that old grout, make sure you have all the tools and materials you'll need to finish the job. To help make sense of what you'll need, think of this project in three parts: scraping and cleaning, regrouting and cleanup.

When you're choosing grout-removal tools, stick with steel to be safe. Many special grout scrapers equipped with carbide tips work well and stay sharp for a long time, but if you slip, the carbide can damage your tile or tub. Steel utility knife blades, on the other hand, may dull quickly, but they're less likely to scratch the tile. Buy a knife with easy-to-change blades, and also buy plenty of spare blades. They're ideal for cleaning out narrow joints. A grout saw (Photo 2) with a notched steel blade is also handy for snagging chunks of grout.

As for grout, buy a 10-lb. bag—you may have some left over, but that's better than running out. Grout comes in two forms: unsanded and sanded. Your choice depends on the width of the gaps between the tiles. For joints up to 1/8 in., choose the unsanded variety. For wider joints, choose sanded to avoid cracking. Whatever type you need, look for a "polymer-modified" mix. The extra ingredients help prevent future cracking and staining. It's almost impossible to match new grout to old, but don't worry. By scratching out the topmost layer from all the grout lines and adding new, you'll get a fresh, consistent color.

To apply the grout, buy a rubber grout float and a grout sponge. In case the grout starts hardening too quickly, you'll also want to

Pro tip

When you're shopping for grout, stick with brands that offer color-matching caulks. Factory-matched caulk/grout combinations blend almost perfectly.

STIFF BRUSH

3 Clean out all of the dust and loose debris from the grout joints using a stiff brush and vacuum.

buy a plastic scouring pad. Last, buy a tube of tub-and-tile caulk that matches the grout color.

Slice out caulk and scratch out grout

Before you begin your attack, take a minute to protect your tub against scratches and debris that can clog your drain (Photo 1). Tape a layer of plastic sheeting to your tub's top edge. Next, lay a drop cloth on top of the plastic to protect the tub and cushion your knees. Then remove the faucet hardware or protect it with masking tape.

Getting rid of the old caulk and grout requires plenty of elbow grease, but it's not difficult work, especially if you take your time. Begin by cutting out the old caulk (Photo 1) and then move on to the grout (Photo 2). When you're using a utility knife, switch blades as soon as the edge stops digging and starts skating on the grout (Photo 2). At times, you may have more success with the grout saw.

Whatever tool you choose, the goal remains the same: to remove about 1/8 in. from the top (or more, if the grout comes out easily).

When you're done, remove dust and debris, which can weaken the bond between the tile and the new grout (Photo 3).

Mix the grout and pack the joints

Once the grout is mixed, the clock starts ticking toward the moment when it will harden on the wall...or in the bucket. Pro tilers can mix and use a 10-lb. bag of grout before it hardens, but to play it safe, mix up a few cups at a time and work in sections. A smaller batch will allow you plenty of time to apply it and clean the excess from one wall at a time. When you run out, rinse the container before mixing a new batch.

Before you make a batch from a bag, shake the bag to redistribute any pigment and Portland cement that might have settled out in shipment. After it's been dry mixed, scoop out a few cups (one cup equals about a half pound) into a bucket. The instructions on the bag indicate how much water to add per pound of mix. To ensure a strong mix, start with about three-quarters of the specified amount of water and gradually pour in just enough to make the grout spreadable. Aim for a fairly stiff consistency, somewhere between cake icing and peanut butter (Photo 4, inset). Don't worry if the grout looks a little lumpy. After it's mixed, allow it to sit, or slake, for 10 minutes. During this time, the remaining dry specks will absorb moisture. Give the grout one last stir (restirring also keeps the mix from hardening in your bucket) and it's ready for application.

Focus on one wall at a time. Scoop out a dollop and press it out across the tiles at a 45-degree angle (Photo 5). It's OK to be messy. The goal is to pack as much grout into the joints as you can. Press hard and work the float in several directions.

Immediately after you fill the joints, rake off the excess grout. Hold the float on edge, like a snowplow, and cut off most of the excess (Photo 6). Move the float across the joints diagonally to prevent the edge from dipping into the joints and pulling out too much grout. Work quickly before the grout starts to harden.

The time between scraping and sponging varies from job to job. Depending on your mix, the humidity or the temperature,

DRILL SET ON "SLOW"

POLYMER-MODIFIED GROUT

HOLDS PEAKS

PAINT-MIXING PADDLE

4 Mix the grout with water in a tall bucket using a paint-mixing paddle. Mix slowly until the grout becomes a thick paste.

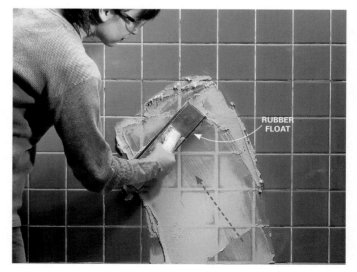

RUBBER FLOAT

5 Spread grout at an angle to the grout lines with a rubber float. Press hard on the float to pack the joints full of grout.

6 Scrape off excess grout by tipping the float on edge and pushing it diagonally across the tile. Work quickly.

TILE SPONGE

SCOURING PAD

DIRTY "FIRST RINSE" BUCKET

CLEAN WATER

7 Wipe off excess grout with a damp sponge as soon as the grout lines are firm. To keep the rinse water clean, dip the sponge in the "dirty" bucket and wring it out. Then dip it in the "clean" bucket and wring it over the dirty bucket.

the grout may take anywhere from five to 20 minutes to firm up. Begin sponging as soon as the grout feels firm and no longer sticks to your finger.

Using a well-wrung tile sponge, wipe away the bulk of the unwanted grout with short, gentle, circular strokes (Photo 7). Turn the sponge so that you're using a clean edge with each pass. Rinse and wring it out in the "dirty" bucket, then dip the sponge in a "clean" bucket, and finally wring it out again over the "dirty" bucket. This two-bucket technique helps keep your sponge and rinse water clean so that you can remove grout more effectively. Wring out as much water as possible. Too much water can pull cement and pigment from your fresh grout lines.

In addition to wiping away the excess, the sponge works for fine-tuning the shape of your grout lines. To shave down any high spots and make the lines slightly convex, run the sponge across the joint until the grout lines appear uniform. (If you find a low spot, use your finger to rub in a little extra grout.)

Pro tip

You can buy a cheap grout float for less than $5. But spend a few bucks more for a quality job. A better float will scrape off excess grout more cleanly. And that will save you lots of sponge work.

Finally, scrape out any globs of grout that may have gotten into the joints you intend to caulk (Photo 8). This includes all corners and the tub/tile joint. You could do this chore later, but it's a lot easier now, before the grout is rock hard.

The sponge-wiped walls may look clean at first, but as the surface moisture evaporates, the remaining grout particles will create a light haze. Give the grout an hour or two to dry, then buff off any residual haze with a soft towel (Photo 9).

8 Scrape grout out of the inside corners and tub/tile joint so that you can seal these joints with caulk later on.

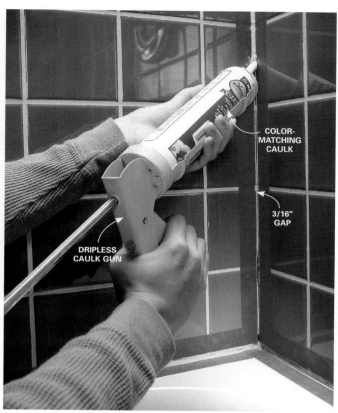

COLOR-MATCHING CAULK

3/16" GAP

DRIPLESS CAULK GUN

10 Apply painter's tape to control your caulk lines. Apply the caulk, smooth the joint with your finger and immediately remove the tape.

Finish up with neat caulk joints

Let the grout dry overnight before applying the caulk along the tub/tile joint and inside corners. For clean, precise caulk lines, run painter's tape along the inside corner and at the tub/tile joint (Photo 10). Just remember to remove the tape as soon as you finish smoothing. If you wait too long, the caulk will skin over or stick to the tape and you'll pull out the caulk when you try to remove the tape. Depending on the caulk, your bath should be ready for an inaugural shower in 24 hours.

To reduce mold growth, seal grout lines for extra stain and water resistance. Give the grout a week or two to cure completely before sealing. Remember that sealers wear off in time, so you'll need to reapply it every year or so. If you don't want to apply a sealer, wiping your walls down with a squeegee after each use works almost as well.

Pro tip

When you cut the caulk tube's spout, cut close to the tip. That leaves a smaller hole in the spout—and a smaller hole means neater caulking.

HAZE

9 Buff the haze off the tile after the grout dries (several hours). Use an old terry cloth towel.

Prevent frozen pipes

13 tips to prepare your plumbing for winter

We all know that water expands when it freezes. That's not a problem with the ice cubes in your freezer, but if that ice forms in your plumbing, it's a potential disaster. A frozen pipe can crack, spewing hundreds of gallons of water into your home. Fortunately, you can take steps to help prevent a catastrophe and put your mind at ease.

3 DISCONNECT HOSES
A water-filled hose left out in cold weather will freeze. If the hose is still connected to the faucet, ice can back up into the pipe inside your house, causing the pipe to crack. Disconnect all hoses from their faucets, drain them and store them for the winter.

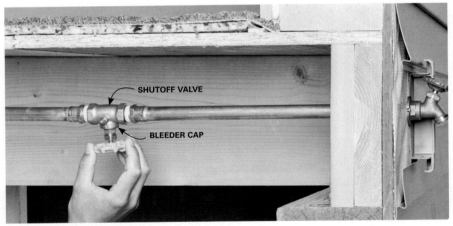

SHUTOFF VALVE

BLEEDER CAP

1 SHUT OFF OUTDOOR FAUCETS
Turn off outdoor faucets at their shutoff valves. Open the faucet and then open the bleeder cap on the shutoff valve to drain any water out of the pipe. If you don't drain the pipe, it can still freeze and crack. Leave the bleeder cap open with a bucket underneath to catch any drips. If the dripping continues, your shutoff valve needs to be replaced.

4 COVER HOSE BIBS
Insulated covers slow the heat loss from a pipe as it travels through the wall out into the cold. They provide some protection for very little cost (about $3 at home centers).

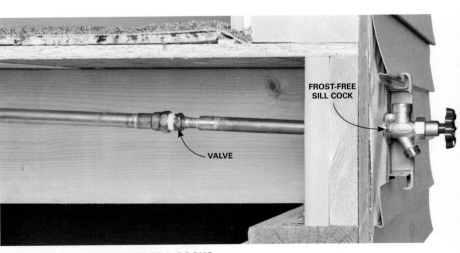

FROST-FREE SILL COCK

VALVE

2 INSTALL FROST-FREE SILL COCKS
Unlike a typical faucet, the working parts of a frost-free sill cock—valve, seat and washer—are located up to 18 in. inside the wall instead of right at the faucet. When the sill cock is properly installed, with a slight downward pitch, water drains from the pipe every time you turn off the knob at the faucet. Frost-free sill cocks are available at home centers.

5 GET AN EARLY WARNING
A Wi-Fi thermostat lets you control and monitor your home's temperature using your smartphone. If the temperature in your house drops, you'll get an email or text alert. Other types of alert systems are also available. Some send alerts to your cell phone via a phone jack in your house. Others send an alert to a landline or cell phone. For more on these devices, visit familyhandyman.com and search "Wi-Fi thermostat."

RIM JOIST INSULATION

7 SEAL AROUND RIM JOISTS

The rim joist is a likely area for cold air intrusion. Seal cracks or holes using expandable foam and then insulate between the floor joists. Be sure that you don't insulate a pipe from the heat in the rest of the house. Also, inspect around holes where cables, wires or pipes pass through an exterior wall. Insulate where you can, and seal drafts with caulk or expandable foam. After insulating, be sure you have combustion air for the furnace coming in through a makeup air pipe.

THERMOSTAT

6 INSTALL HEAT CABLE

Heat cables are a perfect solution for vulnerable pipes. They have an integral thermostat that senses pipe temperature, turning the heat on and off as needed to keep the pipe from freezing. You'll need an accessible outlet to plug in the cable. Heat cables are available at home centers.

MAIN SHUTOFF

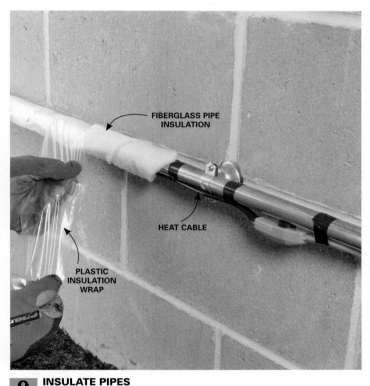

FIBERGLASS PIPE INSULATION

HEAT CABLE

PLASTIC INSULATION WRAP

8 IF YOU LEAVE TOWN, SHUT OFF THE WATER

If you're leaving town for a few days or more, turn the water off at the main shutoff. That way, if a pipe does freeze and crack, you'll have far less damage. Shut off your automatic icemaker so it doesn't continually try to make ice, burning out the motor. Even if the ice bin is full, the ice will evaporate and the icemaker will try to make more.

9 INSULATE PIPES

If you have pipes in an unheated area, such as a crawl space, an attic or a garage, use heat cable and cover it with pipe insulation. Pipe insulation alone does little, as it's only a matter of time before cold air can reach the pipe. In fact, insulating pipes without also using heat cable can prevent warm air from getting to them. Various types of pipe insulation are available at home centers.

Keep your house from falling apart!

Stop lurking leaks

Find and fix minor drips before they cause major damage

Tiny leaks that go unnoticed for years can do just as much harm as big, sudden leaks. By keeping walls and floors constantly damp, these lurking leaks rot framing, destroy walls and ceilings, ruin flooring and feed mold. Given enough time, a tiny drip will cause hundreds or even thousands of dollars of damage.

Here we'll show you how to recognize and find the most dangerous slow leaks. We'll also outline the solutions to these leaks. For detailed leak fixes, visit familyhandyman.com.

Stop toilet flange leaks

Toilet flange leaks

These leaks occur where the toilet meets the waste pipe below. They allow water to seep out at every flush, which will wreck flooring, rot the subfloor and joists, and damage the ceiling below (right photo).

Signs of trouble:
- Water seeping out around the base of the toilet.
- Loose or damaged flooring.
- Stains on the ceiling below.
- A toilet that rocks slightly when you push against it. This movement will eventually break the wax seal between the toilet and the closet flange.

How to find the source:

If you have ceiling stains, measure from stacked walls (right photo) before you go through the hassle of removing the toilet. If the stain is near the toilet, a leaking flange is the most likely source. Remove the toilet (far right photo) and look for these leak sources:
- The flange is level with or below the surrounding floor surface.
- Cracks in the flange.
- Bolts or the slots they fit into are broken.
- The flange is loose, not screwed solidly to the subfloor.

How to fix it:
- If you don't find any of the problems listed above, reinstall the toilet with a new wax ring.
- If the flange is too low, install a plastic flange riser over the existing flange.
- If the flange or bolt slots are broken, install a metal repair flange.
- If the toilet rocks because the floor is uneven, slip toilet shims under the toilet when you reinstall it.

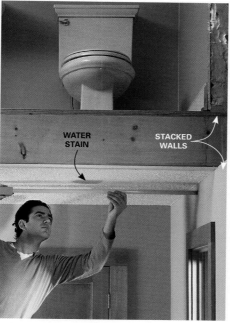

LOCATE THE SOURCE

Take measurements from stacked walls to find the source of a ceiling stain. In most cases, the stain occurs close to the source.

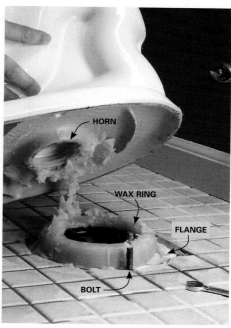

CHECK FOR FLANGE LEAKS

Unscrew the toilet bolt nuts and remove the toilet. Scrape away the wax and look for leaks. Also check for cracks around the toilet's horn.

Figure A
Toilet leaks

Toilet leaks can come from the water supply or tank, but the most damaging leaks occur at the flange and wax ring.

Stop tub and shower leaks

Splash leaks

Splash leaks are simply water escaping past a shower curtain or a shower door. Plumbers tell us it's the most common type of bathroom leak. Although it may sound minor, this leak causes major damage when water seeps into the subfloor where flooring meets the tub or shower. Before long the vinyl flooring or tiles begin to loosen. Even worse, the plywood subfloor delaminates and rots, requiring a huge, expensive tearout and replacement project.

Signs of trouble:

► Curling vinyl flooring or loose tiles next to the tub.
► Peeling paint or flaking, chalky-looking wood finish near the shower.
► Water stains on the ceiling or joists below.
► Mold spots on the wall or floor near the tub or shower.
► If you use a curtain, look for standing water on the floor after you shower.

How to find the source:

► If you have a shower door, splash water all around the door and frame. Leaks around the frame may take five minutes or longer to show up.
► If the door has rubber gaskets or a rubber door sweep, check them for gaps.
► Also check for any gaps in the caulk where the shower or tub meets the flooring.

How to fix it:

► Be sure to overlap sliding doors correctly when you close them. The inner door should be closest to the faucet.
► If you have a shower curtain rather than a door, make sure you close it completely when you shower, or add a splash guard.
► Seal a leaking frame by running a small bead of caulk around the inside of the frame. Force the caulk into any gaps between the frame and the shower surround. Quickly wipe away all the excess caulk. When the caulk dries, test for leaks again.
► Replace any worn gaskets or door sweeps. Bring the old one to a home center or plumbing supply store and look for a matching replacement.
► If the old caulk along the floor shows gaps, scrape it out and run a new bead.

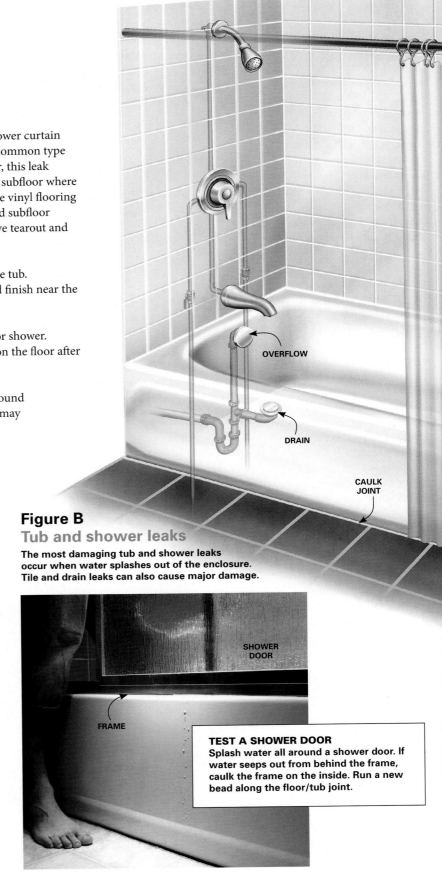

OVERFLOW

DRAIN

CAULK JOINT

Figure B
Tub and shower leaks

The most damaging tub and shower leaks occur when water splashes out of the enclosure. Tile and drain leaks can also cause major damage.

SHOWER DOOR

FRAME

TEST A SHOWER DOOR
Splash water all around a shower door. If water seeps out from behind the frame, caulk the frame on the inside. Run a new bead along the floor/tub joint.

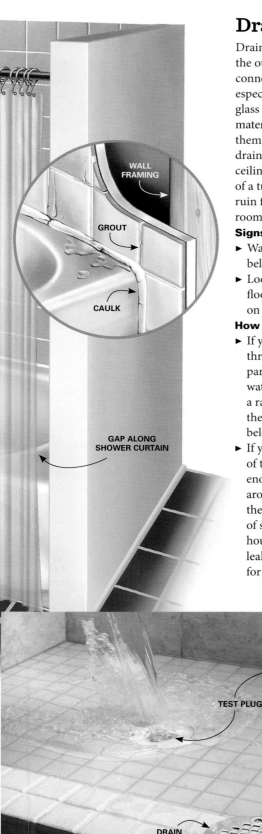

WALL FRAMING

GROUT

CAULK

GAP ALONG SHOWER CURTAIN

Drain leaks

Drain leaks allow water to sneak around the outside of the drain where it's connected to the tub or shower. This is especially common with plastic or fiberglass tubs and shower pans, since these materials flex slightly when you stand on them, often breaking the seal around the drain. These leaks can stain or destroy the ceiling below or rot floor joists. In the case of a tub set on a concrete slab, the leak will ruin flooring in the bathroom or adjoining rooms.

Signs of trouble:
▶ Water stains on the ceiling or joists below.
▶ Loose flooring near the tub or damp floors in adjoining rooms (if the tub is on a concrete slab).

How to find the source:
▶ If you can see the underside of the drain through an access panel or open ceiling, partially fill the tub and then release the water. In a shower, plug the drain with a rag and then release the water. Check the drains and traps for leaks from below through the access panel.
▶ If you don't have access to the underside of the drain, plug the drain and add enough water to form a small puddle around the drain (bottom photo). Mark the edge of the puddle by setting a bottle of shampoo next to it. Then wait an hour. If the puddle shrinks, the drain is leaking. Don't rely on your tub stopper for this test; it may leak. Remove the

stopper and insert a 1-1/2-in. test plug ($5 to $10 at home centers). Remove the grate and use a 2-in. plug for a shower.

How to fix it:
▶ To repair a tub drain, unscrew the drain flange from above. Then clean the flange and apply silicone caulk. Also remove the rubber gasket that's under the tub's drain hole and take it to a home center to find a matching gasket. Slip the new gasket into place and screw in the drain flange. For more information, visit familyhandyman.com and search for "bathtub drain."
▶ If you have access to a shower drain from below, tighten the ring nut that locks the drain to the shower pan. If that doesn't work, replace the drain assembly ($15). If you don't have access beneath the drain, cut a hole in the ceiling below or replace the drain assembly with a WingTite drain ($35; plumbrite.com).

Tile leaks

Tile leaks occur when water seeps through deteriorating grout or caulk and gets into the wall behind the tile (Figure B, inset). Depending on the materials used to set the tile, this can lead to tile falling off the wall, severe rotting of the wall framing, and damage to the subfloor, joists or ceiling below.

Signs of trouble:
▶ Loose tiles.
▶ Persistent mold.
▶ If the shower is against an exterior wall, you may find an area of peeling paint outside.
▶ Stains on the ceiling under the shower.

How to find the source:
▶ Examine the grout and caulk joints for gaps. You almost always find mold here.
▶ If you have loose tile behind the tub spout or faucet, open the access panel behind the faucet and look for dampness or stains.

How to fix it:
▶ Remove the old grout, caulk and loose tiles.
▶ If the surface behind the tile is still solid, you can reattach tiles, regrout and recaulk.
▶ If more than a few tiles are loose or if the wall is spongy, you'll have to install new backer board and tile, or a fiberglass surround.

TEST PLUG

TEST A DRAIN
Plug the drain with a test plug and add water. After an hour, check to see if the water level has dropped.

DRAIN GRATE

Stop sink leaks

Sink rim leaks

Sink rim leaks allow water to seep under the rim or the base of the faucet. They will gradually destroy your cabinets and countertops in kitchens and bathrooms.

Signs of trouble:

► Puddles, dampness or water stains inside the cabinet.
► Loose plastic laminate near sink.
► A loose faucet base.
► Deteriorating caulk around sink.

How to find the source:

► If you have a plastic laminate counter-top, examine the underside of the countertop using a flashlight. Look for swollen particleboard or other signs of water damage.
► Dribble water around the sink rim and look for leaks (right photo).

How to fix it:

► Tighten the faucet base by turning the mounting nuts underneath it.
► If the sink rim is caulked, scrape away the old caulk and recaulk.
► Tighten the clips under the sink rim that clamp the sink to the countertop.

TEST FOR RIM LEAKS
Dribble water around the sink rim and faucet base with a sponge. Then look for leaks below using a flashlight.

Drain leaks

Drain leaks in kitchens and bathrooms usually occur at the drain or at the slip joints in the drainpipe. Hidden behind boxes and bottles, these leaks can damage flooring, cabinets and even ceilings below before you notice them.

Signs of trouble:

► Puddles, water stains or a dank odor in the cabinet.
► Loose or damaged flooring in front of the sink.

How to find the source:

► Fill the sink bowls, then as they drain check all joints from the sink to the wall with a dry tissue (see bottom photo, p. 25).
► Run and drain the dishwasher and check the waste hose connection.

How to fix it:

► For a slip joint leak, first tighten the slip nut. If that doesn't work, disassemble the joint, coat the washer with Teflon joint compound and reassemble.
► For a leak from the basket strainer, tighten the ring nut under the sink. If the leak continues, disconnect and remove the basket strainer. Reassemble it using plumber's putty as a sealant under the basket's rim.

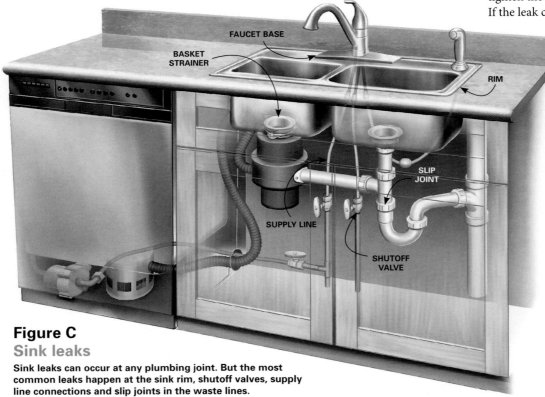

Figure C
Sink leaks

Sink leaks can occur at any plumbing joint. But the most common leaks happen at the sink rim, shutoff valves, supply line connections and slip joints in the waste lines.

Test for hidden leaks

The vast majority of leaks occur at or near plumbing fixtures like tubs, sinks and toilets. But if you suspect a leak in the water supply system, there's a simple way to check it—even if the pipes are hidden inside walls. First, turn off all your faucets. If you have drippy faucets or a toilet that runs between flushes, close the shutoff valves. Then go to your water meter and check the position of the "1-cubic-foot" dial. Check the dial again two hours later. If the dial has moved, you have a leak in the water supply.

Turn off all the faucets and check the 1-cu.-ft. dial on the water meter to test for hidden leaks.

Two slow leaks that signal catastrophe

If you notice puddles near your water heater, check the pressure relief valve and the drain valve.

If either is dripping, replace the valve. If not, the tank is leaking and you need a new water heater. Don't delay. Tank leaks often start slow and then suddenly burst days or weeks later, causing a major household flood.

The same goes for washing machine supply hoses. If you notice a tiny leak in the hose itself or at the crimped metal fittings at the ends, replace the hose. Otherwise the hose may eventually burst, releasing a continuous flow of water.

CHECK FOR SUPPLY LEAKS
Don't rely on your sense of touch to find tiny leaks. Wipe each connection with a dry tissue. Then look for a wet spot on the tissue.

Supply leaks

Supply leaks under the kitchen sink or bath vanity can go unnoticed for a long time since they're usually at the back of the cabinet. Water can run down the pipes into the floor or subfloor, rotting the sink base, the floor and the framing.

Signs of trouble:
▶ Puddles, dampness or water stains inside the cabinet.
▶ Stains on the ceiling below.

How to find the source:
▶ Dab shutoffs and connections with a dry tissue or paper towel and look for wet spots (bottom photo).
▶ Run the dishwasher and check for leaks under it.

How to fix it:
▶ If the valve stem on a shutoff valve drips, tighten the packing nut. If the leak doesn't stop, replace the valve.
▶ For other leaks at the shutoff valve or at the faucet, try tightening the compression nut first. If that doesn't stop the leak, disassemble the fitting, coat the ferrule or gasket with Teflon joint compound (available at home centers and hardware stores) and reassemble the connection.

MOLD

Instant fixes for roof leaks

If you have water stains that extend across ceilings or run down walls, the cause is probably a roof leak. Tracking down the leak is the hard part; the fixes are usually pretty easy. We'll show you some simple tricks for finding and repairing most of the common types of roof leaks. But if you live in the Snow Belt and in the winter you have leaks only on warm or sunny days, you probably have ice dams.

Finding the leaks

When you're trying to track down a leak, start by looking at the roof uphill from the stains. The first thing to look for is any roof penetrations. Items that penetrate the roof are by far the most common source of leaks. In fact, it's rare for leaks to develop in open areas of uninterrupted shingles, even on older roofs. Penetrations can include plumbing and roof vents, chimneys, dormers or anything else that projects through the roof. They can be several feet above the leak or to the right or left of it.

If you have attic access, the easiest way to track down a leak is to go up there with a flashlight and look for the evidence.

If running water doesn't reveal the exact location of the leak, don't be timid. Start removing shingles in the suspect area. With them removed, there'll be evidence of the leak and you'll be able to track it down right to the source. You'll see discolored felt paper or water-stained or even rotted wood directly below and around it.

There will be water stains, black marks or mold. But if access is a problem or you have a vaulted ceiling, you'll have to go up onto the roof and examine the suspect(s). The photos on the following pages will show you what to look for.

If the problem still isn't obvious, enlist a helper and go up on the roof with a garden hose. Start low, soaking the area just above where the leak appears in the house. Isolate areas when you run the hose. For example, soak the downhill side of a chimney first, then each side, then the top on both sides. Have your helper stay inside the house waiting for the drip to appear. Let the hose run for several minutes in one area before moving it up the roof a little farther. Tell your helper to let you know when a drip becomes visible. You'll be in the neighborhood of the leak. This process can take well over an hour, so be patient and don't move the hose too soon. Buy your helper dinner.

1

Plumbing vent boots

Plumbing vent boots can be all plastic, plastic and metal, or even two-piece metal units. Check plastic bases for cracks and metal bases for broken seams. Then examine the rubber boot surrounding the pipe. That can be rotted away or torn, allowing water to work its way into the house along the pipe. With any of these problems, you should buy a new vent boot to replace the old one. But if the nails at the base are missing or pulled free and the boot is in good shape, replace them with the rubber-washered screws used for metal roofing

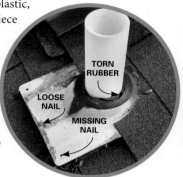

PROBLEM: When gasket-type plumbing vent flashing leaks, the culprit is usually a cracked gasket or missing or loose nails.

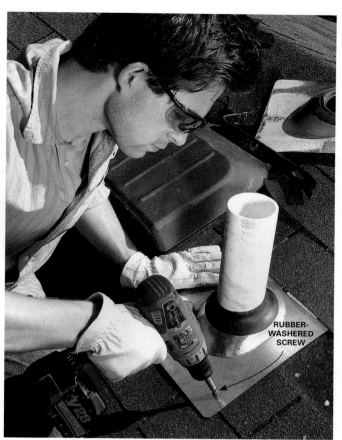

SOLUTION: Replace the old boot. Screw the base to the roof with rubber-washered screws. Don't use nails. They'll only work loose over time.

systems. You'll find them at any home center with the rest of the screws. You'll have to work neighboring shingles free on both sides. If you don't have extra shingles, be careful when you remove shingles so they can be reused. Use a flat bar to separate the sealant between the layers. Then you'll be able to drive the flat bar under the nail heads to pop out the nails.

2

Roof vents

Check for cracked housings on plastic roof vents and broken seams on metal ones. You might be tempted to throw caulk at the problem, but that solution won't last long. There's really no fix other than replacing the damaged vents. Also look for pulled or missing nails at the base's bottom edge. Replace them with rubber-washered screws.

In most cases, you can remove nails under the shingles on both

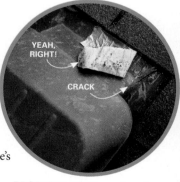

PROBLEM: Plastic roof vents can crack and leak. Duct tape is *not* the solution this time!

SOLUTION: Replace the old vent. If you're careful, you won't have to remove any shingles to slip out the old one and slide the new one into place.

sides of the vent to pull it free. There will be nails across the top of the vent too. Usually you can also work those loose without removing shingles. Screw the bottom in place with rubber-washered screws. Squeeze out a bead of caulk beneath the shingles on both sides of the vent to hold the shingles down and to add a water barrier. That's much easier than renailing the shingles.

3

Leaky walls and dormers

Water doesn't always come in at the shingled surface. Often, wind-driven rain comes in from above the roof, especially around windows, between corner boards and siding, and through cracks and knotholes in siding. Dormer walls provide lots of spots where water can dribble down and enter the roof. Caulk can be old, cracked or even missing between the corner boards

PROBLEM: Water that sneaks behind walls and dormers dribbles down into your house just like a roof leak.

and between window edges and siding. Water penetrates these cracks and works its way behind the flashing and into the house. Even caulk that looks intact may not be sealing against the adjoining surfaces. Dig around with a putty knife to see if the area is sealed. Dig out any suspect caulk and replace it with a siliconized latex caulk. Also check the siding above the step flashing. Replace any cracked, rotted or missing siding, making sure the new piece overlaps the step flashing by at least 2 in. If you still have a leak, pull the corner boards free and check the overlapping flashing at the corner. Often, there's old, hardened caulk where the two pieces overlap at the inside corner.

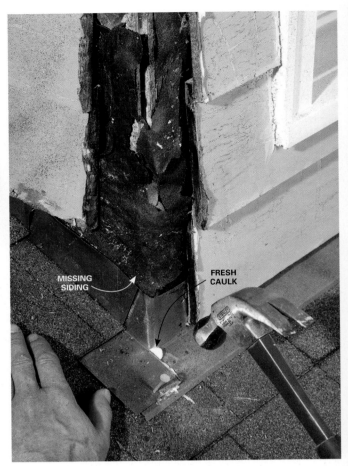

SOLUTION: Recaulk the corner flashing. Lift the overlapping section, clean it thoroughly and add a generous bead of fresh caulk underneath. Make sure the gap at the corner is filled with caulk.

4

Step flashing

Step flashing is used along walls that intersect the roof. Each short section of flashing channels water over the shingle downhill from it.

But if the flashing rusts through, or a piece comes loose, water will run right behind it, and into the house it goes. Rusted flashing needs to be replaced. That means removing shingles, prying siding loose, and then removing and replacing the

PROBLEM: Unnailed step flashing can slip down and channel water into the wall.

step flashing. It's that simple. But occasionally a roofer forgets to nail one in place and it eventually slips down to expose the wall.

SOLUTION: Push a loose piece of step flashing right back in place and then secure it with caulk above and below.

⑤ Small holes

Tiny holes in shingles are sneaky because they can cause rot and other damage for years before you notice the obvious signs of a leak. You might find holes left over from satellite dish or antenna mounting brackets or just about anything. And exposed, misplaced roofing nails should be pulled and the holes patched. Small holes are simple to fix, but the fix isn't to inject caulk in the hole. You'll fix this one with flashing.

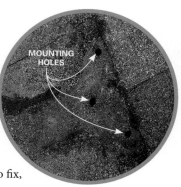

PROBLEM: Leftover mounting holes can let in vast amounts of water.

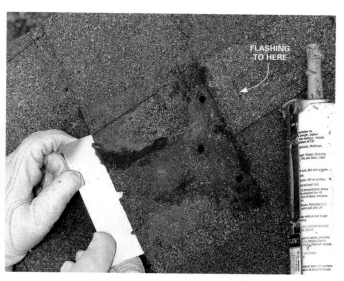

SOLUTION: Seal nail holes forever. Slip flashing under the shingle and add a bead of caulk under and over the flashing to hold it in place.

Minor leaks can cause major damage

Have a roof leak? Well, you'd better fix it, even if it doesn't bother you much or you're getting a new roof next year. Over time, even small leaks can lead to big problems, such as mold, rotted framing and sheathing, destroyed insulation and damaged ceilings. The flashing leak that caused this $950 repair bill was obvious from the ceiling stains for more than two years. If the homeowner had dealt with it right away, the damage and subsequent repairs would have been minimal.

Pro tip: Don't count on caulk!

Rarely will caulk or roof cement cure a roof leak—at least for very long. You should always attempt a "mechanical" fix whenever possible. That means replacing or repairing existing flashing instead of using any type of sealant. Only use caulk for very small holes and when flashing isn't an option.

Great goofs

Look out below!

A few years ago, my wife and I bought a 100-year-old house. This house needed every fix-up project you could imagine, but we thought we'd better tackle the leaky roof first. The house had one layer of shabby-looking shingles. To save time and money, we decided to skip the tear-off and just add a second layer of shingles. After carrying the first bundle up the ladder, I slammed it down onto the roof. I couldn't believe my eyes. It broke right through the roof and fell onto the floor below. That's how I found out that some of the wood beneath the old shingles was rotting. A whole new roof was the only project we did that year!

—Jason Schmidt

How to save a flooded carpet

CARPET CLEANER

Rent a commercial extractor or a carpet cleaner to suck out as much moisture as possible. Move slowly and do several passes in different directions.

Call in the pros

If you had a sewer backup, washing machine drain-water spill or river flood, you need professional help. Pros are the only ones with the proper equipment to get your basement dry and disinfected in the shortest possible time.

To find a certified water restoration professional, search online for "water damage restoration." Look for IICRC (Institute of Inspection, Cleaning and Restoration Certification) credentials in the ad (Servicemaster is one company that is fully certified). Or search for IICRC online.

Be aware that pros can give you a rough price estimate (the average cost of a basement cleanup is $2,500), but the final cost depends on how long it takes them to dry out your basement. There are just too many variables beyond their control (inside and outside temperature and humidity levels) to give you a set price up front. Be wary of any company that gives you a set price over the phone.

Q **My basement flooded and I've got wet carpet. Is it possible to save it?**

A You'll have to go by these rules: If the floodwater was clean (broken pipe, burst washing machine supply hose or a foundation leak), you can probably save the carpet (the pad is iffy). But you've got to act fast. If the carpet isn't dry within 72 hours, it'll start to grow mold. However, if the floodwater was dirty (sewer backup or washing machine drain water), you need to call in the pros.

We'll assume the basement was flooded with clean water, the water is now shut off and the cost of the carpet is less than your insurance deductible (or that you simply want to do it yourself to avoid a claim). Before you set one boot on that squishy carpet, heed this warning: You must turn off the power to the basement. If you're not positive which breakers power the basement receptacles, flip the main circuit breaker in the garage panel. If your electrical panel is in the basement, call an electrician to turn off the power.

Next, remove any extension cords and power strips from the floor and unplug or switch off all electrical appliances (washer, dryer, HVAC). Ask the electrician (if you hired one) to repower the upstairs (to keep the fridge going) and inspect the basement receptacles to determine whether it's safe to repower them. If not, you'll have to buy several GFCI-equipped extension cords and run power from upstairs receptacles.

Then it's time to extract the water from the carpet. Don't waste your time with a wet/dry shop vacuum—it simply doesn't have enough power. Instead, rent an extractor (if available) or carpet cleaner, an air mover fan or two, and a large commercial dehumidifier. Rent the largest dehumidifier available. The big ones can remove up to 30 gallons per day, compared with 4 gallons for the largest home units.

Extraction is 1,200 times more effective than dehumidification. You'll want to move the extractor slowly across the carpet to suck up as much water as possible. Don't rush this step! Once the water is out, peel back the carpeting (watch out for those rusted sharp nails on the tackless stripping) and remove the wet pad. Cut the pad into strips, roll it up and haul it outside. If the weather is hot, dry and sunny, you can try drying it yourself by rolling it out on your driveway. If that works, you can reinstall it by taping it back together. Just be aware that new carpet pad is cheap, so don't waste a lot of time trying to dry the old stuff.

Lay the carpet back on the floor and fire up the air movers and rental dehumidifier. Keep the basement temperature at or below 75 degrees F. You might think hotter is better because it will dry everything faster. But a higher temp will accelerate bacterial growth and turn your basement into a petri dish.

While the carpet is drying, check the condition of the wall insulation. If you don't have insulation and you dry out the basement quickly, you don't have to replace the drywall. But if the insulation is wet, it's gotta go (wet insulation cannot be saved). Snap a chalk line, cut the drywall with a recip saw and toss the wet stuff. Replace the insulation and install new drywall.

Finally, if your appliances or furnace was under water, call in appliance and HVAC specialists before plugging any of them back in.

Save your stuff

Most people leave their valuable items in the basement while they dry out the carpet. Big mistake. The longer your items sit in the basement, the more moisture they'll soak up. And that means mold. So get them out of the basement fast!

- ▶ Move all electronic gear upstairs (high humidity can corrode electronic components).
- ▶ Take photos and artwork off the walls and move them to a dry location.
- ▶ Place valuable wet books in your freezer until the "freeze-drying" effect removes all the water from the pages.
- ▶ If you can't move furniture out of the basement, place aluminum foil under the legs.

COMMERCIAL DEHUMIDIFIER

COMMERCIAL AIR MOVER FAN

Rent a commercial dehumidifier and air mover fan ASAP. Position the machines on opposite sides of the room to pick up and remove most of the moisture.

How to waterproof a basement

Install a basement drain system

Do April showers bring a wet basement along with those May flowers? Then it might be time to consider installing a drain system. A wet basement not only prevents you from enjoying additional space in your house but also can turn your basement into a giant petri dish perfect for growing unhealthy molds and fungi.

Installing a drain system is filthy, backbreaking work, but it's not complicated. With a little instruction from our drain tile experts, you can do a first-class job. And DIY pays off big: Pros charge $5,000 to $8,000 for a typical job (120 linear feet of drain tile). You can install yours for less than $1,500 in materials and tool rentals.

Before you get started

It's always best to stop water from entering your basement in the first place, so before you run to the rental center for your jackhammer, be sure to address the exterior issues. The grade next to the house should slope down away from the building by least 6 in. for the first 10 ft. Consider installing gutters, or make sure the existing gutters are working properly. And check that your irrigation system isn't adding to the problem by spraying water right up against the side of the house.

If your basement is finished, with stud walls and insulation covering the foundation walls, you can still install a drain system. When you break out the concrete, leave small sections of floor intact so the wall doesn't drop down. A 4 x 4-in. section every 6 ft. is enough to support the wall. If there are obstacles along the wall (like a furnace), plan to tunnel under them.

You'll find most of the materials you'll need at a home center. Order the rock from a landscape supplier. You'll also need a pickup to haul the dirt to the landfill.

Always check with your local building official. Explain your project, and see if any permits or inspections are required in your area. Sometimes, a building official who has been around for a while may have information on how your house was built or what issues you may run into in your area.

Radon

A drain tile system creates a perfect pathway for dangerous radon gas to escape. If you've never tested for radon, it's smart to do so before you install a drain system. That way, you can plan for a radon mitigation system as well. To learn more, search for "radon" at family-handyman.com.

1 GET READY FOR DUST
Instead of just covering your stuff with sheets of plastic, isolate your work area with a wall of plastic sheeting. Make sure to fill in the spaces between joists.

16" TO 18"

2 BUST UP THE FLOOR
Remove 16 in. to 18 in. of concrete along the wall with a rented electric jackhammer. Start by chipping in a straight line along the entire length of the wall, then come back and bust it into manageable chunks.

RUBBER FEED BUCKET

3 DIG A TRENCH ALONG THE WALL
Dig the trench as deep as the bottom of the footing. Instead of lugging pails of soil up the stairs, buy buckets that will fit through your basement windows.

Control the dust

There's no getting around it: Busting up concrete is a dirty job. Shut down your furnace or central air conditioning while you're working, and cover all return air vents until you're finished cleaning up. Instead of covering your furnishings with plastic, move everything out of the area and drape plastic from the ceiling to create an isolated work space (Photo 1). If you have an unfinished ceiling, be sure you run the plastic up into every joist space. Set a fan in the window to exhaust the heavy dust while you run the jackhammer. And wear a dust mask and hearing protection.

Bust up the floor

The pros use electric jackhammers, because the air that runs pneumatic jackhammers kicks up a lot more dust. You can get one from a rental center for about $75 a day. Start by hammering a line about 16 in. to 18 in. away from the wall (Photo 2).

Once the perimeter is done, come back and break the row of concrete into manageable chunks. Each section will break free easier if it has room to pull away, so remove the sections as you go. If you're working alone, make the most of your rental time; just set the chunks aside until you're done with the hammer. Don't forget to bust up a larger area for your sump basin.

Dig the trench

Once the concrete is removed, dig down to the bottom of the footing but not below. If you compromise the soil under the footing, you could end up with cracks in your wall, or worse.

Five-gallon buckets are OK for hauling out debris, but many pros use rubber feed buckets (typically used for farm animals) because they fit through small basement windows and are less likely to bang up trim (Photo 3). You can get them at farm supply retailers for about $14. And when it's time to haul the debris away, you may find that the landfill considers it to be "clean fill." You may be able to dump it for free!

Install the basin

It's best to locate your basin in an unfinished area of the basement so you can have easy access to the sump pump. If you never plan on finishing the basement, locate the basin in the same area where you want the water to drain out of the house so you don't have as much plastic pipe to install. Dig the hole so the top of the basin will sit flush with the finished concrete.

Many basins come with flat "knockout" areas meant to make cutting the hole easier. Don't assume the location of these knockouts will work for your system. Because the pipe will be slightly sloped down toward the basin, the longer the drain is, the lower the pipe will be when it reaches the basin. You never want standing water in your drainpipes, so make sure to choose a model that is deep enough. Pros typically use 30-in.-deep basins. They use 36-in.-deep models for systems longer than 120 ft., and they install two basins if the drain is longer than 180 ft.

Set the basin in place, and then mark the locations for the holes where the pipes will meet the basin. Keep in mind there will be a thin layer of rock (one layer thick) under the pipe near

Figure A
Drain detail

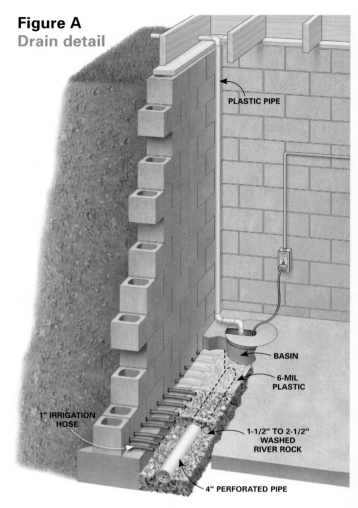

PLASTIC PIPE

BASIN

6-MIL PLASTIC

1" IRRIGATION HOSE

1-1/2" TO 2-1/2" WASHED RIVER ROCK

4" PERFORATED PIPE

Figure B
Sump basin detail

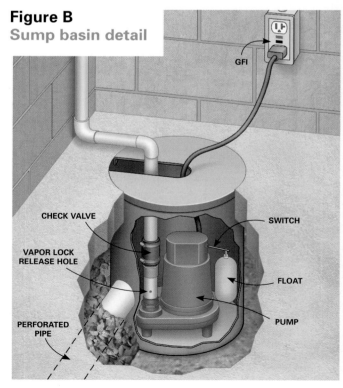

GFI

CHECK VALVE

SWITCH

VAPOR LOCK RELEASE HOLE

FLOAT

PERFORATED PIPE

PUMP

the basin. Cut the holes using a reciprocating saw, jigsaw or hole saw. The holes don't have to be perfect.

Don't haul out all the dirt right away; you'll need some to fill in around the basin. Once it's permanently in place, fill in around it, tamping the dirt with a 2x4 as you go. **Caution:** Never drill holes in the bottom of the basin! If you have a high water table, water could come up from the bottom, and your pump will run nonstop, attempting to dry out the neighborhood.

Drill holes in block

If your basement walls are made from concrete block, drill 1-in. holes in each block core and into each mortar joint (see Figure A). This will allow the water that collects in the cores and between the blocks to flow into the drain. Drill the holes as close to the footings as you can. You may find that the bottom blocks are filled with concrete. In that case, you'll have to remove any existing walls and install foundation wrap (see p. 36). Cut down on dust by laying a shop vacuum hose next to the hole as you drill.

Install the pipe

Before you lay the pipe in the trench, shovel in a bottom layer of 1-1/2-in. to 2-in. washed river rock (a layer of smaller rock can become clogged with minerals and sediments). The pipe should slope toward the basin at least 1/4 in. for every 10 ft. Rake the rock around to achieve this pitch.

Lay your irrigation pipe on top of the rock. Don't use ordinary flexible drainpipe because it clogs easily. The pros prefer to lay down a 4-in.-diameter Schedule 10 perforated pipe. Buy the kind

RIVER ROCK

4 **LAY IN THE PIPE**
Lay the pipe with the holes face down. Add or remove rock to slope the pipe so water flows to the sump basin. There's no need to cement the pipe connections.

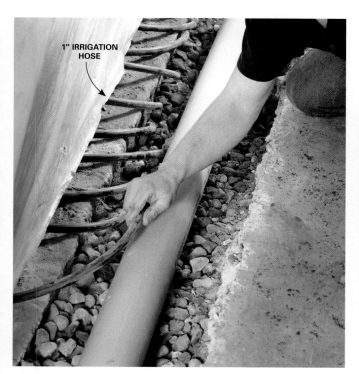

1" IRRIGATION HOSE

5 **INSTALL HOSE IN THE BLOCK WALLS**
Drill 1-in. holes in each block core and each mortar joint. Then insert sections of 1-in. irrigation hose from the holes into the gravel to carry away the water.

6-MIL PLASTIC

HAND FLOAT

6 **CAP OFF THE TRENCH WITH CONCRETE**
Lay plastic over the rock and cover it with concrete. Smooth out the concrete with a float. Wait 20 minutes, and work it smooth with a steel trowel.

of pipe with rows of 1/2-in. perforation holes only on one side, not all around the pipe.

Lay the pipe with the holes facing down (Photo 4), so the minerals and sediment in the water can flow down around the pipe and settle into the ground. This way, the water that does rise up into the pipes from underneath will be relatively clean. Clean water will add years to the life of the whole system. Start at the basin, and push the male end of the pipe into the basin about 4 in. Use PVC or ABS elbows at the corners. It's not necessary to cement the sections together.

Divert the water into the drain

Once your pipe is installed, it's time to install the 1-in. irrigation hose that will carry the water from the blocks to the trench (Photo 5). Softer hose, like garden hose, can get crushed flat by the new concrete, so stick with irrigation hose. Cut the hose with a hacksaw or reciprocating saw. Make sure each section of hose runs several inches past the footing.

Cover it back up

Once the hoses are in or the foundation wrap is in place, it's time to cover it up. Fill in the trench with river rock up to the bottom of the existing slab, and then cover the rock with at least a 6-mil thickness of plastic for a vapor barrier (Photo 6).

To cut down on dust, mix your concrete outside. Bagged concrete mix for slabs and sidewalks works just fine. Slide a 3-ft. section of 2x4 along the floor to "screed" the new concrete flush with the floor, and then smooth it out with a hand float. Wait 20 minutes, then smooth it with a finishing trowel. Use the float to completely fill the gap under any existing walls.

Hook up the pump

Pros prefer submersible pumps that have a vertical float switch on them because they're more reliable than pedestal or float switch pumps. Install a 6- to 8-in. section of pipe on the pump, then a check valve. Make sure the check valve doesn't interfere with the pump switch. Above the check valve, attach another section of pipe long enough to reach above the top of the basin.

Drill a 1/4-in. to 3/8-in. vapor lock release hole in the section of pipe that's just below the check valve (see Figure B). This allows the pump to get up to speed before trying to force open the check valve, which may have many gallons of water pressing down on it. Angle the hole so water sprays down while the pump is working. It's best if you have a dedicated outlet for your pump. Extension cords get unplugged, and other appliances hooked up to the same circuit could trip a breaker.

The pipe that exits the basement needs to be located in an area that slopes away from the house. If that means running a pipe

If you have a solid concrete foundation

If you have poured concrete walls rather than block, you'll need to install a foundation wrap to let the water into the drain as shown below. Foundation wrap is made from tough plastic and consists of rows of dimples that allow water to flow behind it. Platon by CertainTeed is one example. Home centers can order it if they don't stock it.

Cut the sheets into strips with a utility knife. Bend the strips at 90 degrees and let the bottom half run past the footing. The length of the wrap that's up against the wall depends on your situation. At a bare minimum, run the wrap up 4 in. above the top of the concrete on a poured wall, or up 4 in. past the holes you drilled in the block wall. If you're working along stud walls, try to tuck the wrap behind the bottom plate.

EXISTING WALLS

FOUNDATION WRAP

Install foundation wrap

Set foundation wrap over the footing and up the wall. If you have stud walls along the foundation, tuck the wrap up behind the studs if possible. On solid concrete walls, foundation wrap allows water to trickle down the wall surface and into the drain system.

back across the basement, consider burying the waste pipe in the trench and having it come back up where you want it. If your pipe is going to discharge above grade and you live in a cold climate, run the pipe no more than 8 in. past the siding. This will keep it from freezing up in the winter.

With few exceptions, basement drain water cannot be dumped into city sewer systems. Most systems can be drained into storm sewers as long as they're above grade when they do. Ask your building official what the rules are in your area.

Can you count on your sump pump?

A dead pump can lead to disaster. Here's how to avoid trouble

A sump pump is one of the most important (and most ignored) disaster prevention devices in a home. When this simple system fails, the results can be catastrophic, leading to thousands of dollars in damage, daily disruptions caused by major repair work and higher insurance premiums for years to come. So spending some time and money on avoiding failure makes a lot of sense. Here we'll show you how.

What causes primary pumps to fail?

The most common reason for pump failure is a power outage, not some problem with the pump itself. Common events besides power outages can also cut off the supply of electricity. For example, lightning can trip GFCI outlets, or someone can unplug the pump and forget to plug it back in.

Assuming the power stays on, sometimes the pump itself fails. Many inexpensive sump pumps are simply too small to handle the flow from a major downpour or rapid snowmelt. And because inexpensive pumps are built with less durable materials, they lose pumping efficiency. So the pump runs more often and burns out early. Or the motor runs but the pump doesn't eject water.

Float switches are also a frequent cause of pump failure. "Wide angle" tethered float switches, the kind that free-float around the sump basket, are the biggest troublemakers. They swirl around the sump basket, making them far more likely to get trapped against the pump, discharge pipe or power cord. Once trapped, they can't switch on the pump. Inexpensive switches can also simply wear out or cause motor burnout.

Backup systems

Some homeowners keep a replacement pump on hand in case their pump dies.

Water-powered backup

A water-powered backup pump uses water pressure to siphon water out of your sump. Most use 1 gallon of city water for every 2 gallons of sump water they remove. So a pump that's capable of removing 1,500 GPH will use 750 GPH of city water. And that's created a lot of controversy. In fact, a few municipalities prohibit their use due to already severe water shortages. So check with local ordinances before buying a water-powered sump pump. In an area with high water costs, the water bill can run as high as $170 a day. But keep that in perspective. If your power goes out for a couple of days, you'd happily pay a $300 water bill to avoid a flood.

Water-powered pumps require at least 40 psi and a 3/4-in. feed line to achieve maximum pumping rates. And they require a separate drain line and some type of backflow prevention to prevent cross-contamination with potable water.

Water-powered pumps come in two styles: in-sump and above-sump. An in-sump pump (one choice is the Liberty No. SJ10 SumpJet pump; $200 at home centers and online) is always immersed in drain water, which raises the risk that drain water could contaminate the drinking water supply. To prevent that, most local codes require the installation of an expensive reduced pressure zone (RPZ) backflow prevention valve ($200). RPZ valves must be professionally installed and tested annually by a licensed plumber. That adds an annual cost to the system. So check with your local building inspection department before you buy an in-sump system.

An above-sump unit (one choice is the Basepump RB750-EZ; $300 at basepump.com) mounts well above the sump, which reduces the risk of drinking water contamination. Therefore, many plumbing inspectors require only a less expensive atmospheric vacuum breaker (AVB), which costs about $40.

Advantages
► No limit to run-time; works as long as you have water pressure
► No battery replacement costs
► No routine maintenance

Disadvantages
► If you have a well, this setup won't work during a power outage
► More difficult installation because it requires a new water line, backflow preventer and new drain line
► Annual fee for RPZ valve testing (if required by local code)
► May be expensive to run in areas with high water costs

That's a good idea (home centers often sell out of pumps during storms or floods). But having a replacement handy won't help you if you're on vacation during a power outage or if your pump dies while you're slumbering through a stormy night. That's the beauty of backup systems: No matter what the reason for the pump failure, a backup system will save the day. Here are your options:

Sizing a pump

Whether you're buying a replacement pump or a backup system, you'll have to determine the pump capacity. Here's how: Disconnect your existing pump, pull it out of the basket, and check the GPH rating on the label or check the pump's specifications on the manufacturer's site. Buy a new pump with at least that much capacity. If your existing pump sometimes can't keep up with the incoming water, select a model with a higher GPH rating.

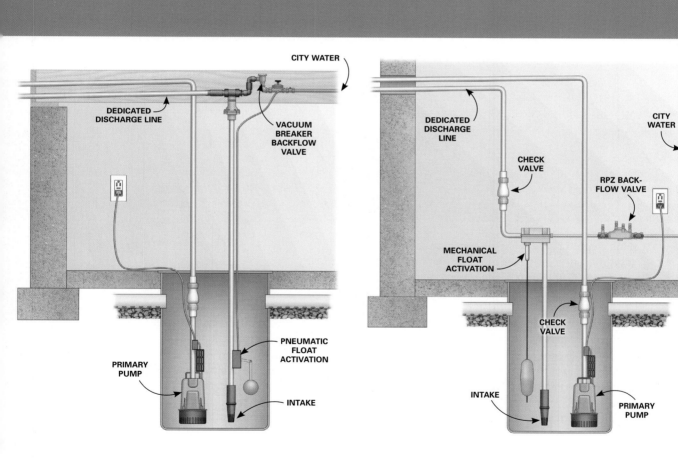

Figure A
Above-sump water-powered pump

This pump operates like an in-sump unit, using city water to pump sump water. Both kinds of water-powered systems require a separate discharge line.

Figure B
In-sump water-powered backup

When the primary pump fails, a water-powered pump uses city water pressure to siphon water out of the sump. With an in-sump version, your local inspector may require an RPZ valve to prevent contamination of drinking water.

Generator-powered sump pump

During a power outage, a generator can pay for itself in a dozen ways. One of those ways is powering a sump pump. A typical sump pump draws about 9 amps, so it won't add much load to the generator. But a generator isn't a perfect substitute for a backup system. A battery- or water-powered system kicks in automatically, whether you're home or not and no matter what the failure. A portable generator works only if you're around to connect it. And a generator (standby or portable) won't help if your primary sump pump is kaput.

Know when your pump is dead

Too often, homeowners don't discover a sump pump failure until they see the damage. But there are ways to avoid that:

If you buy a new AC sump pump run by a controller, it'll have some type of alarm to let you know if the pump fails or the power goes out. The same holds true for most new battery-powered systems.

▶ **Local alarm.** Detects water at the top of the sump basket using either a probe or a float and sounds an audible alarm (such as the BWD-HWA Basement Watchdog Water Sensor and Alarm; $15 at home centers). Local alarms are great if someone is home at the time of the failure.

▶ **Verbal message via landline.** Detects water at the sump and dials a preprogrammed phone number and plays a recorded message. Also sounds an audible alarm. Must have a landline.

▶ **Text messaging.** Detects water at the sump and sends a text to three different cell phones. Requires an adequate Verizon signal at the sump pump and a monthly fee. Find a dealer at blueangelpumps.com.

Battery backup systems

CHARGER

BATTERY-POWERED PUMP

BATTERY

Manufacturers of battery backup systems usually sell three models: good, better and best. The "best" units come with a larger battery and a more sophisticated battery charger. The larger battery gives you a longer run-time, and the better charger prolongs the life of the battery.

So how long will a battery backup system keep your basement dry? That depends on how much water is entering your sump basket (which determines how often the pump will run). Here's an example: one manufacturer's system comes with a 40-amp/hour battery that's projected to last up to 53 hours (pumping at the rate of 2,300 GPH once every five minutes). But, if you have serious water problems such that the pump runs once a minute, that same battery will last only 12 hours. That's hardly enough battery capacity to get you through an extended power outage. In that case, buy a system with a larger battery, or a system with a charger large enough to keep two batteries fully charged.

If you have minor seepage and rarely experience power outages, you're probably safe buying a less expensive battery backup system. Then again, that $400 savings could cost you

big-time if just one 100-year storm knocks out your power and turns a sump trickle into a flood.

Advantages of battery backup systems
▶ Simple installation—connect to existing discharge pipe or run a separate pipe
▶ Unlike water-powered systems, battery backup systems work when there's no water supply

Disadvantages
▶ Battery may run down before power comes back on
▶ Battery water levels must be checked every few months
▶ Battery terminals must be cleaned twice a year
▶ Battery must be replaced every five years (and costs about $100).

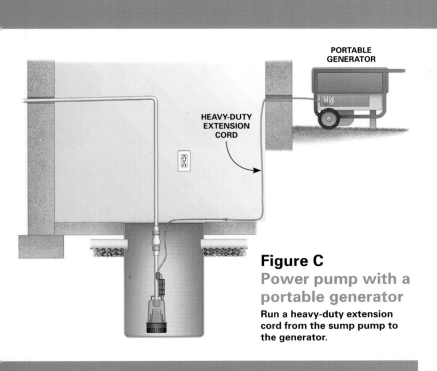

PORTABLE GENERATOR

HEAVY-DUTY EXTENSION CORD

Figure C
Power pump with a portable generator
Run a heavy-duty extension cord from the sump pump to the generator.

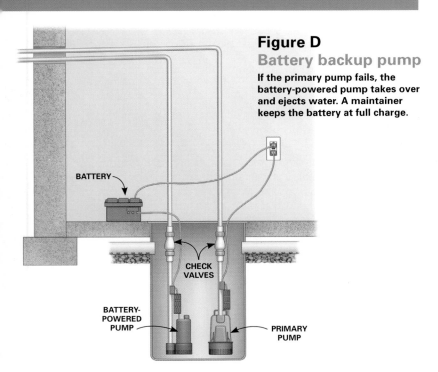

Figure D
Battery backup pump
If the primary pump fails, the battery-powered pump takes over and ejects water. A maintainer keeps the battery at full charge.

BATTERY

CHECK VALVES

BATTERY-POWERED PUMP

PRIMARY PUMP

How to buy a primary sump pump

Home centers sell a confusing array of sump pumps that range from $50 to $250. But don't despair. We've reviewed all the specs, talked to the engineers and boiled it down to five simple buying tips:

1. Horsepower means nothing. It's the pumping volume in gallons per hour (GPH) that counts. Check the capacity of your current pump. If your current pump keeps up with the flow during the heaviest rainstorms, buy that capacity again. If not, buy a pump with a higher GPH rating. To find your current pump's rating, locate its make and model number on the label and find the specs on the manufacturer's Web site.

2. Check the "head" on the manufacturer's GPH rating. Head is the height that water has to be lifted from the pump to the horizontal discharge pipe. More height means harder work for the pump. The GPH rating on most good-quality pumps includes the head (typically 10 ft.). But some manufacturers rate pump capacity without head ("3200 GPH at 0 head" for example). That gives an unrealistic—and misleading—estimate of pump capacity.

3. Spend at least $125 to get a quality sump pump. Look for a caged or vertical float switch, a motor with a UL and a CSA rating, and a pump made with a stainless steel, cast aluminum or cast iron impeller and pump body. Avoid pumps made from epoxy-coated parts.

4. Buy an energy-efficient pump. Once you find a pump with the correct GPH rating, look for a model that consumes the fewest amps. This isn't about saving electricity; high-amp pumps run hotter and burn out the float switch faster.

5. If your sump accumulates gravel or sand, buy a "top suction" pump that's "solid passing" to prevent a stall/burnout caused by trapped gravel. Or raise a "bottom suction"-style pump on a few bricks to keep it off the bottom of the sump.

While you're at the home center, buy a new male fitting to fit the pump outlet; pipe primer and cement; a new check valve and rubber couplers.

Chapter Two

AVOID APPLIANCE BREAKDOWNS

REFRIGERATOR

Extend the life of your fridge

If you're like most other homeowners, cleaning the refrigerator condenser coil is at the bottom of even your "low-priority" list. You know that a dirty coil wastes electricity, but the annual electrical savings probably isn't enough to motivate you. Need a better reason? You're killing your fridge. A dirty condenser coil makes the compressor run longer and hotter, and that dramatically reduces its life span. With some refrigerators costing $1,000 or more, it's time to get with the program and clean the beast. We'll show you how to do the job in half the time by blowing the coil clean, rather than brushing it.

You'll need an air compressor, a wand-style compressed air gun, a vacuum cleaner with a hose, a box fan, a pleated furnace filter (not the cheap fiberglass kind), nut drivers and a paintbrush.

Start by converting your box fan into a dust collector. Tape the furnace filter onto the intake side of the box fan. Seal off any open grille area on the fan with masking tape so all the air has to get pulled through the filter. Then pull the refrigerator away from the wall and unplug it. Seal the sides of the refrigerator to the floor with masking tape to prevent dust from blowing out sideways. Next, remove the back access panel fasteners and grille with a nut driver and set the grille aside. Unsnap the grille in the front of the fridge to expose the condenser coil.

Set the fan/filter unit behind the fridge and turn it on to its highest speed. Then aim the compressed air gun at a corner of the condenser coil and blow it clean (Photo 1). Continue cleaning until no more dust comes out the back of the fridge. Let the box fan run for a while to remove any airborne dust. Then shut it down and toss the filter.

Move to the back of the fridge and clean the condenser fan blades (Photo 2). Then suck up any remaining dust and cobwebs from the back side. Reinstall the access panel, plug in the fridge and push it back into place.

1 BLOW THE DUST OFF THE COIL
Tape a furnace filter to the intake side of a box fan and place it close to the rear of the fridge. Then shoot one-second bursts of compressed air into the condenser coil. Allow time between each burst so the fan can collect the dust cloud from the back of the fridge. Then move the wand to the next dirty section and do some more quick bursts.

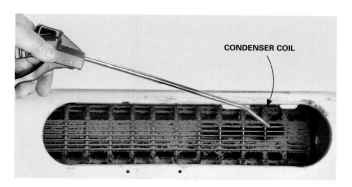

CONDENSER COIL

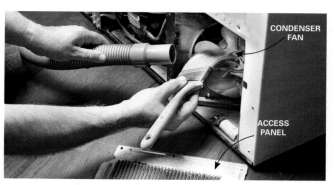

CONDENSER FAN

ACCESS PANEL

2 BRUSH AND VACUUM
Brush the dust off the condenser fan blades with an old paintbrush and suck up all the crud with the vacuum cleaner hose. Then clean the access panel grille and compressor.

Fix a bottom-freezer leak

If you discover water on your kitchen floor near the refrigerator, first check for leaks in the water line to the icemaker. If the water line and valve are dry, chances are you have a clogged evaporator drain line. The water is from frost and ice buildup on the evaporator coil that melts off during the defrost cycle. Normally this water just drains into a pan in the bottom of the refrigerator. Then, the condenser fan motor blows warm air across the pan and the water simply evaporates.

But if the drain line clogs, the water overflows and seeps down the interior walls of the freezer and onto the floor. You can fix the problem yourself in just a few hours and save the cost of a service call. All you need is a pair of tweezers and a short piece of flexible 1/4-in. O.D. tubing from any hardware store. Here's how to remove the clog.

To reach the drain, you'll first have to remove the access panel from the back of your bottom freezer. This refrigerator has been cut so you can see where all the components are. But every refrigerator is different, so search online for instructions on how to remove the access panel on your particular refrigerator.

Start by removing all the frozen food from the freezer. Put it in a cooler. Then remove the freezer drawer and slides (Photo 1). Next remove the access panel (Photo 2). Clean debris from the evaporator gutter and drain (Photo 3). Then pour hot water into the gutter to melt the ice and snake the drain with the tubing (Photo 4). Then flush water through it again. If it flows, you're done and can reassemble everything. If it still doesn't flow, call a pro.

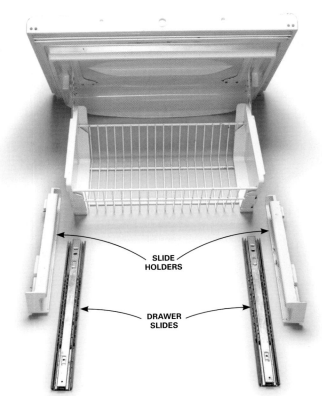

SLIDE HOLDERS

DRAWER SLIDES

1 **REMOVE THESE COMPONENTS FIRST**
Pull the freezer door all the way out and lift if off the slides. If the slides prevent you from removing the access panel, unscrew or unsnap them and remove them. If the drawer slide retainers block access to the access panel, remove the screws and lift off the retainers.

ACCESS PANEL

WE CUT THIS SO YOU COULD SEE!

2 **REMOVE THE ACCESS PANEL**
Use a nut driver to remove the access-panel retaining screws and pull the panel forward. Disconnect any lights or sensors attached to the panel. Then set the panel aside.

3 **REMOVE DRAIN DEBRIS**
Pluck the clog out of the drain with a pair of tweezers.

4 **SNAKE THE DRAIN**
Thread flexible 1/4-in. tubing down the drain and rotate it as you push it to break the clog. Stop pushing when you hear it hit the drain pan under the refrigerator. Flush the drain with hot water and make sure it all goes into the drain pan (remove the bottom front grille and shine a flashlight through the opening to see the drain pan).

Refrigerator diagnostics

A refrigerator that makes a buzzing or humming sound and doesn't keep the food cold may have a blown compressor (big bucks) or just a bad overload or compressor relay.

We had this exact problem with a refrigerator and called Costas Stavrou, our appliance consultant. To avoid the cost of a service call, Costas suggested we first try unplugging the refrigerator for about 20 minutes to allow enough time for the compressor to cool and any on-board computers to reset. When we plugged it back in, the problem returned. So he suggested we buy both an overload and a compressor relay (or a universal relay kit) from the appliance parts store and install it (photo, right). If the problem went away, it would be an inexpensive fix. Unfortunately, the compressor noise returned (meaning it was toast). We had to buy a new refrigerator, but at least we didn't have to waste money on a service call.

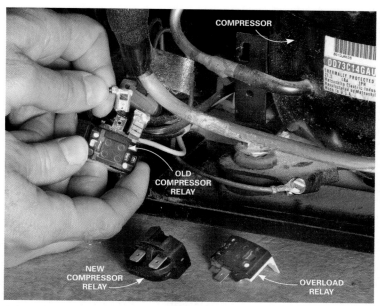

TRY A NEW OVERLOAD OR COMPRESSOR RELAY
Pull the fridge away from the wall, unplug it and remove the service panel. Swap in the new compressor and overload relays. Then plug it back in to see if the problem is gone.

Repair a leaking water dispenser

If you have a water dispenser in the door of your refrigerator and notice water on the floor when you fill a glass, the vinyl tubing that runs under the refrigerator could be leaking. To find out, pull the refrigerator forward a little. Then tip it back and prop up the front feet on blocks of wood. Look underneath and ask someone to dispense a glass of water. If the tube's leaking, you'll see it.

The fix is simple. Photos 1 – 3 show the steps. Cut out the section of damaged tubing and take it with you to the home center or hardware store. Buy a new section of vinyl tubing and one or two quick-connect couplings. If you don't have a quick-connect coupling on one end of the damaged tube as shown in Photo 1, then cut the tubing in two spots and join it with two new quick-connect couplings.

The tubing for icemakers can also get damaged and leak. So if you ever notice water on the floor under your refrigerator, check for a leaking tube and repair it using the process we show here.

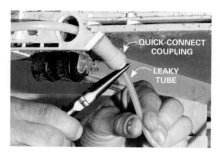

1 DISCONNECT THE LEAKING TUBE
Disconnect one end of the leaking tube by pressing in on the inner ring with needle-nose pliers to release the tube. If there isn't a quick-connect coupling, simply cut the tube with a sharp utility knife.

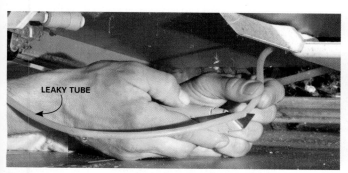

2 CUT OUT THE DAMAGED SECTION OF TUBE
Cut off the damaged tubing with a sharp utility knife. Don't use a side cutters; it'll distort the tubing and prevent a good seal with the quick-connect coupling.

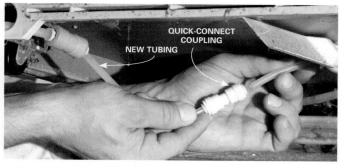

3 SPLICE IN A NEW SECTION OF TUBING
Quick-connect couplings simplify this repair. Just push cut ends of the tubing into the coupling for a leak-free connection.

Fix a broken water dispenser switch

So the kids were really thirsty and jammed their glass into the water dispenser on the refrigerator door. Now the paddle is hanging by a wire, and you're expecting an expensive repair bill. No way! You can do this repair yourself with ordinary hand tools in about an hour. A replacement paddle/switch costs about $75. We'll show you how to make the repair on a Whirlpool refrigerator. Repairs on other makes are similar.

Open the fridge door and write down the model and serial number of the fridge. Then contact a local appliance parts dealer or search online (repairclinic.com is one online source for discounted parts) to buy a new switch and paddle.

Start by unplugging the refrigerator. Then remove the drip tray to expose the trim panel screws. If you don't see any screws, unsnap the panel using a plastic putty knife and paint can opener (Photo 1). Lift the trim panel off the door. Next, remove the microswitch (Photo 2). The switch retaining pegs are usually broken, so replace them with screws (Photo 3). If the paddle is broken, first disconnect the water tube. Then remove the metal paddle retainer plate and swap in a new paddle (Photo 4).

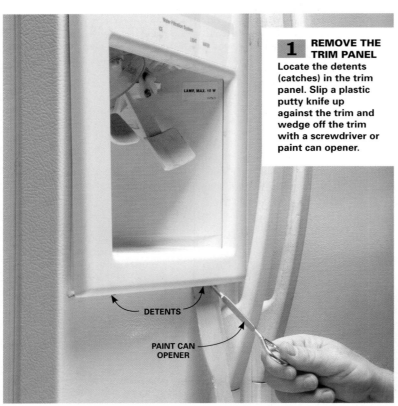

1 REMOVE THE TRIM PANEL
Locate the detents (catches) in the trim panel. Slip a plastic putty knife up against the trim and wedge off the trim with a screwdriver or paint can opener.

DETENTS

PAINT CAN OPENER

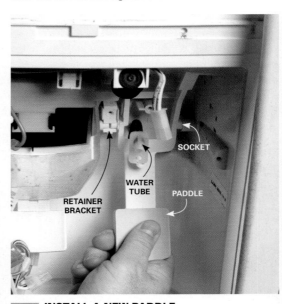

2 REMOVE THE MICROSWITCH
Pull the snap retainers away from the switch and slide it off the pegs.

BROKEN PEG

SNAP RETAINER

SWITCH

PEG

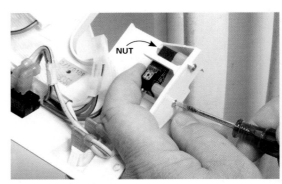

NUT

3 REPLACE THE PEGS
Drill out the pegs and replace them with two No. 4 x 1-1/4-in. machine screws. Slide new switch onto the screws and tighten the nuts.

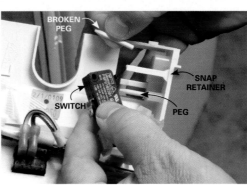

SOCKET

WATER TUBE

PADDLE

RETAINER BRACKET

4 INSTALL A NEW PADDLE
Remove the metal retainer plate (not shown). Replace the broken paddle with a new one. Reattach the water tube.

Problem: Fridge or freezer won't cool

1 Remove cover to inspect the evaporator and to access the evaporator fan. The screws may be covered with plastic plugs that you pry out.

2 If your refrigerator has a fan cover, remove the screws that hold it in place. Then remove the cover to reach the fan.

3 Replace the evaporator fan if it's noisy or doesn't spin. First unplug the refrigerator. Then remove the screws that hold the fan to the wall of the freezer.

There are several possible causes when a refrigerator doesn't keep your milk cold or your ice cream frozen. Before you attempt more complex repairs, try these simple fixes:

► Be sure the fridge is plugged in and getting power. The light should come on when you open the door.

► Check the thermostat to make sure it hasn't been turned way down by mistake.

► Be sure the vents on the back of the freezer compartment aren't blocked by boxes of ice cream or frozen vegetables—the vents have to be clear for cold air to circulate.

► Vacuum the coils under or behind the fridge. Clogged coils can cause poor cooling.

► Check to make sure nothing is stuck in the condenser fan and that it spins freely (models with coils on the back won't have a fan). To do this, unplug the fridge and pull it out. Clean the fan blades and spin the fan by hand to see if it's stuck (Photo 5 shows the

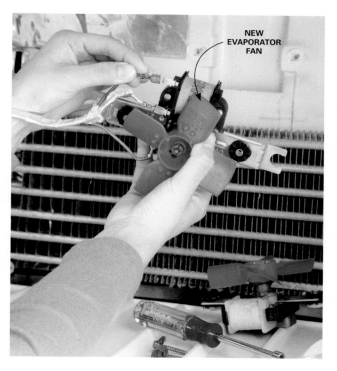

4 Replace the old fan with a new one. Remove the mounting bracket from the old fan and attach it to the new fan. Unplug the wires and switch them from the old fan to the new fan. Reinstall the fan and replace the cover.

condenser fan location). Plug in the fridge and make sure the fan runs when the compressor is running. If the fan doesn't run, see Photos 5 and 6, which show how to replace it.

Replace the evaporator fan

Here are some troubleshooting tips to help you zero in on the problem. If you can hear the compressor running but the fridge isn't cooling, the problem is most likely either frost-clogged evaporator coils or a stuck or broken evaporator fan. Evaporator fans often squeal or chirp when they start to go bad. You'll know it's the evaporator fan if the noise gets louder when you open the freezer door. The evaporator coils and fan are located behind a cover in the freezer compartment. Photos 3 and 4 show how to replace the fan if it's necessary.

If you remove the cover inside the freezer and find the coils completely filled with frost, take everything out of the freezer and fridge, unplug it and let it thaw for 24 to 48 hours. Keep a few towels handy to soak up water that may leak onto the floor. When all the frost is melted away, plug the fridge back in. If it works, the problem may be a defrost timer, defrost heater or defrost thermostat. Replacing these parts isn't difficult, but figuring out which is faulty requires troubleshooting that we won't cover here. Call a pro if you suspect a problem with these parts.

Normally the condenser fan and compressor, located near the floor on the back of most refrigerators, come on when the thermostat calls for more cooling. If you don't hear the compressor running after the door has been left open for a while, it could mean the condenser fan is stuck or worn out or that the relay or compressor is bad.

Replace the condenser fan

Pull the fridge away from the wall, unplug it and remove the thin panel on the back near the bottom to access the compressor and condenser fan. Next plug the fridge in and wait for the compressor to come on. The fan should also come on. If the compressor runs but the fan doesn't, or if the fan is noisy, you need a new fan. If neither runs and the compressor is hot, unplug the fridge and point a fan or a hair dryer set to "no heat" at the compressor. Wait for the compressor to cool and try again. If the compressor runs but the fan doesn't, the fan is bad. Unplug the refrigerator and replace the fan (Photos 5 and 6). If neither runs, then you may need a new relay or compressor. Call an appliance repair technician to find out.

5 **REPLACE THE CONDENSER FAN** if it's noisy or doesn't run. Depending on your fridge, you may have to remove the fan bracket first, and then unscrew the fan from the bracket.

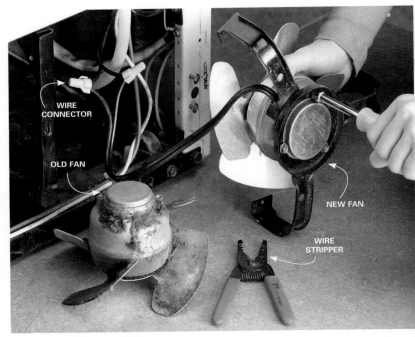

6 **INSTALL THE NEW FAN.** Cut the wires close to the old fan. Strip the wires and connect the new fan with wire connectors. Screw the new fan to the bracket and reinstall the fan and bracket in the fridge.

Replace a broken icemaker

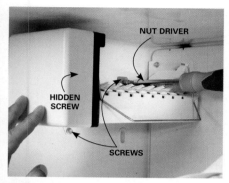

1 Use a nut driver or a long screwdriver to remove the screws that hold the icemaker in place.

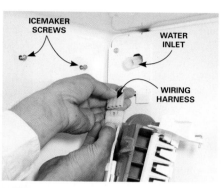

2 Line up the wiring harnesses and plug them together before screwing the icemaker in place.

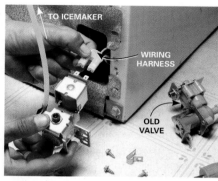

3 Remove the old inlet valve and plug in the new one, then attach it to the frame.

If your icemaker stops working, there's no need to call the appliance repair service. First, locate the saddle valve that's clamped to the house water supply and turn it off and on a few times to break up any mineral buildup clogging the valve. If that doesn't work, unplug the refrigerator and remove the icemaker (Photo 1) to make sure the water inlet at the back of the refrigerator isn't plugged with ice (just heat it with a hair dryer if it is). However, if the water supply isn't blocked and the refrigerator is older, it's time to replace the icemaker. According to appliance repair pros, most icemakers break down long before the refrigerator. The good news is that most replacement kits are in the $100 to $125 range, and installing one is simple.

Locate the model number on the wall of the refrigerator just inside the door, then buy a new icemaker at an appliance store or online (search "appliance parts").

Unplug the refrigerator and turn the water off, then take the old icemaker out and disconnect the wiring. Plug the new icemaker in (Photo 2), hold it in position and screw it to the refrigerator wall.

Pull the refrigerator out from the wall, disconnect the water supply from the inlet valve at the bottom of the refrigerator, then replace the old inlet valve (Photo 3). Inlet valves should be replaced when the icemaker is replaced, and are usually included with replacement kits. If not, order it separately.

Before you push the refrigerator back, turn the water on and check for leaks.

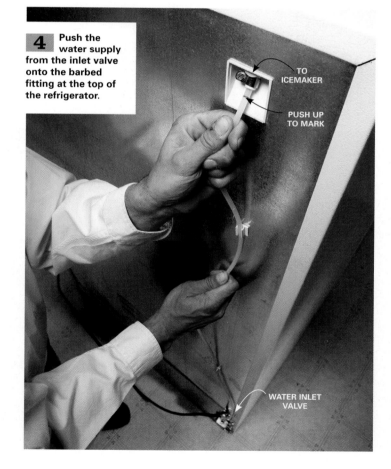

4 Push the water supply from the inlet valve onto the barbed fitting at the top of the refrigerator.

Upgrade an icemaker supply line

Inexpensive plastic water lines and saddle valves sold for icemakers can eventually clog or leak, causing water damage.

You can replace your plastic water line with a copper tee fitting, a high-quality shutoff and a braided steel supply line in a half hour for about $30—and never have to worry about leaks again. Braided steel is a tough, non-kinking alternative to 1/4-in. flexible copper or plastic.

Turn off the house water supply and drain the water from the entire system. Remove the saddle valve and cut out the copper underneath it (Photo 1). You may need to cut more, depending on how much play you have in the water line, to make room for a repair coupling and additional copper if needed.

Unscrew the packing nut from the shutoff and remove the handle and core before soldering. Jiggle the water lines to get all the water out, then clean and flux the fittings and solder everything together (Photo 2).

Allow the pipe to cool for several minutes, then reattach the shutoff handle. Close the shutoff and turn the house water back on to check for leaks. Attach the braided water line (Photo 3), then run the water into a bucket or sink for a few minutes to flush out any corrosion or bits of solder. Finally, fish the water line through the floor or wall to the back of the refrigerator (Photo 4).

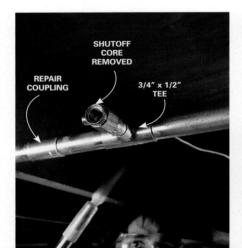

NEW STAINLESS STEEL SUPPLY LINE

1 Unscrew the valve and slide it aside. Cut the water line to make room for a new tee fitting.

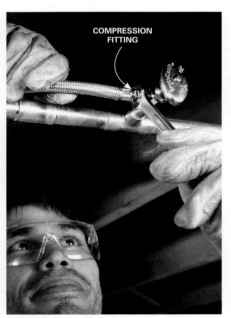

2 Clean, flux and assemble the copper fittings and the shutoff valve, then solder the joints.

3 Hand-tighten the water line to the shutoff, then turn the nut another half-turn with a wrench.

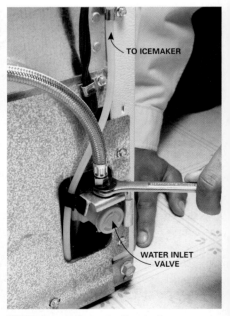

4 Attach the water line to the water inlet valve at the back of the refrigerator.

Roll-on stainless steel

Apply Liquid Stainless Steel to your kitchen appliances and you'll have the stainless steel look without having to buy new (it's great for giving aging appliances a face-lift!). The water-based latex paint is made with stainless steel and applied with foam brushes and a roller (included with paint purchase). A topcoat gives the surface a durable satin or gloss finish (your choice). We were very impressed with our refrigerator's new look.

The paint can be used on stoves, refrigerators, dishwashers and toasters—just clean them, tape off areas you don't want covered and start painting. You can apply both coats and the satin or gloss topcoat in a morning. The paint can also be used on kitchen cabinets, tables and chairs (after priming). One quart, which is enough to cover an average-size refrigerator with the required two coats, costs $70. The topcoat costs $30 per quart. Retailers are listed online, or buy the products directly from the manufacturer. Thomas' Kitchen Art, liquidstainlesssteel.com

Two turns of a wrench will correct a crooked fridge door

A sagging refrigerator or freezer door doesn't just look bad. It can cause the door gaskets to seal poorly, and that means your fridge will work harder to keep the milk cold. It can also lead to frost buildup in the freezer. To realign the door, just pry off the hinge cap and loosen the hinge screws. Then align the door with the top of the refrigerator. Adjust only the top hinge to straighten an upper door. To realign the lower door, adjust the middle hinge. Moving the middle hinge will affect the upper door, so you may have to adjust the top hinge afterward.

LOOSEN

LIFT

1

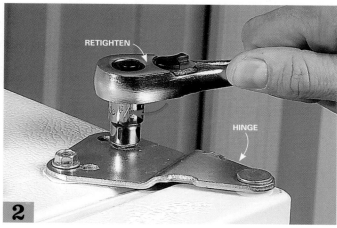

RETIGHTEN

HINGE

2

Pull out a fridge without wrecking the floor

Lay down a cardboard runway before dragging out your fridge. For the ultimate floor protection, use 1/8-in. hardboard (sold at home centers). A pair of shims create a ramp for easier pulling.

1/8" HARDBOARD

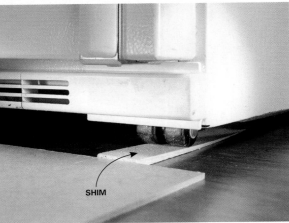

SHIM

Diagnose and replace a bum circuit board

If your refrigerator isn't keeping food cold, the cause could be a burned circuit board or a sticking circuit board relay. Before calling for repair service, try this trick. Unplug the fridge and roll it out. Remove any metal cover plates or cardboard access panels on the back and look for a circuit board. Examine the board for burn marks. Replace it if you see any (Photo 2).

If the board looks good, locate the largest relay on the board (look for the largest rectangular plastic box). Then plug in the fridge (don't touch any wires!) and tap the relay (Photo 1). If the compressor starts, the circuit board is the problem. Replace it.

If there are no burn marks and the tapping doesn't work, or the compressor makes a humming or clicking sound and then shuts off, the problem may be a relay located on the compressor itself. To learn how to do that fix, go to familyhandyman.com and search for "refrigerator compressor."

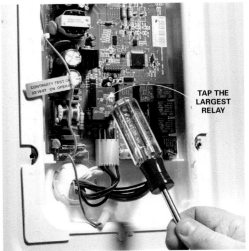

1 RATTLE THE RELAY
Tap lightly on the compressor relay to rattle the electrical contacts inside. If the fridge starts, you need a new circuit board.

TAP THE LARGEST RELAY

2 SWAP OUT THE CIRCUIT BOARD.
Move the press-on connectors to the new board one at a time. Press each connector onto the header pins until it's firmly seated.

PUSH-ON CONNECTOR

HEADER PINS

NEW CIRCUIT BOARD

Extend the life of your water heater

Water heaters often work perfectly for a decade or more without any care, so they're easy to neglect. But a few minutes of TLC once a year pays off by extending the tank's life span and maintaining your water heater's efficiency and safety.

Before you do any maintenance, close the shutoff valve on the cold water supply pipe that feeds the water heater. Then turn on the hot water at any faucet to release the pressure inside the heater's tank. Leave the faucet on until you finish your work. If you have an electric heater, turn off the power at the main panel. With a gas heater, turn the gas control dial to "off."

First, test the pressure-relief valve located on the top or side of the water

Tip

Set your water heater's dial to 120 degrees F. If the dial doesn't have numbers, check the water temperature with a cooking thermometer. Higher temperatures increase sediment buildup and the risk of scalding injuries.

heater (Photo 1). This safety valve opens automatically if the pressure inside the tank gets too high. (Excess pressure can actually cause the tank to explode.) If the valve doesn't release water when you lift the lever, replace the valve.

Replacement is simple; unscrew the discharge pipe and then unscrew the old

valve. Wrap the threads of the new valve with thread sealant tape and screw it into the tank. If your valve is several years old and has never been tested, it might leak after you test it. In that case, replace the valve.

Next, drain the tank to flush out sediments that have settled to the bottom of the tank. Sediment buildup shortens the life of your water heater and adds to your energy bill by reducing its efficiency. Draining 2 or 3 gallons of water is usually enough to flush out sediments, but always let the water flow until you no longer see particles in the bucket.
Caution: The water is scalding hot.

Don't worry about any gurgling or groaning noises coming from the heater; it's just air entering the system as water drains out. If the drain valve won't close tightly when you're done, drain the tank completely, unscrew the old valve and screw in a new one. To restart the water heater, open the shutoff valve and let the hot water run at any faucet to purge air from the system. Then turn on the power or relight the pilot.

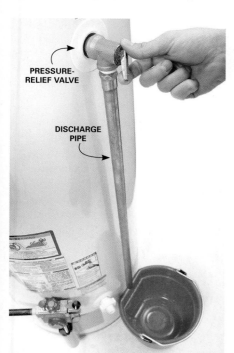

PRESSURE-RELIEF VALVE

DISCHARGE PIPE

1 Place a bucket below the discharge pipe and gently lift the lever on the pressure-relief valve to test it.

DRAIN VALVE

2 Open the drain valve slowly and let the water run until it's clear and free of sediments. **Caution: The water is hot!**

Flush a water heater

Double the life of your water heater

Have you flushed your water heater lately? This boring but important chore should be done at least once a year to remove sediment that accumulates on the bottom of the tank. That's especially true if you live in a hard-water area. The task is easy to blow off because it's out of sight—but skipping it is costing you a lot. Sediment buildup reduces the heating efficiency of your water heater.

All about sediment

One sign of excessive sediment buildup is a popping or rumbling sound coming from your water heater. That's the sound of steam bubbles percolating up through the muck. On a gas water heater, the sediment creates hot spots that can damage the tank and cause premature failure. On an electric water heater, sediment buildup can cause the lower heating element to fail. So flushing offers a payback in lower energy bills and extended heater life.

However, if you've never flushed your water heater, or haven't done it in years, you could be in for a nasty surprise. As soon as you open the drain valve, the sediment will likely clog it and prevent

you from closing the valve all the way after it's drained. Then you'll have sediment buildup and a leaking water heater. We'll show you the best way to drain the sediment out of even the most neglected heater and save the cost of a service call. You'll need some plumbing parts from a home center, a garden hose, a wet vacuum, pliers and a pipe wrench.

Buy the parts

Not only will an old drain clog up, but you won't be able to suck debris through its small opening. The key is to build a new drain valve with a 3/4-in. full-port brass ball valve with threaded ends, a 3-in. x 3/4-in. galvanized nipple, and a 3/4-in.

MIP x G.H. garden hose adapter.

Then build a shop vacuum adapter. If your shop vacuum has a 2-1/2-in. hose, buy a converter to reduce it to 1-1/4-in. Then assemble a vacuum hose-to-plumbing adapter (Photo 1) with a 1-1/4-in. x 1-1/2-in. female PVC trap adapter, a 3/4-in. MIP x 1/2-in. barb fitting, a second 3/4-in. x 3-in. nipple and a 24-in. piece of 1/2-in. I.D. vinyl tubing.

Start the draining process

Shut off the gas or electricity to the water heater and open a hot water faucet and let it run full blast for about 10 minutes to reduce the water temperature in the tank.

1 BUILD A SHOP VACUUM ADAPTER
Glue a 1-1/2-in. PVC x 3/4-in. FIP adapter (A) onto a female PVC trap adapter (B). This allows you to attach your vacuum to 3/4-in. pipe (see below). The barbed fitting (C) connects to tubing (Photo 4).

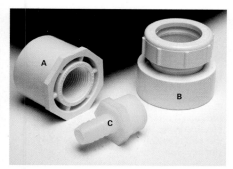

TPR VALVE

VACUUM HOSE 2-1/2" TO 1-1/4" REDUCERS

VACUUM ADAPTER IN TPR PORT

2 APPLY SUCTION
Remove the temperature pressure release valve and screw in the vacuum adapter. Attach the shop vacuum hose and fire up the vacuum.

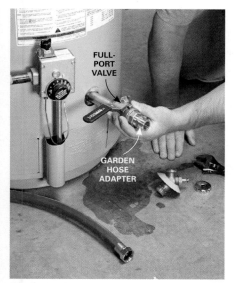

FULL-PORT VALVE

GARDEN HOSE ADAPTER

3 SWAP VALVES
Unscrew the old drain valve and install the full-port valve (closed position). Attach one end of the garden hose to the valve and run the other end into a colander and on to the floor drain.

4 SUCK OUT THE SEDIMENT
Remove the full-port valve and suck out the remaining sediment with your shop vacuum adapter and vinyl tubing.

Then shut off the cold water valve at the top of the tank and attach a garden hose to the existing drain valve and route it to a floor drain. (Use a kitchen colander to catch the sediment so it doesn't clog the floor drain.) Then open a hot water faucet on an upper floor and the water heater drain valve. Let the tank drain until sediment clogs the valve and reduces the flow. Then close the upstairs hot water faucet and water heater drain valve.

Next, remove the clogged drain valve and swap in the new full-port valve. But first, remove the blow-off tube and the temperature pressure release (TPR) valve and apply suction to the tank so you won't get soaked when you yank the old drain valve (Photo 2). Then swap the valves (Photo 3). Remove the vacuum hose from the TPR port and finish draining the tank.

Most of the sediment will flush out through the full-port valve. To remove the rest, open the cold water valve at the top of the tank in short bursts to blast it toward the drain. If you still can't get the last bit out, try vacuuming it (Photo 4).

When you're done, close the ball valve and leave it in place. But remove the lever handle to prevent accidental opening. Then reinstall the TPR valve and blow-off tube. Refill the water heater and turn on the gas or electricity, and you'll be back in hot water without all the noise.

YUCK! This is what the sediment looks like.

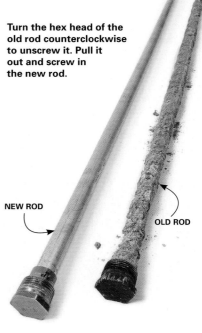

SHUTOFF VALVE

OLD ANODE ROD

"CHEATER" PIPE

1-1/16" SOCKET

Turn the hex head of the old rod counterclockwise to unscrew it. Pull it out and screw in the new rod.

NEW ROD

OLD ROD

5-year repair

Replace an anode rod

Most water heater tanks are steel with a thin glass lining to protect the metal from corrosion. Since the lining eventually cracks, tanks have a second line of defense against rust: a long metal "anode rod" that attracts corrosive elements in the water. When the rod itself becomes so corroded that it can no longer do its job, the tank soon rusts out, leaks and needs replacement. However, if you replace your anode rod before it fails, about every five years, you can double the life of your water heater.

Rods are made from magnesium, aluminum or aluminum/zinc alloy. Aluminum replacement rods cost about $30 each at home centers. In most cases, the hexagonal head of the rod is visible on the top of the water heater. If you don't see the hex head, check your owner's manual. The rod may be under the water heater's sheet metal top or connected to the hot water outlet nipple. (Some newer plastic-lined tanks have no anode rods to replace.)

Before you get started, close the shutoff valve, turn on the hot water at a faucet to

relieve pressure, and turn off the electricity or gas to the heater. Open the drain valve near the bottom of the tank and drain out about 2 gallons of water.

Caution: The water is hot!

If the hex head is set below the top of the heater, you'll need a 1-1/16-in. socket to reach it. If it protrudes above the top, you can use any type of wrench. Chances are your old anode rod will be frozen in place by corrosion. Douse the head with a spray lubricant such as WD-40 and give it a few minutes to penetrate. You may

also have to slip a "cheater" pipe over the wrench handle to increase your torque. The weight of the water in the tank is usually enough to keep the entire heater from turning. But if it begins to move, have a helper (or two) hold it in place.

When the threads break free, stop turning and look for water around the hex head. If you see leakage, drain the tank further. If you don't have enough overhead clearance to pull the rod out of the tank, bend it as you remove it. Then when you buy a new rod, choose a flexible, "segmented" version. Smear Teflon pipe thread sealant on the threads of the new rod before you install it. Don't use tape, since it can reduce the effectiveness of the rod. Before you turn on the water and electricity or gas, drain another gallon out of the tank to flush out any remaining debris.

TEMPERATURE DIAL

A slight turn of the dial makes water heaters safer

Water heaters set too high send thousands (mostly children) to hospitals each year with burns from water from a faucet. Most safety experts recommend a setting of 120 degrees F. But finding that setting on the dial isn't easy—most dials aren't labeled with numbers. If the stickers on the water heater don't tell you how to set the temperature and you can't find the owner's manual, use this method:

Run hot water at the tap closest to the water heater for at least three minutes. Then fill a container and check the temperature. If the water is above 120 degrees F, adjust the dial, wait about three hours and check again. Repeat until you get 120-degree F water. For a final test, check the temperature the following morning, before anyone uses hot water.

COOKING THERMOMETER

Stop a water heater drain valve leak

You're supposed to flush your water heater regularly to remove sediment from the bottom of the tank. But many homeowners don't do it until they hear rumbling from the tank. After the flush, they discover that the drain valve leaks. If the drain valve is brass, you can usually replace the washer. It's a fairly easy but time-consuming fix because you have to shut off the water and drain the tank. If you have a plastic drain valve, your best bet is to replace the entire valve. You guessed it; you'll have to drain the tank for that fix, too. So how do you stop the drip until you get around to fixing the valve? Simple—buy a brass garden hose end cap and screw it onto the valve threads.

GARDEN HOSE END CAP

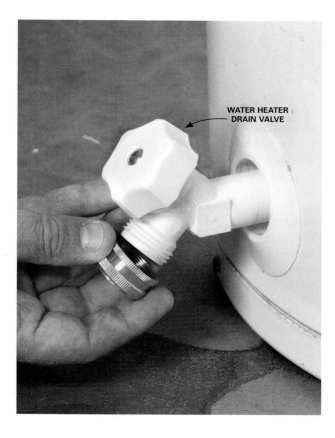

WATER HEATER DRAIN VALVE

THERMOCOUPLE BULB

PILOT LIGHT

LONG-REACH LIGHTER

Fix a water heater pilot light

No hot water? If you have a natural or propane gas water heater, chances are the pilot has gone out. The pilot is a small flame that ignites the gas burner on your water heater (photo above). When it goes out, first try relighting it, following the directions on the water heater label. If the pilot doesn't relight, or if it goes out right after lighting, by far the most common cause is a bad thermocouple (photo right). The good news: You can usually replace a thermocouple for about $12 and in less than an hour. You'll get your hot water going without waiting for a pro to show up, and save the cost of a service call.

To replace the thermocouple, follow the photo series. Be sure to turn off the shutoff valve in the gas line (Photo 1, inset); that is, one quarter turn so that the handle is at a right angle to the pipe. Since working room is tight around the burner, we recommend that you simply unscrew the three nuts at the control valve and pull out the entire burner assembly. You'll see either a slot or clips that hold it in place (Photo 2). Then either unscrew the thermocouple end or pull it out (depending on the water heater) and take it with you to an appliance parts store to find a match. Position it exactly like the old one. When relit, the pilot flame should wrap around the thermocouple bulb.

To reattach the three lines to the gas valve, thread the nuts into place with your fingers and hand-tighten them. Then snug them up with a quarter to half revolution with a wrench. The metals are soft, so don't overtighten.

Be sure to test for gas leaks. You must have the pilot lit and the burner on for this

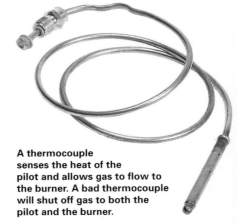

A thermocouple senses the heat of the pilot and allows gas to flow to the burner. A bad thermocouple will shut off gas to both the pilot and the burner.

test so that gas is flowing through the large tube. Reopen the shutoff valve, relight the pilot, then turn the control valve to "on." When the gas burner comes on, use a 50/50 dish soap/water mix to test the screw joints for air bubbles that indicate leaks.

CONTROL VALVE

GAS LINE

THERMOCOUPLE LINE

PILOT LINE

BURNER ACCESS COVER

SHUTOFF VALVE

Note: Some gas water heaters have a "closed" burner chamber, which is difficult to access. We recommend that you call a service pro to fix this type. Also, some gas water heaters don't have pilots. Let the pros fix these as well.

1 Turn off the control valve and the shutoff. Remove the burner access covers and unscrew the nuts on the gas, pilot and thermocouple lines.

BURNER

SLOT

2 Pull out the burner assembly. Pull out the old thermocouple. Buy a new one that matches the old one in size and length.

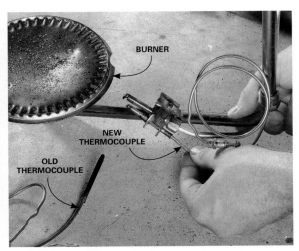

BURNER

NEW THERMOCOUPLE

OLD THERMOCOUPLE

3 Install the new thermocouple exactly like the old, slide the burner assembly back in and reattach the three lines to the control valve.

*A one-hour DIY fix
that saves $75*

Fix an electric water heater

If your electric hot water heater is slow to heat, runs out of hot water faster than it used to, or doesn't deliver any hot water at all, there's a 90 percent chance that simply replacing one or both of the heating elements will solve the problem. The fix is straightforward, and replacement elements are inexpensive ($8 to $20) and readily available at home centers, hardware stores and appliance parts dealers.

We'll show you how to test the heating elements, remove one if it's bad, and install a new one. Just keep in mind that water heaters have a typical life span of 10 to 15 years. If your heater is approaching old age, replacement may be smarter than repair.

Of course, there are other potential causes of a lack of hot water. Before you test the elements, check to make sure the circuit breaker is on and not tripped. Also press the reset button on the high-temperature cutoff located just above the upper thermostat. Resetting either the circuit breaker or the high-temperature cutoff may resolve the problem, but the fact that they were tripped in the first place may indicate an electrical problem. If they trip again, test the heating elements.

If the heating elements are good, the problem could be with the thermostats or cutoff switch. Testing is complicated, but since they're inexpensive—about $20 for both thermostats and the cutoff switch—you could simply try replacing them.

Figure A Electric water heater

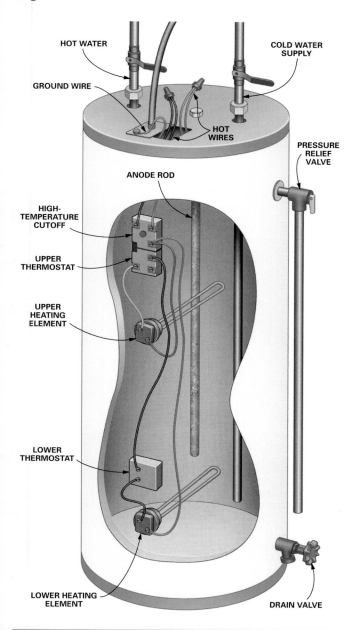

HOT WATER

GROUND WIRE

COLD WATER SUPPLY

HOT WIRES

ANODE ROD

PRESSURE RELIEF VALVE

HIGH-TEMPERATURE CUTOFF

UPPER THERMOSTAT

UPPER HEATING ELEMENT

LOWER THERMOSTAT

LOWER HEATING ELEMENT

DRAIN VALVE

What's inside and how it works

Most residential electric water heaters have two heating elements: one near the top of the tank and one near the bottom. Power enters the top and runs to the high-temperature cutoff switch, and then to the thermostats and elements. The top and bottom elements are controlled by separate thermostats. When the water on the top of the tank is hot, the top element turns off and the lower one heats. The upper and lower heating elements never come on at the same time.

Test the elements

You don't need electrical experience to check and replace the heating elements. But you do need to make very sure the power is off before you perform any tests or repairs.

First, find the circuit breaker in the main electrical panel that's labeled for the water heater and switch it off. Then go back to the water heater and test for power with the noncontact voltage detector. Make sure the tester is working by putting the tip into an outlet you know has power. The tester should indicate power by lighting up or beeping.

Now test the wires leading into the water heater. If they're covered by metal conduit, the tester won't read voltage. Instead you'll have to remove the metal thermostat cover on the side of the water heater, pull out the insulation and hold the tester near the wires leading into the top of the high-temperature cutoff switch (see Figure A).

COVER PLATE

1 REMOVE THE COVER PLATES
Turn off the power at the circuit breaker and remove the metal covers to expose the thermostats and elements. Make sure the power is off by touching the electrical connections with a noncontact voltage detector.

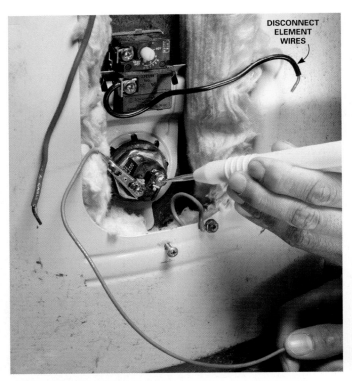

DISCONNECT
ELEMENT
WIRES

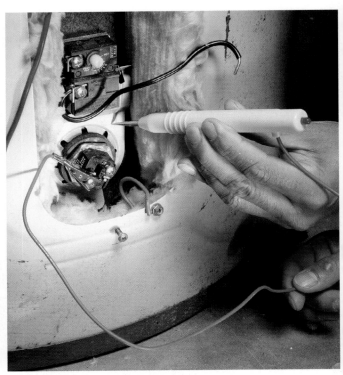

2 **TEST CONTINUITY FOR A BURNED-OUT ELEMENT**
Clip the alligator clamp onto one of the element screws and touch the other screw with the tester probe. If the tester doesn't light, replace the element.

3 **TEST FOR A SHORT CIRCUIT**
Clip the alligator clip to one of the element screws and touch the tester probe to the element mounting bracket. Repeat on the other screw. If the tester light comes on either time, there's a short. Replace the element.

Test both hot wires. Then hold the tester against the metal water heater shell. If the tester doesn't light up, it's safe to test the elements.

Test for a burned-out element

For this you'll need a continuity tester ($5 to $10). It's basically a lightbulb and battery with two wires attached. Touching the end of each wire to a continuous circuit will cause the bulb to light. You'll find both of these tools near the electrical testers in any hardware store or home center. You may also find a continuity tester called a "water heater tester" near the replacement elements.

If you own and understand a volt-ohm meter, you can test with it instead. To expose the elements for testing, remove the two metal covers, the insulation and the plastic covers on the side of the water heater.

First perform a continuity test to see if an element is burned out. Electricity won't flow through a burned-out element. Disconnect the wires from the terminal screws. Then connect the alligator clip to one terminal and touch the probe to the other one (Photo 2). The tester should light up, indicating a complete circuit. If there's no light, the element is bad.

Test for a shorted element

Next, test to see if the element is shorted out. If the element has a short, power will flow through the metal tank of the water heater. With the wires still disconnected, touch one probe (or connect the

The secret of the red button

Rarely, both elements will test OK, but you're still not getting hot water. Try pushing the button on the "high-temperature cutoff," located just above the upper thermostat. It may solve the problem, but if the problem recurs, check your heating elements.

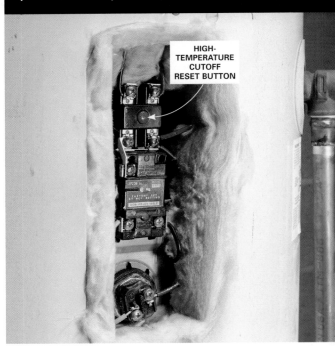

HIGH-
TEMPERATURE
CUTOFF
RESET BUTTON

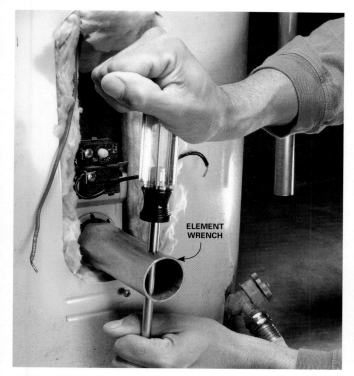

ELEMENT
WRENCH

4 **REMOVE THE BAD ELEMENT**
Drain the water from the tank and unscrew the old element using a heating element wrench. You'll need a long, sturdy Phillips screwdriver to turn the socket. If it won't unscrew, use a cold chisel and hammer to loosen the threads.

alligator clip) to one screw terminal and touch the other tester probe to the element mounting bracket (Photo 3). Repeat the test on the second terminal. If the tester lights on either test, the element has a short; replace it. Test both terminals on both elements.

Replace an element

To replace an element, start by draining the tank. With the power still turned off, close the cold-water inlet valve (Figure A). Open the hot water faucet in the kitchen. Then connect a garden hose to the drain valve and open it to drain the tank. For thread-in–type elements like we show here, you'll need a water heater element wrench ($5 at home centers and hardware stores).

Try unscrewing the bad element by turning it counterclockwise (Photo 4). If it's stuck, you can try breaking it free with a cold chisel and ball peen hammer or a small maul. Set the chisel at an angle against the nut so that pounding on it will turn the nut in a counterclockwise direction. Then install the new element, using the wrench to tighten it, and reconnect the wires (Photo 5). Close the drain valve and fill the tank before switching on the circuit breaker.

If testing reveals the elements are good, the thermostat may be faulty. The thermostat testing procedure is complex, so we recommend simply replacing the thermostat(s). You don't have to drain the tank to replace a thermostat. Simply remove the old thermostat—they're usually held by a metal clip—transfer the wires to the corresponding terminals of the new thermostat, and attach the new thermostat.

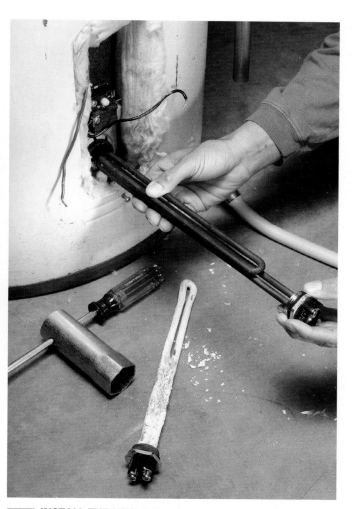

5 **INSTALL THE NEW ELEMENT**
Thread the new element into the water heater and tighten it with the heating element wrench. Reconnect the wires, making sure the connections are tight. Replace the insulation and metal covers.

Buying heating elements

Replace your heating element with one of the same wattage. If your old element isn't labeled with the wattage, refer to the nameplate on the water heater or your instruction manual, or search online using the model number from the nameplate.

Heating elements are held to the water heater either with a large thread and nut as shown here or by four bolts and nuts. Most home centers stock the version we show, but you can buy an adapter kit if you're replacing the four-bolt version.

Simple U-shape elements are the cheapest. More expensive low-density elements are usually folded back like the one shown in Photo 5. These provide the same amount of heat but spread out over a larger surface area, which lowers the surface temperature, making them less prone to mineral buildup.

If your old element was caked with minerals, replace it with a low-density element for more efficient operation and longer life.

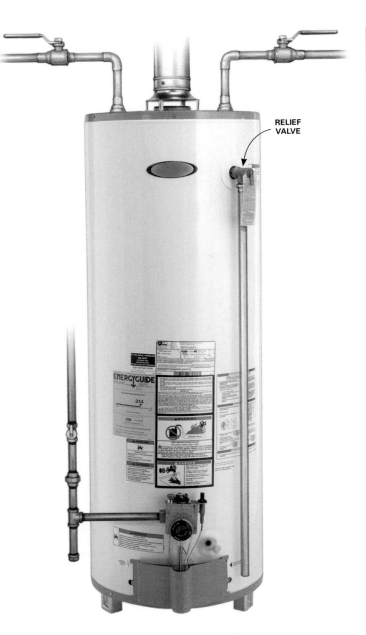

RELIEF VALVE

Never, ever plug the relief valve

As water heats up, it expands with tremendous force—enough to fracture the tank and launch the water heater through the roof (seriously, that does occasionally happen). The temperature and pressure relief valve prevents this by opening if the tank pressure becomes too high. But when a relief valve lets off a little pressure (or just leaks), some homeowners "fix" it by plugging the valve or the pipe connected to it. A very, very bad idea. Furnace boilers also have relief valves, and blocking them is just as dangerous.

The ever-flowing water heater

When the plumber replaced one of the heating elements in my electric water heater, I watched carefully, knowing that the other element would eventually need replacing too. Sure enough, a year later the other element went. I checked it with an ohmmeter, confirmed my diagnosis and headed to the plumbing supply store. When I returned home, I killed the power supply at the electrical panel and at the wall switch. Feeling proud and confident, I dragged the garden hose into the house, connected it to the heater and ran it into the floor drain to empty the heater—just like the plumber had done. Then I sat and waited for the water to stop flowing. After about an hour of a good, steady flow, it occurred to me to SHUT OFF THE WATER SUPPLY! Fifteen minutes later and hundreds of gallons of water poorer, I replaced the element.

—**Dianna Tucker**

Washing machine won't drain?

If the water won't drain out of your washing machine, either something is stuck in the drain hose or pump, or the pump is broken. Both fixes are simple if you're even just a little bit handy with tools. We're showing the repair on a Maytag washing machine.

Start by unplugging the machine and emptying the water. Bail the water out of the tub, or you can drain the tub using gravity by placing the drain hose on the floor near the drain or in a bucket. Clamp the hose to prevent any remaining water from running out (Photo 3). Once the washer's empty, support the front of it on paint cans or stacked 2x4s. Photo 1 shows where to find the screws that hold the front panel in place. Remove the panel and you'll see the pump. The pump has a translucent housing, so you might even see the offending piece of clothing wrapped up in the pump. Photo 3 shows what to do if the pump is clogged. If you don't see the clog in the pump or in the hose near the pump, then it could be stuck in the outlet where the hose connects to the bottom of the tub. To find out, loosen the clamp that holds the hose to the bottom of the tub and remove the hose. Have a bucket and sponge handy, though. Any water that's left in the machine will run out. When you locate the piece of clothing, pull it out with needle-nose pliers.

If nothing is clogging the hose or pump, the pump could be shot, although in most cases you'll hear noise from a bad pump, and it'll start to leak if you don't replace it right away. Photo 4 shows how to remove the pump. Buy a new one to match. You can find a new pump online or go to your local appliance parts center. You'll need the brand and model number for proper part identification. Model numbers are usually stamped on a small metal plate located under the tub lid or on the top, side or back of the machine. Copy down all the plate information, or snap a photo, and use it to access online parts suppliers, or take it along to the parts distributor. Install the new pump by attaching it with screws and connecting the hoses, and then reinstall the belt.

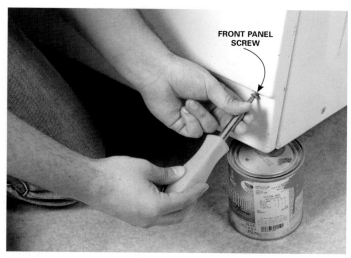

FRONT PANEL SCREW

1 REMOVE PANEL SCREWS
Unplug the washer. Then prop up the washer and remove the two screws that secure the front panel.

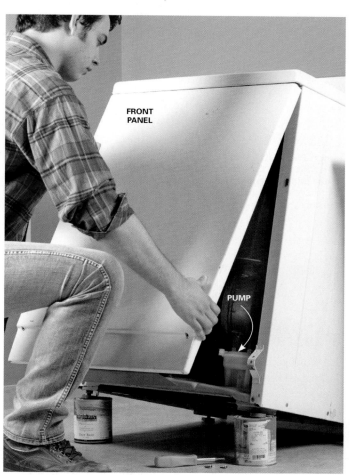

FRONT PANEL

PUMP

2 REMOVE THE FRONT PANEL
Pull the lower edge of the panel outward and "unhook" the top. On a Whirlpool washer, you'll have to remove the entire shell to access the pump.

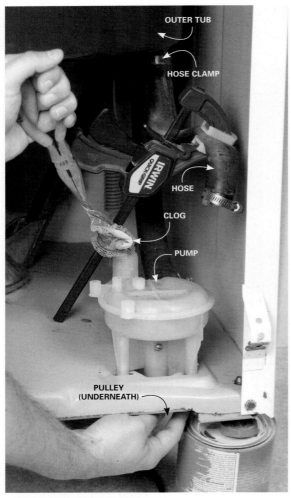

OUTER TUB

HOSE CLAMP

HOSE

CLOG

PUMP

PULLEY
(UNDERNEATH)

PUMP

PULLEY

BELT

3 **PULL OUT THE CLOG**
Remove the belt from the pulley on the bottom side of the pump. It's spring-loaded, so it comes off easily. Then remove the hose, and if the clog is visible, pull it out. Twist the pulley to unwind the fabric as you pull it out.

4 **REMOVE THE PUMP**
If the impeller inside the pump is damaged (reach your finger inside to feel for broken fins) or if the pump leaks or makes noise, you'll have to replace it. Remove the three screws that hold the pump to the washer. Buy a new pump and install it.

Great goofs

F is for flub—and flood

I couldn't get the valves that fed my washing machine to stop leaking, so I replaced the entire faucet assembly. The installation went fine. I reconnected the washer hoses, double-checked for leaks and washed my first load of clothes. Satisfied with my leak-free connections, I went upstairs.

Everything worked perfectly—until I returned to the laundry room and found myself standing in a pool of soapy water. Unfortunately, I'd forgotten to put the drain line back into the laundry tub and an entire washer's worth of dirty water had poured onto my floor. Talk about washed up!

—**William C. Sinclair**

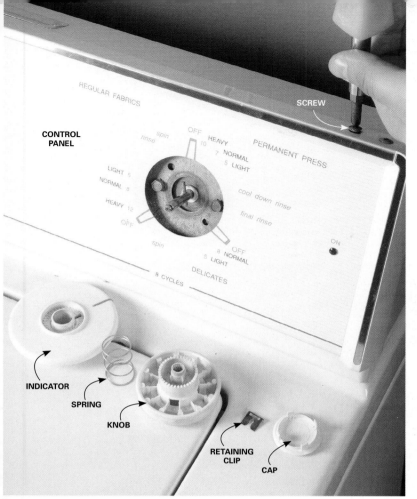

CONTROL PANEL

SCREW

REGULAR FABRICS

spin
rinse
OFF
HEAVY
10
7 NORMAL
5 LIGHT
PERMANENT PRESS

LIGHT 5
NORMAL 8
HEAVY 12
OFF

cool down rinse
final rinse

spin
OFF
8 NORMAL
5 LIGHT
ON

DELICATES

8 CYCLES

INDICATOR

SPRING

KNOB

RETAINING CLIP

CAP

1 **ACCESS THE CONTROLS**
Unplug the washer. Then remove the screws that hold the control panel in place and tip the top of the panel forward.

Washer stuck on one cycle?

If your washing machine is stuck on one cycle and doesn't advance, the timer is broken. Replacing a timer is simple, but it's not cheap. A new one will run about $120. Still, that's less than a new washer.

Photos 1 and 2 show how to remove the old timer. To start, unplug the machine and remove the control knob. On this Maytag washer, you pry off the plastic disc in the center of the knob to reveal a clip that holds the knob. Arrange the parts in order as you take them off so reassembly will be easier. Photo 3 shows how to install the new timer. Contact the manufacturer of your washer or the local appliance repair parts store to find a new timer.

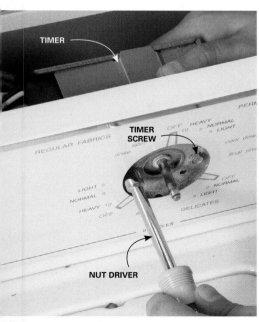

TIMER

TIMER SCREW

REGULAR FABRICS

NUT DRIVER

2 **REMOVE THE TIMER**
Use a nut driver to remove the screws that hold the timer to the front panel. Pull the timer back and out.

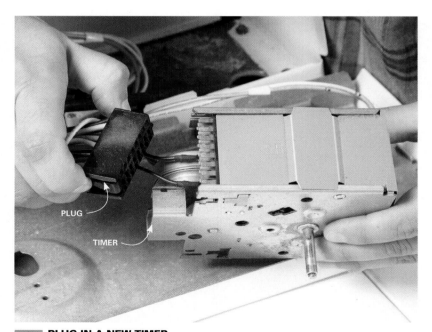

PLUG

TIMER

3 **PLUG IN A NEW TIMER**
Press in on the plastic retainer clips on each side of the plug and pull the plug from the timer. Push the plug into the new timer and put everything back together in the reverse order.

Front-loading washer won't drain?

If your front-loading washing machine doesn't drain, there could be an easy fix, especially if you own a newer Maytag washer. Even though some instruction manuals don't mention it, there's a filter near the water pump that catches stuff before it gets into the pump and causes damage. If the filter gets clogged, it can prevent your machine from draining. In some cases, a code number will show up on the digital display. If you look up the code in the instruction manual, it will indicate a problem with suds or tell you to check the filter. On Maytag front loaders, it's easy to avoid these problems by cleaning the filter every six months. On newer Maytag machines, you can access the filter easily by removing the front panel (Photo 1). On Frigidaire and some other brands, the filter is part of the pump and you'll have to remove a hose or the entire pump to clean it.

1   REMOVE THE FRONT PANEL
Tilt washer back and slide blocks under the front legs for easier access to the screws. Remove the screws and lift off front panel.

2   TWIST OFF THE FILTER
If your washer has a filter that's separate from the drain pump, you'll see it alongside the pump. Unscrew the filter by turning it counterclockwise. Clean it out and reinstall it.

For better performance, check the water temperature

Fill the washer as usual, but before the cycle starts, check the water temperature with a thermometer.

Water coming from the cold water tap can be pretty chilly during the winter (or year-round if you have a well). According to washing machine manufacturers, if the water is colder than 65 degrees F, the additives in laundry detergent won't work as well—and powder detergents won't fully dissolve. Cold water for washing should be in the 65- to 85-degree F range or clothes won't get completely clean.

To find out if your clothes are getting a good wash, check the water temperature with a cooking thermometer (one that registers low temperatures) when you do a cold, a warm and a hot wash. If the water temperature is below 65 degrees F for cold water washes, boost it by selecting warm water for part of the initial fill cycle. If the warm water wash is below 85 degrees F (a common problem during winter or when the washing machine is at the opposite end of the house from the water heater), try the hot water setting instead for all or part of the wash cycle. Or run the hot water tap into the laundry tub until it gets hot, then turn on the washer.

Always leave rinse settings on cold, no matter what washing temperature you choose. Cold water rinses are just as effective as warm, and you'll save a lot of energy.

Faster flow for a slow-filling washer

If your washing machine fills with a slow trickle, you might need a fill/inlet valve. But chances are you have a simpler problem: plugged inlet screens. These screens catch debris in the water supply and protect a washer's internal parts. Often, screens clog after a remodeling project or after work by city crews on water mains. Any work on water lines can loosen sediment in pipes and lead to plugged screens.

Cleaning the screens is a simple job. The only tricky part is removing the screens without wrecking them (Photo 1). Don't just yank them out. Gently squeeze and twist as you pull. You'll distort the screens a little, but you can mold them back into shape with your fingers.

If your screens are cemented in place by mineral deposits, you may not be able to remove them without damage. A new pair of screens will cost about $5 at an appliance parts store. Clean the screens with running water or blow out debris with an air compressor. You may have to pick and scrape away stubborn particles with a utility knife.

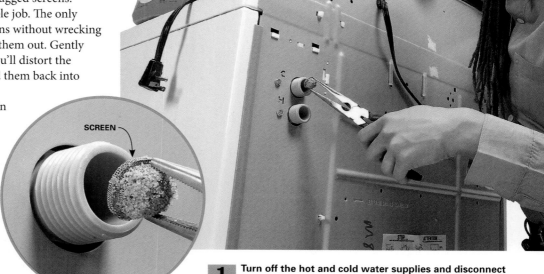

SCREEN

1 Turn off the hot and cold water supplies and disconnect the hoses. Use a pair of needle-nose pliers to gently remove the screens for cleaning.

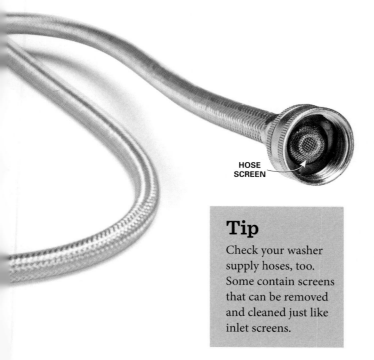

HOSE SCREEN

Tip

Check your washer supply hoses, too. Some contain screens that can be removed and cleaned just like inlet screens.

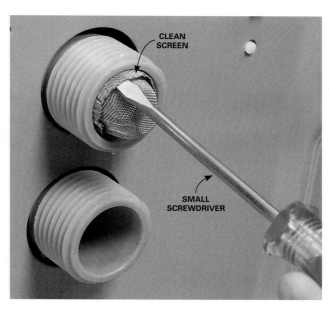

CLEAN SCREEN

SMALL SCREWDRIVER

2 Work the clean screen back into the inlet by pressing around the rim of the screen with a small screwdriver. Reconnect the hoses, turn on the water and check for leaks.

Preventive maintenance:

Avoid a flood with steel-belted washer hoses

If your washing machine is connected to bare rubber hoses, you're risking thousands of dollars' worth of water damage. Under constant water pressure, these hoses are prone to leaks or even bursting. That's why building codes say that the water supply should be shut off when the washer isn't in use—unless it's connected to no-burst hoses. No-burst hoses are encased in a woven metal sleeve that prevents weak spots in the rubber from developing into leaks. The hoses cost about $10 each at home centers, and installing them is as easy as connecting a garden hose.

1 INSTALL THE VALVES
Screw the new motorized valves onto the manual shutoff valves. Then attach the washing machine hoses. Tighten until snug with slip-joint pliers.

Avoid flooding disasters

Flooding from washing machines happens far more often than you think. In fact, washing machine floods hold a prominent place in the "Top 10" list of homeowner's insurance claims.

Even if you've already switched out your rubber hoses for "no-burst" braided hoses (you did that, right?), you're still at risk. The machine's water valve, drain hose and pump can fail and cause major damage. This is especially important if your washing machine is located on an upper floor, in a finished room or in a condo, where major flood damage can cost tens of thousands of dollars.

A washing machine valve shutoff kit (one choice is FloodStop No. FS3/4H-90; from amazon.com) puts all that concern to rest. When the floor-mounted sensor detects puddling, it instantly shuts off the water valve. The unit installs in less than 30 minutes with just slip-joint pliers (no soldering required). Here's how.

Turn off the water to the washing machine and remove the fill hoses from the valves. Then install the new motorized valves (Photo 1). Then mount the controller close to the nearest electrical receptacle and connect the wires (Photo 2). Locate the flood sensor below the washing machine (Photo 3). For additional protection, buy a few more sensors and daisy-chain them onto the first sensor. Then wet them and adjust the sensitivity at the controller.

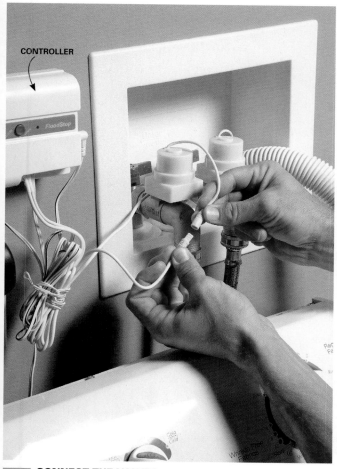

CONTROLLER

2 CONNECT THE VALVES
Plug the valve connectors into the wiring harness from the controller. It doesn't matter which wire goes to which connector plug.

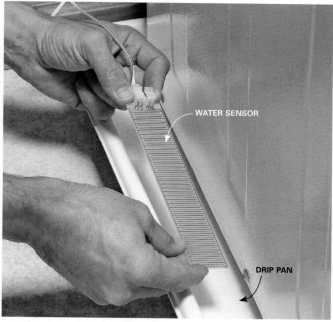

WATER SENSOR

DRIP PAN

3 PLACE THE FLOOD SENSOR
Slide the floor sensor into the washing machine drain pan (if you have one) or lay it on the floor below the washing machine.

Clean out the lint

Built-up lint inside dryer cabinets causes thousands of fires every year. Lint escapes through tiny gaps around the edges of the dryer drum and falls into the cabinet, especially when the exhaust vent or vent cap is clogged and airflow is restricted. The lint can get ignited by electric heating elements, gas burners or even a spark from the motor, and the flames then travel through the lint-lined exhaust vent. To make sure this doesn't happen in your house, check the exhaust vent and the inside of the cabinet frequently.

To clean the exhaust duct, shut off the gas and unplug the dryer, then pull the dryer away from the wall and disconnect the duct from the dryer. Use a brush and a vacuum to remove the lint in the duct. If you have a flexible duct (especially the plastic type!), replace it with rigid metal duct.

To clean inside the dryer, unplug it and turn off the gas, then open either the top or the front. The procedure is the same for gas and electric dryers. For dryers with a top lint filter and a solid front panel, remove the lint filter and take out the two screws on the side of the filter opening. Pull the top forward (Photo 1). Disconnect the door-switch wires in the front corner, remove the front screws and drop the panel forward (Photo 2). The drum will tip as the panel drops, but this won't damage anything. Just hold it up while you clean.

Brush and vacuum under the drum and at the top and back of the dryer. Clean thoroughly around the heating element, but work gently around wires and mechanical parts. Use a long brush to clean the vent, then vacuum it from the top and back (Photo 3).

Finally, reassemble the dryer. Put the front into the drum and lift, then drop the front into the catches near the bottom while holding it tight against the sides. Reattach the front screws and wires, then set the top back down.

If your dryer has a lint filter at the top:

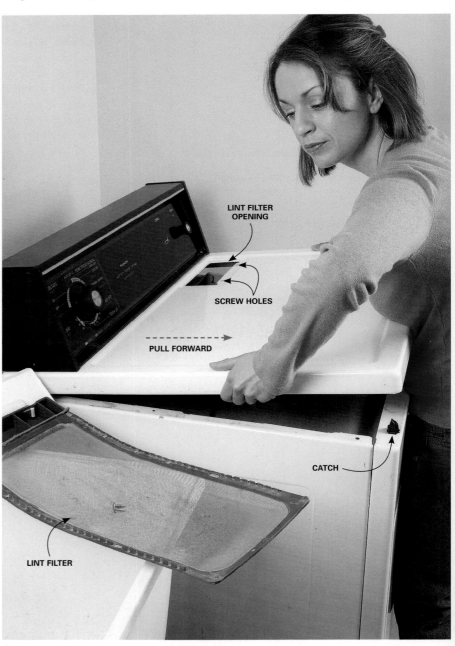

LINT FILTER OPENING

SCREW HOLES

PULL FORWARD

CATCH

LINT FILTER

1 Remove the screws under the lint filter, then jerk the top forward and lift it up to release it from the catches at the corners.

2 Remove the two screws near the top, then tip the front forward and lift it clear of the bottom catches and the drum.

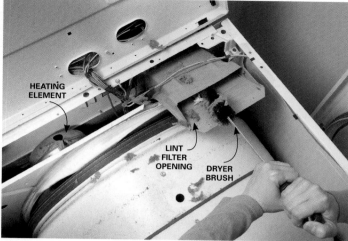

3 Brush out the lint inside the lint filter opening and vacuum all around the drum.

HEATING ELEMENT

LINT FILTER OPENING

DRYER BRUSH

If your dryer has a front access panel:

For dryers with a removable front panel, release the metal catches (or remove screws) and pull the panel off (Photo 1). Remove the screws that hold the vent in place, then clean out the lint with a vacuum and brush (Photo 2).

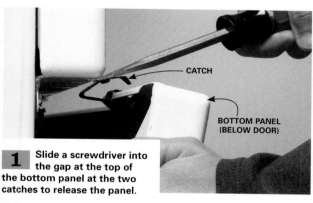

CATCH

BOTTOM PANEL (BELOW DOOR)

1 Slide a screwdriver into the gap at the top of the bottom panel at the two catches to release the panel.

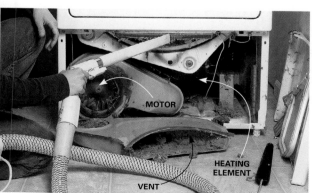

MOTOR

HEATING ELEMENT

VENT

2 Vacuum out the motor, the vent and the inside of the dryer. Clean carefully around wires and small parts to avoid breaking them.

DRYER FILTER

Clean the lint filter

A common cause of poor drying is a clogged lint filter. The filter may look clean, but it may actually be covered by a nearly invisible film caused by dryer sheets. This film reduces airflow and forces the thermostat to shut off the heat before your clothes are dry. Pull out the filter and scrub it in hot water with a little laundry detergent and a stiff kitchen brush.

Also check the outside dryer vent for any lint that may have built up there. The louver door–style vent covers are notorious for lint buildup, which traps heat and turns the heat off in the dryer. Pull the cover completely off to get to these clogs.

Pro Tip

Test your filter by pouring water into it. If the filter holds water, it's past time to clean it.

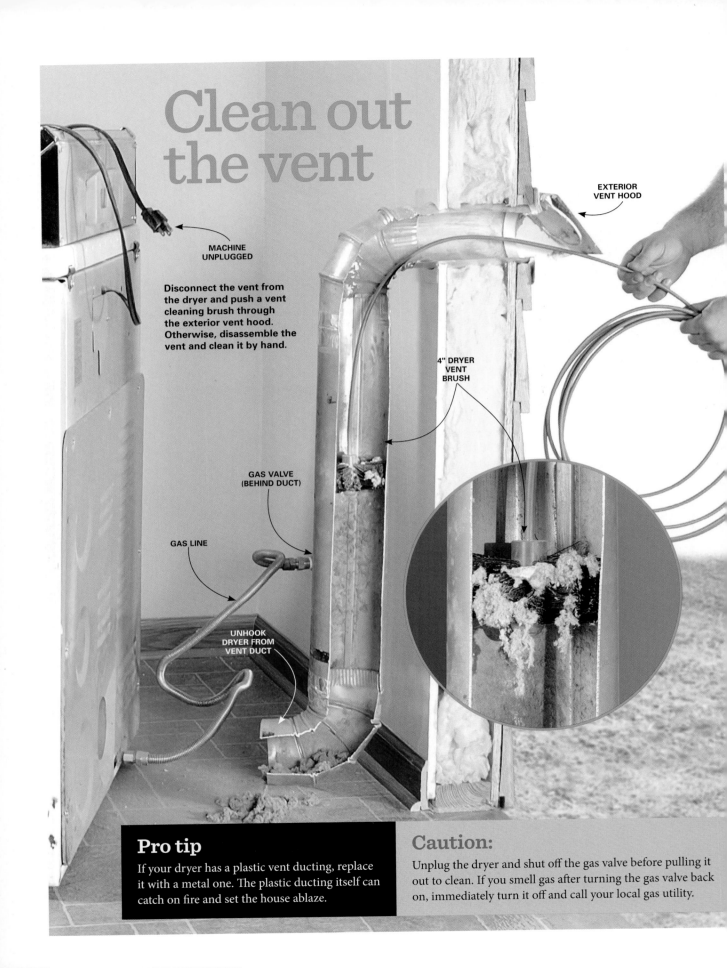

Clean out the vent

EXTERIOR VENT HOOD

MACHINE UNPLUGGED

Disconnect the vent from the dryer and push a vent cleaning brush through the exterior vent hood. Otherwise, disassemble the vent and clean it by hand.

4" DRYER VENT BRUSH

GAS VALVE (BEHIND DUCT)

GAS LINE

UNHOOK DRYER FROM VENT DUCT

Pro tip

If your dryer has a plastic vent ducting, replace it with a metal one. The plastic ducting itself can catch on fire and set the house ablaze.

Caution:

Unplug the dryer and shut off the gas valve before pulling it out to clean. If you smell gas after turning the gas valve back on, immediately turn it off and call your local gas utility.

1 Cut the old caulk with a utility knife and pull out the vent from the outside.

METAL TAPE

NEW CAULK

2 Insert the duct from the dryer into the new vent duct and wrap the joint with metal tape.

Replace a broken dryer vent cap

Dryer vent caps are deliberately lightweight so they'll open easily, but this flimsiness also means they'll break easily. The caps, especially the type with multiple small flaps, also clog easily with lint. (Avoid this type unless you're conscientious about cleaning it.)

To replace an old vent cap, first pull apart the duct at the last joint inside the house. If they don't pull apart easily, look for small screws holding the sections of pipe together. Next, remove the screws or nails used to attach the cap to the siding and cut through the caulk around the edges (Photo 1). Pull out the cap, scrape away old caulk and dirt, and then wipe the siding clean so new caulk will stick.

Cut the new vent pipe to the same length as the old one, then slide it through the wall. Screw the cap to the siding and caulk around the edges with paintable caulk.

Finally, join the old duct inside the house to the new vent (Photo 2). Vent caps are available at home centers.

Crushed and clogged

Metal "semirigid" duct is a safe option for dryer venting. Building codes and dryer manufacturers typically allow lengths up to 8 ft. But be careful not to crush it. The dent in this duct caused lint buildup and blockage, which led to an expensive dryer breakdown. It could have caused a dangerous dryer fire.

SEMIRIGID FLEXIBLE DUCT

RIGID METAL "PIPE"

Quick fix for a dryer door

If your dryer door won't stay closed, chances are the latch is either bent or missing, or the strike is worn. The fix is cheap and easy. Buy the parts from any appliance parts store. Then grab pliers, a couple of small, straight-slot screwdrivers and a roll of masking tape.

Grab the bent or broken latch and yank it out. Then install the new one (Photo 1). Next, protect the door's finish with tape and remove the old strike (Photo 2). Snap in the new strike and you're back in the laundry business.

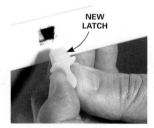

NEW LATCH

1 POP IN THE NEW LATCH
Line up the replacement latch with the hole and push in firmly until the locking tabs seat.

2 PRY OUT THE OLD STRIKE
Jam a small screwdriver into the strike and bend the metal locking tab inward. Pry upward with a second screwdriver to pop it out.

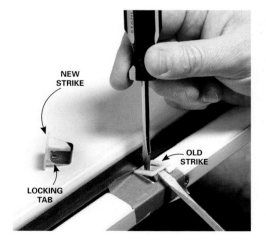

NEW STRIKE

OLD STRIKE

LOCKING TAB

You can solve most problems yourself—
no experience necessary!

Dryer repair guide

If your dryer breaks down, here's the first thing to know: You can solve most dryer troubles yourself. There's no need to find a technician, schedule a service call or pay a couple hundred dollars for repairs.

The fixes we show here correct about 90 percent of dryer breakdowns. Most repairs take about an hour, but set aside extra time to locate replacement parts. To find parts, search online for "appliance parts." Aside from basic tools like a socket set and screwdrivers, you may need a continuity tester or multimeter to diagnose the problem.

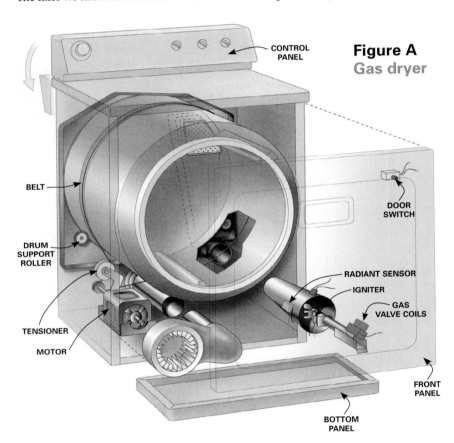

Figure A
Gas dryer

CONTROL PANEL

DOOR SWITCH

BELT

DRUM SUPPORT ROLLER

RADIANT SENSOR

IGNITER

GAS VALVE COILS

TENSIONER

MOTOR

FRONT PANEL

BOTTOM PANEL

Using a continuity tester

Our photos show using a multimeter to diagnose trouble. But a continuity tester will also work for all the troubleshooting. To use a continuity tester, simply attach the clamp to one contact point and touch the probe to the other. If the light glows, you've got continuity. If not, you've got trouble.

Tip

The first step in any appliance repair is to make sure it's getting electricity. Unplugged cords and tripped breakers are a leading cause of appliance "breakdowns."

Caution

Don't get shocked! Unplug the dryer before you do any disassembly, diagnostic or repair work. On a gas dryer, also turn off the gas supply shutoff valve.

Dryer disassembly

Most dryer repairs require some disassembly of the outer cabinet so you can get at the parts inside. If your dryer's lint filter is inside the front door (Figure A), disassemble it this way: First, remove the screws at each corner of the control panel. Flip the panel up and back to expose the screws in the top panel. Remove the screws, then pull the top toward you and lift it off. To open the bottom panel, release the spring catches by shoving a putty knife into the slot just above them. With the bottom panel open, you can remove the front panel by removing two screws at the top and two at the bottom.

If your filter slides into the top of the dryer, remove the screws alongside the filter slot. Using a putty knife, release the two spring catches located under the top panel at the front. Tilt the top panel up like a car hood and remove the screws that hold the front panel in place.

Dryer won't start

If your dryer seems absolutely dead when you turn it on, chances are the door switch is bad or the plunger is broken or bent. Door switches wear out from normal use, but repeatedly slamming the door can speed up their demise. Start by checking the plunger located on the door. If it's missing or bent, replace it. If the plunger checks out, the next step is to remove the top cabinet panel to gain access to the door switch.

Test the switch for continuity. If the switch is good, test the thermal fuse mounted on the blower housing. If you have a gas dryer with the lint filter in the door, access the thermal fuse by opening the bottom panel. If the filter slides into the top of the machine, remove the entire front panel. On an electric dryer, remove the rear service panel. If you don't get a continuity reading from the thermal fuse, do NOT simply replace it. A blown thermal fuse is a warning that you have other serious problems— either a malfunctioning thermostat or a clogged vent. Fix those before replacing the fuse.

DOOR SWITCH

Pull the wires off the door switch. Open and close the door while testing for continuity. If you don't get continuity, replace the switch.

Dryer thumps, rumbles or chirps

The drum support rollers are worn. Replace all of them ($25; shown below). If the noise continues, replace the tensioner roller (p. 47). Since it takes longer to disassemble the machine than to actually replace the rollers and belts, we recommend replacing both of them at the same time—total parts cost is $45.

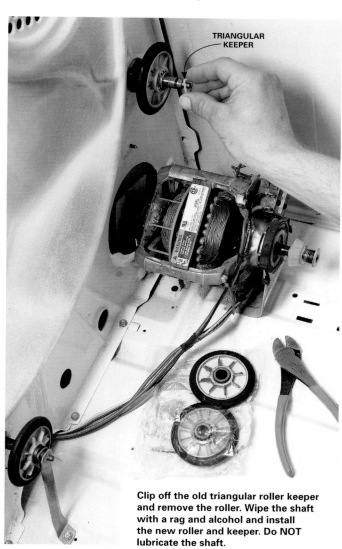

TRIANGULAR KEEPER

Clip off the old triangular roller keeper and remove the roller. Wipe the shaft with a rag and alcohol and install the new roller and keeper. Do NOT lubricate the shaft.

No heat

If you have an electric or gas dryer that tumbles but won't heat, check the thermal fuse for continuity. If the thermal fuse checks out, move on to the radiant sensor if you have a gas dryer. It monitors the igniter and powers up the gas valve coils when the igniter reaches peak temperature. A bum sensor will stop the whole show. Test it for continuity (Photo 1) and replace it if it fails. If the sensor is good, disconnect the electrical connector to the igniter and check it for continuity. Again, replace it if it fails the continuity test. If both the radiant sensor and the igniter pass the test, replace the gas valve coils. To replace them, remove the retaining plate, unplug the sensors and pull them off the gas valve.

If the thermal fuse on your electric dryer checks out, test the heater element for continuity. Replace the element if you don't get continuity (Photos 2 and 3).

THERMAL FUSE

RADIANT SENSOR

IGNITER

GAS VALVE COILS

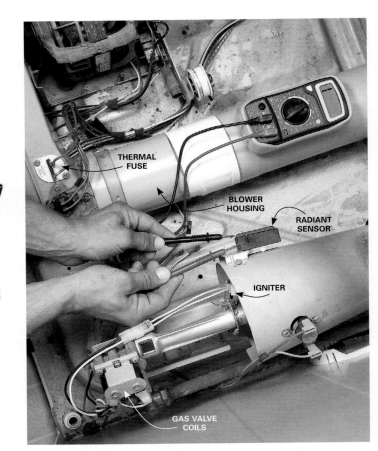

1 On a gas dryer, test the radiant sensor, igniter and thermal fuse by disconnecting the wires and checking for continuity. Replace them if they fail the continuity test.

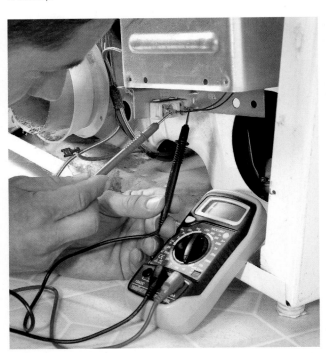

2 Disconnect the wires to the heating element of an electric dryer and test it for continuity. Replace the element if you don't get a continuity reading.

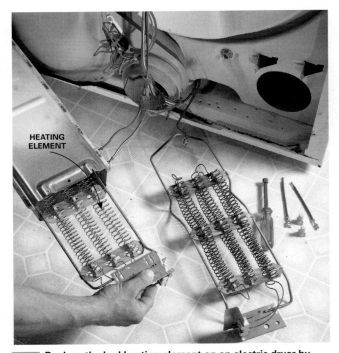

HEATING ELEMENT

3 Replace the bad heating element on an electric dryer by unscrewing the retaining clip at the top of the heater box. Then pull out the box and remove the element retaining screw. Swap the elements and reinstall.

Drum won't rotate, but the motor runs

You're in luck—it's only a broken belt. Remove the front cabinet panel and lift the entire drum out of the cabinet. Now's the time to fire up your shop vacuum and suck out all the lint. Then spin the tensioner roller by hand to see if it runs smoothly and examine it for cracks. Replace the tensioner if it fails either test. Reinstall the drum and wrap the new belt around it (ribs facing the drum). Some tensioners are mounted behind the motor, so they're difficult to see from the front access panel. You'll have to do this by feel. Reach your hands around the blower housing and lift the tensioner up while you route the belt around the motor pulley.

Route the new belt around the drum and toward the motor/tensioner assembly. Reach your hands around the motor and retract the tensioner so you can wrap the belt around the motor pulley.

Great goofs

Attention-getting dryer

I was installing a new, quieter dryer in a client's high-end house. The power cord was unattached and had exposed connectors at one end. Like an idiot, I pushed the plug into the 240-volt outlet to see if the prongs fit. Well, the connectors at the other end were all touching one another and—WHAM!

The loose ends shorted out and knocked me clear over. This in turn set off the house alarm system, alerted the police and set every dog in the neighborhood barking.

It's bad enough to goof—it's far worse to have to explain your screwup to your client and your boss, a crowd of curious onlookers and the police.

—**Ben Rall**

Fourth time's the charm

Our washing machine was on the fritz. It's a heavy stacked unit (dryer on top) that's tucked into a tight wall recess, so it's tough to maneuver. After 45 minutes of pulling and straining, I got it out from the wall and spotted the problem right away—a broken clutch. But because it was too late in the day to get the part and the unit was blocking the hallway to the kitchen, I had to push the whole thing back against the wall.

The next day I did the backbreaking 45-minute thing over again and replaced the clutch. Then I reattached the supply hoses, pushed the unit back into place and started it. Oh, man—water began coming out from underneath the washer! I'd forgotten to reattach the drain hose! Once again, I pulled the whole thing out from the wall. Then I reattached the drain hose, pushed the unit back yet again, started it and hallelujah, it seemed to work fine—no leaks.

The next day my wife discovered hot water coming out during the cold cycle. I'd switched the hot and cold hoses when I reattached them! Which meant I had to....

—John Klube

Hold on!

We wanted to move our washer and dryer down to the basement. Although my wife was due home shortly to help, I decided to get a start on it. I loaded the dryer onto a dolly and rolled it toward the steep, narrow staircase.

I was in trouble immediately. The dryer began to pull me forward, so I dropped to the floor and lodged my feet against both sides of the doorjamb.

Ten minutes later my wife arrived home to find me sprawled at the head of the stairs, sweating and holding on to the dolly with all I had. She began giggling uncontrollably.

One of us had to get below the dryer, but the staircase was too narrow to squeeze past. Luckily, there's an exterior door leading to our basement.

While my wife held the dolly, I rushed outside and frantically cut a hole in the locked door.

The two of us were able to lower the dryer down safely. The basement door still has a big cutout in it; it reminds me to ask for help.

— John McAllister

Splash guard

Got a garbage disposal that spits, um, garbage at you? Forget about replacing the entire unit. You can install a new splash guard (purchase at a home center) in about 20 minutes, and you don't need any special tools.

If your garbage disposal is hard-wired, start by flipping off the circuit breaker. If it plugs in, unplug it. Stack up books or lumber to support the disposal. Then remove the drainpipe and disconnect the quick-connect fitting (Photo 1). Replace the old splash guard with a new one (Photo 2).

The hardest part of reinstallation is hoisting the disposal up and into place with one hand while you try to engage the locking ring with the other. Forget about that. Use our tip in Photo 3.

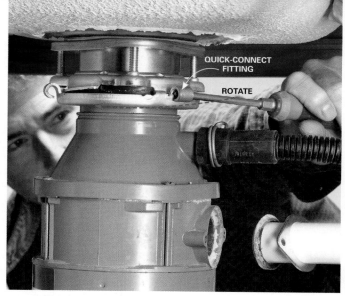

QUICK-CONNECT FITTING

ROTATE

1 DISCONNECT THE DISPOSAL
Jam a screwdriver into the locking ring and rotate it away from you. The disposal will drop onto the books or lumber below. Support it with one hand so it doesn't tip over.

NEW SPLASH GUARD

2 REPLACE THE SPLASH GUARD
Grab the lower edge of the old rubber guard and peel it up and off. Then slip the new one on and push it down until it seats.

3 RECONNECT THE DISPOSAL
Shove several shims between the books or lumber and the bottom of the disposal until the locking ring just touches the sink flange. Then just rotate the ring to lock it in place. Reinstall the drain line, do a leak test and grind away.

HOLD-DOWN PLATE

SHIMS

Clean a stinky garbage disposal

BRUSH OFF THE CRUD AND RINSE
Dip an old toothbrush in antibacterial grease-cutting kitchen cleaner (Clorox Antibacterial Degreaser is one choice) and lift up one corner of the splash guard. Scrub off the crud and rinse with cold water. Repeat with each flap until it's totally clean and rinsed.

GREASE AND FOOD

SPLASH GUARD

Even if you run your garbage disposal until the last shred of food is gone, and you let the water run the recommended time, you can still wind up with an out-of-control science experiment that stinks up your kitchen. Face it; some food is going to stick to the inside of the grinding chamber, and it's going to decay. You can clean the chamber by grinding ice and lemon rinds, adding baking soda or rinsing with vinegar and water. Or you can add commercial cleaners like Disposer Care, which is available at discount stores and most home centers.

However, if you don't clean the underside of the splash guard, you haven't finished the job and may still wind up with a stinker. Cleaning the splash guard is easier than you think. You don't even have to remove it. Just clean it with a toothbrush and cleaner as shown.

Maintain your dishwasher

4 simple steps solve most problems

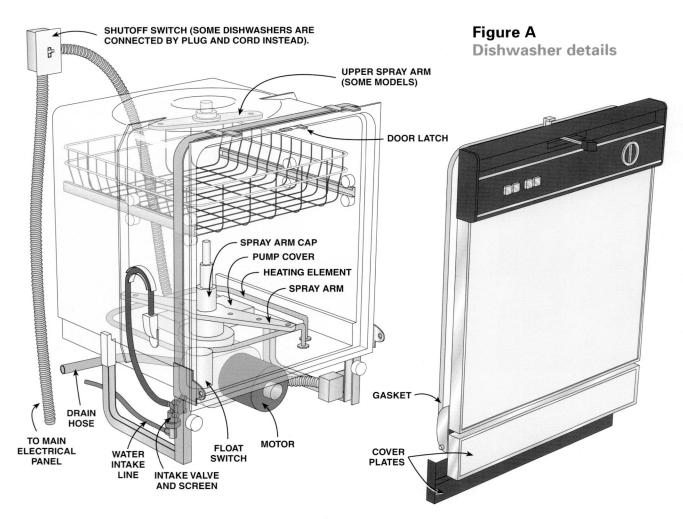

SHUTOFF SWITCH (SOME DISHWASHERS ARE CONNECTED BY PLUG AND CORD INSTEAD).

UPPER SPRAY ARM (SOME MODELS)

Figure A
Dishwasher details

DOOR LATCH

SPRAY ARM CAP
PUMP COVER
HEATING ELEMENT
SPRAY ARM

GASKET

DRAIN HOSE

TO MAIN ELECTRICAL PANEL

WATER INTAKE LINE

FLOAT SWITCH

INTAKE VALVE AND SCREEN

MOTOR

COVER PLATES

Tip

Adding a water softening system can dramatically improve your dishwasher's performance.

Review the basics (5 minutes)

► Are you overloading your dishwasher? Check the manufacturer's instructions to make sure you're loading it right.
► Does silverware drop below the lower basket? The spray arm can't spin if it's obstructed.
► Are you using the proper dishwasher detergent?
► Do you routinely scrape food bits off dishes before loading them into the racks? (Rinsing is not necessary.)
► Are you using a special rinsing agent if your water is hard (highly mineralized)? Hard water can leave a film on the dishes.
► Is the water temperature high enough? This can be a complex issue.

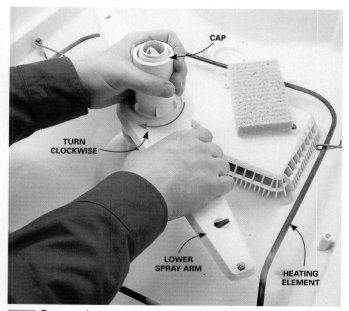

1 Remove the spray arm to clean it. Unscrew the cap, turning it clockwise, and lift off the arm.

Labels: CAP, TURN CLOCKWISE, LOWER SPRAY ARM, HEATING ELEMENT

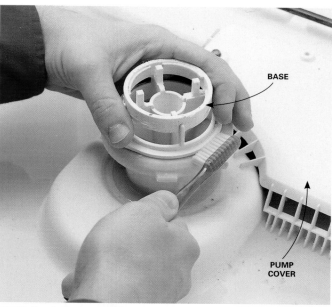

2 Scrub the base and spray arm with a toothbrush and wipe them with a sponge. Grease and debris collect on these parts.

Labels: BASE, PUMP COVER

We recommend that your household water heater be set no higher than 120 degrees F, both to help prevent accidental scalding and to maintain energy efficiency. Many dishwashers have heating elements that boost the temperature to about 140 degrees F. However, some dishwashers don't have a heating booster and require household water at about 140 degrees F. So first check the owner's manual for the recommended water heater setting.

If your dishwasher requires 140-degree F water, check the temperature of your hot water at its current setting. Put a meat thermometer in a glass and fill it at the kitchen faucet with water at its hottest point. If the temperature reads less than 140 degrees F, you'll have to either risk raising the water heater setting (we don't recommend it) or consider buying a different dishwasher. But check the maintenance steps below first to make sure poor cleaning isn't caused by other factors. In any case, consult a service pro before making a buying decision.

Clean the spray arm (10 minutes)

Twirl the spray arm to make sure it spins freely. Also check the holes in the spray arm for debris. If you spot debris or the spray arm doesn't spin, remove the spray arm and clean it (Photos 1 – 3). First take out the wire baskets by removing either a cap or pin at the end of the sliding tracks. Don't fret about a little water on the bottom of the tub. It's supposed to be there. It keeps the seals in the pump and in the motor assembly damp. If they dry out, they'll crack and leak.

The spray arm cap twists off with a clockwise turn, just the opposite of a regular screw (Photo 1). Twist ties, rubber bands and plastic and paper often show up in the spray arm. You might have to use needle-nose pliers to pick them out. The pump usually sucks up most of this stuff, but if you hear a sudden loud grinding sound while running the dishwasher, something like broken glass might be stuck in the pump intake. Unscrew and remove the pump cover (Photo 2) to check it out.

Clean the float switch (5 minutes)

The float switch may not be a problem, but it takes only a few minutes to check it, so open it up and clean it anyway (Photos 4 and 5). Debris can cause the float to stick in the raised position, which prevents the tub from filling. If the water doesn't reach the right level (just covering the heating element), the dishwasher won't clean well.

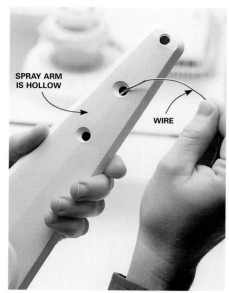

3 Poke a wire into the spray arm holes to clear debris that has collected inside. Then replace the spray arm and cap. Clean the top spray arm as well if the dishwasher has one.

Labels: SPRAY ARM IS HOLLOW, WIRE

See the next section for how to check the water level.

On most models, you'll find the float switch in the lower front of the tub (Figure A, p. 82 and Photo 4). The one shown has a cover, but some don't. You may have to use a small, flexible brush or pipe cleaner to clean those without a removable cover. When clean, the float should slide up and down freely.

How a dishwasher works

A dishwasher doesn't fill like a clothes washer. Instead, 2 to 3 gallons of water flood the lower portion of the tub, where it mixes with the detergent and is pumped through the rotating spray arms onto the dishes. The wash water drains and is replaced by fresh water to rinse the dishes. The cycle often repeats several times. A timer regulates the water volume. A heating element near the bottom raises the water temperature to 140 to 160 degrees F. The element also helps dry the dishes after the wash and rinse cycles are completed.

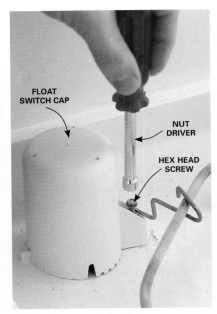

FLOAT SWITCH CAP

NUT DRIVER

HEX HEAD SCREW

4 Unscrew the hold-down screw on the float switch and lift the cap straight up and off.

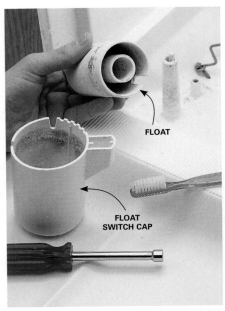

FLOAT

FLOAT SWITCH CAP

5 Clean all accessible parts of the float switch and cover with a toothbrush and sponge. Replace cap.

Dishwasher rack repair

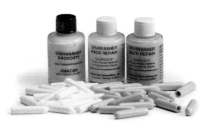

Dishwasher rack tines break off or lose the protective coating at the tips and then you get rust spots on your dishes. New racks are expensive, but you can fix yours in less than an hour and for about $17. Buy a bottle of vinyl repair paint and a package of replacement tips to match your rack color (from any appliance parts store or online). Cut off the rusted tips with a rotary tool and cutoff wheel. Then retip the tines (Photo 2).

To patch a rusted area around a broken tine, first clean off the rust (Photo 1).

1 CLEAN THE RACK
Load a wire brush into a rotary tool and zip off the old rust and vinyl. Keep brushing until you get to fresh metal. Then paint on a new coating.

2 APPLY PAINT AND NEW TIPS
Coat the freshly cut tip with vinyl paint. Then slip a new vinyl tip over the tine. Let it dry and you're good to go.

Problem: Dishes aren't getting clean

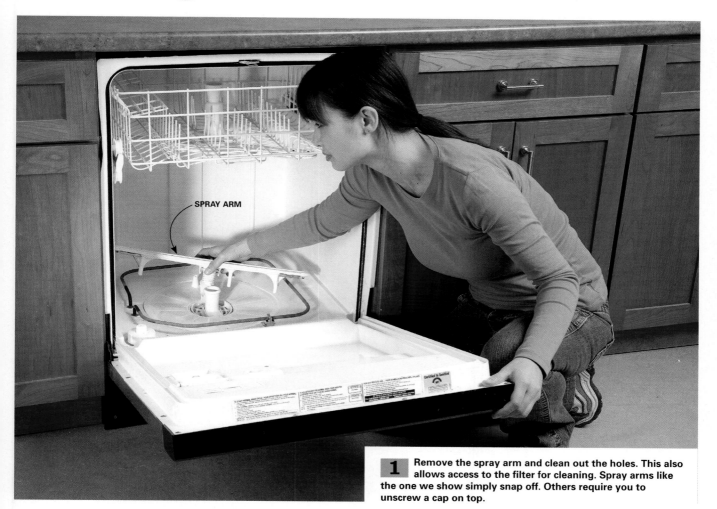

SPRAY ARM

1 Remove the spray arm and clean out the holes. This also allows access to the filter for cleaning. Spray arms like the one we show simply snap off. Others require you to unscrew a cap on top.

If your dishwasher is running but the dishes aren't getting clean, one of these simple fixes could solve your problem. Start by consulting your manual to be sure you're using the right detergent, loading the dishes correctly and maintaining the right hot water temperature. Follow Photos 1 – 5 for repair steps.

Insufficient water in the dishwasher also can cause poor cleaning. If the float gets stuck in the raised position, the dishwasher won't fill with water (Photo 3). Another likely cause is a clogged inlet screen or faulty inlet valve. Photos 4 and 5 show how to clean the screen or replace the valve. To determine if your dishwasher is getting enough water, start a wash cycle. Open the door when you hear the machine stop filling. The water should reach or come close to the heating coil. If not, first make sure the float valve is operating freely (Photo 3). If this doesn't solve the problem, check the inlet valve and screen.

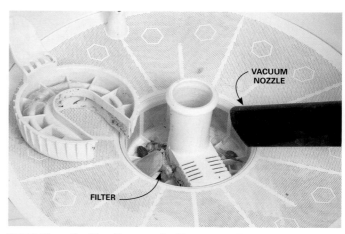

VACUUM NOZZLE

FILTER

2 Clean the filter. Remove the filter screen if possible. Otherwise, use a wet/dry vacuum to suck out the debris.

Replace the inlet valve

Inlet valves that are starting to fail sometimes make a hammering noise. If you hear this, replace the valve. But before you start any work on the dishwasher, unplug it or turn off the power at the shutoff switch or main circuit panel. Test to see if the power is off by turning on the dishwasher and making sure it doesn't run. You'll also have to shut off the water before removing the inlet switch. Usually you'll find a shutoff valve under the kitchen sink or in the basement or crawl space under the dishwasher. Otherwise, close the main water valve.

Photo 4 shows how to remove the inlet valve. Yours may look different. Whether you're replacing the valve or simply cleaning the screen, you'll have to unscrew the brass fitting that connects the water line to the valve. Remove the four screws that secure the valve to the bracket to access the filter screen (Photo 5). Reassemble and reinstall the valve in the reverse order. Wrap Teflon tape around the fitting threads before screwing the fitting into the valve.

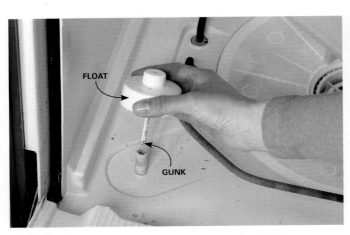

FLOAT

GUNK

3 Make sure the float moves up and down freely. If the float on your dishwasher is removable, take the float apart and clean it.

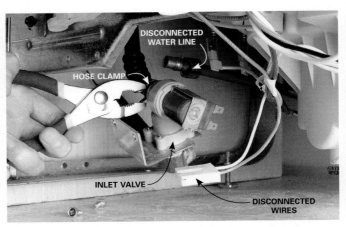

DISCONNECTED WATER LINE

HOSE CLAMP

INLET VALVE

DISCONNECTED WIRES

4 Remove the inlet valve to clean the screen or replace the valve. Unscrew the nut that connects the water line and remove the water line. Remove the screws that connect the valve bracket to the dishwasher frame and lower the valve. Pinch the hose clamp to remove the rubber hose. Unplug the wires.

SCREEN

INLET VALVE

BRACKET

WATER LINE FITTING

5 Check to see if the screen is plugged. Unscrew the water line fitting from the valve. Then unscrew the four screws that connect the valve to the bracket.

Sparkling dishwasher

Add a cup of vinegar to your empty dishwasher and let it run a full cycle once a month or so. Your kitchen may smell a bit like a pickle jar for a few hours, but hard-water lime buildup will be rinsed away, making your spray arm and other dishwasher parts work better.

Under-bed storage rack

If you're getting rid of your old dishwasher, hang on to the lower dish rack. Slip it under a bed for convenient roll-out storage.

But I followed the instructions!

When my garbage disposer went on the fritz, I purchased and then installed a new disposer that same day. Feeling good about conquering a problem without hiring a pro, I did a little victory dance in front of the sink when I turned on the disposer and everything worked perfectly.

That night, my dishwasher quit mid-wash and wouldn't drain. Since this problem was out of my comfort zone, I called for help. When the repairman showed up and looked under the sink, he asked who had installed the disposer. I hung my head and mumbled a quiet expletive, then explained that I'd followed the easy installation directions. "Yeah, but the directions don't mention that you're supposed to remove the factory plug from the drain line that runs to the dishwasher," he said. Sure enough, he unhooked the drain line, popped out the plug and solved the problem. But my oversight wasn't a total bust—the repairman showed me how to tune up and clean the dishwasher.

— **Mark Blair**

Water and ceilings don't mix

The spring and pulley on my dishwasher door broke, so I bought the part to fix it and made the repair in about 30 minutes. As I pushed the dishwasher back into place, I felt pretty good about saving the $100 I would have had to pay a repairman.

Early the next morning, while I was still enjoying a peaceful night's sleep, my wife ran into the bedroom screaming that the basement ceiling was falling down and the basement was flooded. Turns out, when I pushed the dishwasher back in, it pulled the water supply line free. The water ran onto the underlying ceiling all night, ruining everything below. That $100 I saved cost me $1,000 for a new ceiling and flooring.

— **George Louie**

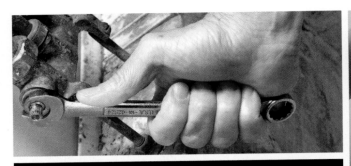

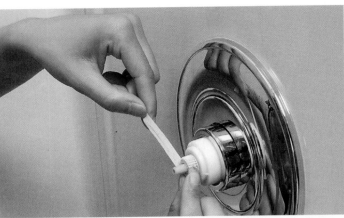

Special Section

PLUMBING FIXES

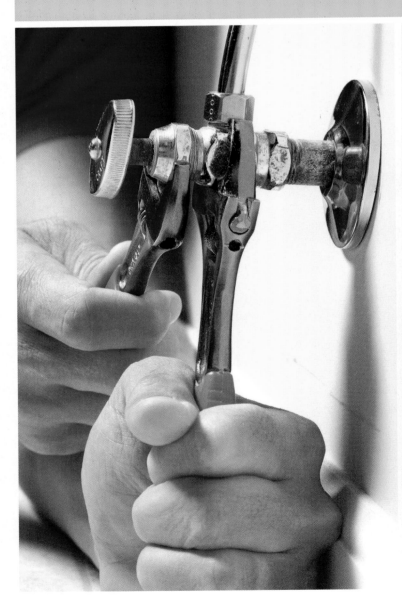

Replacing shutoff valves

If you're servicing or replacing a toilet or sink faucet, the first step is to shut off the water supply valve that feeds the fixture. But the simple task of shutting off the valve can be the start of a whole set of unexpected headaches.

Unless your house is fairly new, chances are you have multi-turn shutoff valves at every toilet and faucet. Shutoff valves perform flawlessly for years. But when they aren't opened or closed for a long time, you may find that the valve handle either won't turn or will turn but won't stop the water flow completely. And even if the valve does shut off the water, it may leak when you reopen it—the last thing you need after a plumbing repair!

You can spend time rebuilding the old valve, but the problems will just reappear years from now. The best way to deal with bad valves is to replace them with modern quarter-turn ball valves. They rarely lock up, leak or wear out and are inexpensive. Best of all, they'll take just an hour or so to install. Here's how to put them in.

Identify the valve connection style

Shutoff valves connect to copper plumbing pipes in one of two ways: compression fitting or sweat fitting. Identify the connection type used in your home by referring to the photos on p. 90. If you have an older home with galvanized pipes, we suggest hiring a plumber to do the switch-out. Unscrewing the old valve and screwing on a new one may seem easy enough. But if the pipe is rusted internally or the threads are rotted, this "simple" plumbing job can turn into a plumbing nightmare. If your home is plumbed with PEX or plastic pipe, these instructions don't apply.

Once you identify the connection type, buy a quarter-turn shutoff ball valve to match the size of the incoming copper pipe and the size of the supply tube connection. If you're replacing a sweat valve, you'll need a torch, flux, solder, emery cloth, wire

brushes and a flame protection cloth to shield the wall. This is also a good time to replace an old supply tube and a corroded escutcheon (wall trim plate).

Prepare for valve replacement

Shut off the water at the main shutoff valve. If you have a gas water heater, turn the knob to the "pilot" position. Shut off the circuit breakers to an electric water heater. Then open a faucet on the lowest level of your house and another faucet on

an upper level to drain the pipes. Then disconnect the supply tube from the shutoff valve. Replace the valve.

After replacement

Close the new valve. Then open the water-main shutoff valve and let the water run until all the air is out of the pipes. Then shut off the upper and lower faucets. Check the new valves for leaks. Turn the water heater gas valve back to "on" or flip on the circuit breakers to the electric water heater.

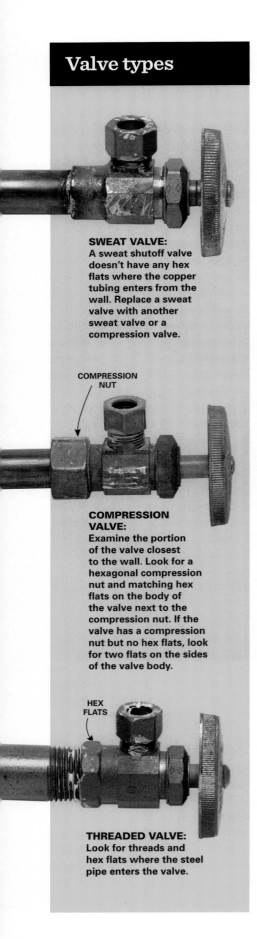

Valve types

SWEAT VALVE:
A sweat shutoff valve doesn't have any hex flats where the copper tubing enters from the wall. Replace a sweat valve with another sweat valve or a compression valve.

COMPRESSION NUT

COMPRESSION VALVE:
Examine the portion of the valve closest to the wall. Look for a hexagonal compression nut and matching hex flats on the body of the valve next to the compression nut. If the valve has a compression nut but no hex flats, look for two flats on the sides of the valve body.

HEX FLATS

THREADED VALVE:
Look for threads and hex flats where the steel pipe enters the valve.

Replace a sweat valve

Hold the valve with pliers, loosen the packing nut and unscrew the entire valve stem. Peek inside and remove the old washer if it's stuck on the seat. Removing the valve stem allows any remaining water to drain out, making the unsweating process easier. Before you do any torch work, make sure there's a fire extinguisher nearby and safeguard the wall with a flame protection cloth. Then remove the old valve (Photo 1) and the remaining solder (Photo 2).

New sweat valve

Clean the tubing with emery cloth. If you're replacing a sweat valve with a compression valve, sand off all traces of solder before adding the new escutcheon, nut and sleeve. Otherwise, remove enough old solder to allow the new sweat valve to slide onto the tubing. Remove the stem and wire-brush the opening in the new quarter-turn valve and apply flux to the valve and the copper tubing. With the flame protection cloth in place, heat the valve just enough to draw in the solder.

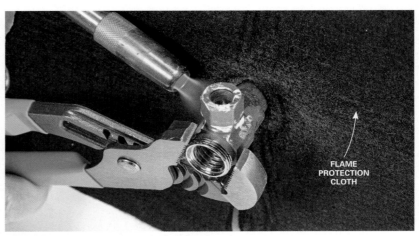

FLAME PROTECTION CLOTH

1 **REMOVE THE OLD SWEAT VALVE**
Drape the flame protection cloth over the copper tubing and tape it to the wall. Adjust the torch to a small flame and aim it toward the body of the valve. As soon as the solder melts, twist and pull the valve off the copper tubing with pliers.

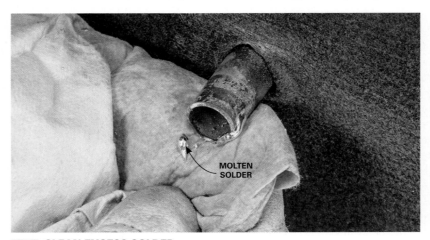

MOLTEN SOLDER

2 **CLEAN EXCESS SOLDER**
Put on a leather glove and grab a damp cotton rag (microfiber cloth will melt). Heat the remaining solder with the torch until it's molten. As soon as the solder melts, wipe away the excess solder with a damp rag. Be sure to wear leather gloves to prevent steam burns.

Remove and replace a compression shutoff valve

To remove a compression-style valve, hold the valve body with an adjustable or open-end wrench, or slip-joint pliers. Grab the compression nut with another wrench and turn it clockwise to loosen it. Then pull the valve off the copper tubing.

Next, remove the old compression sleeve and nut. Grab the old sleeve with pliers, using minimal pressure to avoid distorting the copper tubing. Then rotate and pull it off the tubing. If the sleeve is stuck, saw it (Photo 1) and break it (Photo 2).

Slide the new escutcheon and compression nut onto the copper tubing. Then add the new compression sleeve (Photo 3). Insert the new valve and apply a very light coating of pipe dope to the compression sleeve. Next, screw the compression nut onto the valve until snug. Hold the valve with a wrench or pliers and tighten the nut a one-half to three-quarters turn (follow the manufacturer's tightening instructions). Connect the supply tube and test for leaks.

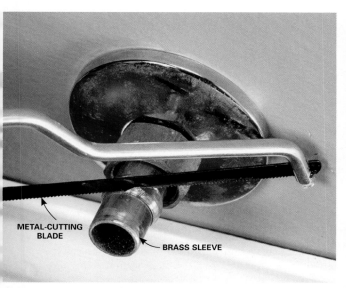

METAL-CUTTING BLADE

BRASS SLEEVE

1 **SAW PARTIALLY THROUGH THE SLEEVE**
Use a hacksaw to cut partially through the sleeve at an angle. Use short strokes to avoid cutting into the copper tubing. Check your progress and stop cutting before you reach the copper.

PREVIOUS SLEEVE DEPRESSION

3 **POSITION THE NEW COMPRESSION SLEEVE**
Slide the new compression sleeve onto the copper tubing. If the old sleeve left depression marks, locate the new sleeve slightly forward of the marks.

2 **TWIST AND BREAK THE SLEEVE**
Insert a flat-blade screwdriver into the cut and twist the screwdriver to break the sleeve. Slide off the old sleeve, old compression nut and the escutcheon (if you're going to replace it).

COMPRESSION NUT

COMPRESSION SLEEVE

New compression valve

Can you use a push-fit valve?

Several companies make quarter-turn push-fit ball-style shutoff valves that install without tools. They're a good alternative to sweat and compression fittings if you have enough tubing projecting out from the wall and if that tubing is in good shape. They make the job even simpler. If your stub-out tubing is perfectly symmetrical, long enough and has a square-cut end, you might be able to use a push-fit valve to replace your old compression or sweat valve.

Most push-fit valves require at least 1 in. of stub-out tubing. So measure the length of the stub-out and refer to the valve manufacturer's length requirements before buying. If your tubing will work, shop for a valve that meets your configuration needs (straight or angled). Push-fit valves are available with and without a permanently mounted supply tube. We don't recommend the permanently installed supply tube version because you have to shut off the water and replace the entire unit if the supply tube ever needs replacement.

Before installing a push-fit valve, remove any burrs from the open end. If you're replacing a sweat valve, remove all traces

AT LEAST 1" STUB-OUT

of solder and ensure the tubing is perfectly round. Then mark the installed length on the tubing and push the valve onto the tubing until it reaches the mark.

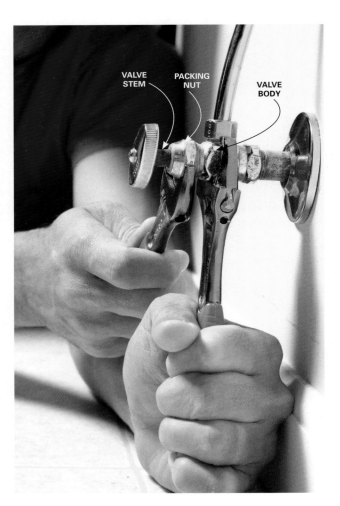

VALVE STEM

PACKING NUT

VALVE BODY

Shutoff valve leaking?

Don't panic. Here's a simple fix that works more than half the time and doesn't cost a dime to try. Many shutoff valves have a packing nut or packing material that surrounds the valve stem. The packing can shrink or get worn over time, causing water to leak out around the valve stem. This usually happens after someone has closed and opened the valve for a repair or for some other reason. The good news is that in most cases simply tightening the packing nut will fix the problem. Go easy, though. If you tighten it too much, the valve won't turn. Quarter-turn shutoff valves don't have a packing nut. If this type leaks around the stem, you'll have to replace it.

TIGHTEN THE PACKING NUT TO STOP THE LEAK
Place one wrench on the valve body and a second wrench on the packing nut. Then turn the packing nut clockwise to tighten while holding the valve in place with the second wrench.

Replace a sink strainer

Kitchen sink basket strainers/drain assemblies work great when they're new. But with daily use and cleaning, the chrome or painted finish starts to wear off. The basket strainer stopper may also start leaking. Once that happens, you can forget about soaking pots and pans overnight. You might think that the solution is to buy a new basket strainer. Good luck finding one that fits and seals. You can buy a "universal" replacement that'll work as a strainer. But it usually doesn't seal well because it's not an exact fit. So your best option is to replace the entire drain assembly.

You can replace the drain assembly yourself, but it's much easier with two people. You'll save about $100 in labor. The hardest part of the job involves removing the old drain locknut. If your locknut comes off easily, you can finish the entire job in less than an hour. However, a drain locknut that's corroded is tougher to deal with. We'll show you two quick ways to conquer stubborn locknuts. And we'll offer some tips on shopping for a new, longer-lasting basket strainer/drain assembly. Let's get started.

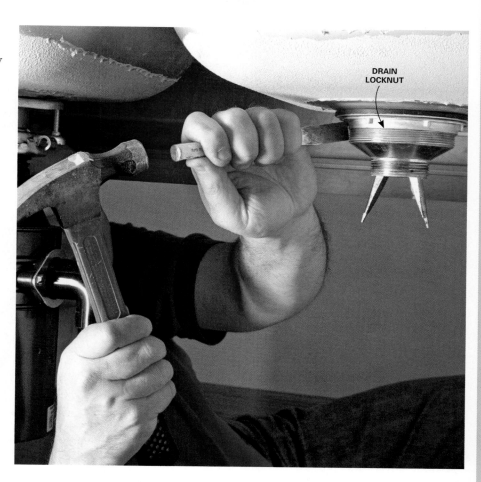

DRAIN LOCKNUT

Remove the drainpipes

Place a bowl under the P-trap. Then use slip-joint pliers to loosen the compression nuts at the drain tailpiece and both nuts on the trap. Completely unscrew the tailpiece nut and swing the P-trap out slightly. Then unscrew the trap nuts completely and remove and drain the entire trap and tailpiece assembly to give yourself more working space.

Loosen and remove the drain locknut

Crawl under the sink and check for corrosion on the large drain locknut. If it's corroded, spray all around the nut with rust penetrating oil and allow it to soak for at least 15 minutes. Then have a friend hold the drain so you can loosen the locknut (Photo 1). Loosen the locknut with a hammer and chisel (Photo 2). If the locknut won't loosen or the entire drain spins and your helper can't hold it, cut it off (Photo 3).

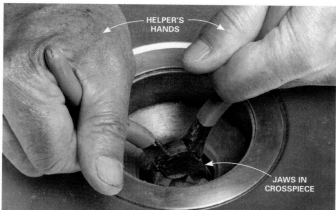

HELPER'S HANDS

JAWS IN CROSSPIECE

1 **HOLD THE DRAIN TO LOOSEN THE LOCKNUT**
Jam needle-nose pliers into the crosspiece section at the bottom of the drain. Have your friend spread the pliers and hold it tightly in the drain to prevent it from turning while you loosen the locknut.

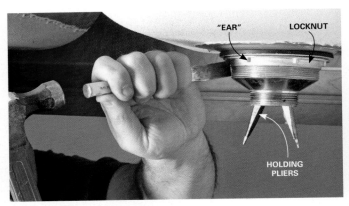

2 LOOSEN THE LOCKNUT

Place the chisel tip against a locknut "ear." Then smack the chisel with a hammer. Move the chisel to the next ear and repeat until the nut spins by hand.

3 DRASTIC MEASURES FOR STUCK NUTS

If all else fails, chuck a metal cutoff wheel into a rotary tool and cut the locknut. Cut until you reach the cardboard ring above the nut. Don't cut into the sink. If the nut still doesn't spin, fit your chisel into the cut area and smack it with a hammer to crack it open. Wear eye protection.

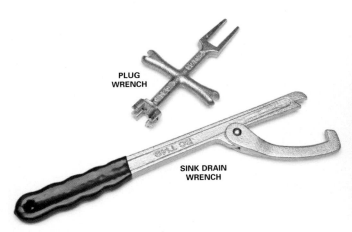

4 NO HELPER? NO PROBLEM!

You can buy these tools for $25 at any home center. Loosen the locknut with the sink drain wrench while you hold the drain with pliers and the plug wrench.

5 INSTALL THE NEW STRAINER

Slide the rubber O-ring on first. Then add the cardboard O-ring and the locknut. Tighten the nut until it starts compressing the rubber O-ring.

If you don't have either a helper or a rotary cutoff tool and you've tried but can't loosen the locknut yourself, there's still another option to try. Head to the home center or hardware store and fork over about $25 for a sink drain wrench to loosen the nut and a plug wrench to help hold the drain (Photo 4). Once you get the locknut off, pull the entire drain up and out of the sink.

Clean the sink flange and install the new drain

Scrape off the plumber's putty or silicone from around the drain flange in the basin and under the sink. If the old drain was caulked with silicone, use silicone remover to clean it. Then apply a fresh bead of silicone around the flange in the basin and insert the new drain. Next, install the new O-ring and locknut in the order shown here (Photo 5). Tighten the locknut until the rubber O-ring compresses slightly. Then reassemble the trap and tailpiece and attach it to the new sink drain. Clean off any excess silicone in the basin with a paper towel. Then clean off the O-ring and locknut.

Test for leaks by filling the sink with water and releasing it while you check the pipes under the sink.

Buying tips

You have to spend at least $50 to get a high-quality strainer/drain assembly with a durable finish and a reliable stopper mechanism. The best strainers have either a spin-lock or a twist-and-drop style stopper. The spin-lock stopper doesn't have any parts that can wear, but screwing it in and out can be annoying. The twist-and-drop style is much easier to use but requires occasional O-ring replacement.

Avoid push-in style strainers that have a nonreplaceable neoprene stopper or a plastic knob. The plastic parts break and can lose their sealing ability if exposed to boiling water.

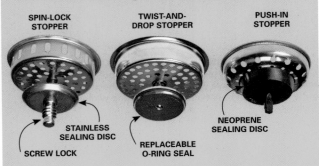

Unclog a toilet

In this article, we'll show you how to avert a morning household disaster by clearing a clogged toilet fast. With a little practice, even a home repair rookie can get most clogged toilets back up and running in minutes, without flooding the bathroom and making the situation worse . . . sometimes much worse!

For about 90 percent of clogged toilets, you only need one special tool—a plunger. Buy one with an extension flange on the rubber bell-shaped end (photo above). It's designed to fit toilets better so you can deliver more "oomph" to the plunge. It'll unplug sink and tub drains too, if you simply fold the flange back into the bell.

Do you have a slow drainer or a no-drainer?

A poor flush means that your toilet drain is either partially or completely plugged. A toilet that's completely plugged—a no-drainer—is obvious. The toilet bowl will fill to the brim with flush water and perhaps overflow. Give the water level 10 minutes or so to drop, then attack the problem with a plunger (Photo 1).

However, most clogged toilets are slow drainers, that is, flush water partially fills the bowl but doesn't rush out and clean away the waste. The water level remains high, then usually drains down to normal height within a minute or two. You might not know the toilet is clogged until you flush it. So if you suspect a problem, test the drainage first as we show in Photo 2. If it doesn't drain, don't flush it. Reach for the plunger.

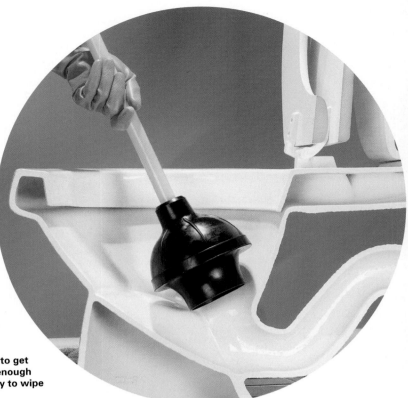

1 Plunge the toilet with the rubber flange pulled out to get a better seal. Push in and out vigorously, keeping enough water in the bowl to cover the plunger. Keep towels handy to wipe up water that splashes out.

Become a master plunger

Photo 1 shows how a plunger fits over and seals the toilet drain. Wear rubber gloves—things can get messy—and follow these plunging tips:

1. Make your first plunge a gentle one. Initially the bell is full of air. A hard thrust will force the air back around the seal and blow water all over the bathroom and you!

2. Once you force out the air, plunge vigorously in and out, maintaining the seal. You'll be forcing water both directions in the drain, which will effectively loosen most clogs. Stick with it, plunging 15 to 20 times if necessary.

3. Be patient. Try alternating between steady strokes and occasional monster heaves.

4. Keep enough water in the bowl so the plunger stays covered. Trying to force air through the toilet trap won't generate much pressure.

Most of the time, this is all it takes to clear the clog. However, if the plunger won't open the drain, or if you can force out the water with the plunger but the toilet still won't flush well, reach for the snake (Photos 3 and 4, p. 97).

2 Don't flush the toilet if you suspect that it's clogged. Instead, remove the tank lid and lift the flapper valve slightly to let a cup or two of water into the bowl to see if the water goes down. Flushing a clogged toilet may flood your floor!

Bore through the clog with a snake

A drain snake is a long wire coil with a corkscrew-like tip that you feed into your pipes until it encounters the clog. Then you turn the snake clockwise, so that the tip screws into or through the clog and breaks it up. Or the debris winds onto the wire so you can pull it out.

Even the least expensive snake will clear a toilet. But the more expensive closet auger (Photo 4) is a special type designed to get around the first bend, keep debris at arm's length, and yet still spin the coil to hook "foreign objects." A rubber sleeve protects the enamel bowl from scrape marks. These snakes are short because most obstructions catch in the first S-bend or at the floor flange. (Plumbers report that the most common foreign objects are toys.)

3

Household snake

Major surgery

If the clog resists all your efforts, you'll probably have to pull up the toilet. This job will take several hours, because you have to turn off and unhook the water supply, partially disassemble the toilet, and unscrew it from its mounting ring. Chances are, you can then get at the problem. Be sure to buy a new wax ring and new mounting bolts to reseal the toilet base to the mounting ring.

However, if other drains in your home are plugged, or if water comes up through them, the problem is probably farther down in the main drainpipes, often out of easy reach. For those clogs, you may need to call a plumber or sewer cleaner.

Do's and Don'ts

1. Avoid chemicals. Don't be suckered into thinking that powerful chemicals will do the messy work for you. They sometimes work, but they're slower. And when they don't work, you have a drain full of corrosive water on your hands.

If you tried chemicals and they didn't work, run as much water into the toilet as possible and let it sit overnight to drain through the clog. Then, when you plunge, wear safety goggles and rubber gloves to keep the water out of your eyes and off your bare skin.

2. Keep the toilet cover down, especially if you have small kids, so toys and hairbrushes won't fall into the toilet.

3. Don't pour hardening compounds down the toilet. These include such things as drywall joint compound, grease, caulk and wax products.

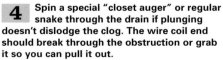

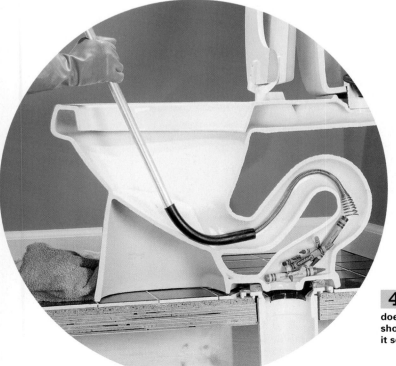

4 Spin a special "closet auger" or regular snake through the drain if plunging doesn't dislodge the clog. The wire coil end should break through the obstruction or grab it so you can pull it out.

Replace a broken or corroded toilet flush handle

A few readers have written to us asking if there's a trick to replacing a toilet flush handle. What's throwing them for a loop is the retaining nut inside the tank—it's a reverse thread. So, if you're in front of the toilet, turn the nut to the left (Photo 1). Remove the old handle and lever and install the new one (Photo 2).

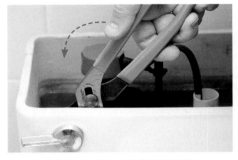

1 LOOSEN THE RETAINING NUT
Grab the nut with pliers and turn to the left to loosen.

2 INSTALL THE NEW HANDLE
Slide the new handle into place. Then thread on the retaining nut. Tighten by turning to the right.

Fix for a running toilet

If you hear your toilet refilling too often, or if you hear the steady hiss of running water, the flapper may be leaking. The flapper (aka "flush valve seal") is the plug that falls against the drain hole (flush valve drain seat) on the bottom of the tank and holds water in until the next time you flush. When flappers or flush valve seats wear out, water trickles out, causing the water valve to open to refill the tank. Usually the fix is simple. Remove the old flapper and take it with you to the hardware store or home center to find a matching replacement.

Occasionally a new flapper doesn't solve the problem. If you've tried replacing the flapper but the toilet still runs, the flush valve seat is probably rough or pitted. You can replace the entire flush valve, but it's a big job. Here's an easier fix. Look for a flapper kit that contains a flush seat repair. We show a Fluidmaster 555C kit, but others are available. The kit contains a flapper and matching seat that you adhere to the damaged seat with the adhesive provided, as shown.

Start by closing the valve on the water line to the toilet by turning it clockwise. Then flush the toilet and hold the flapper open to allow the water to drain from the tank. Use a sponge to mop out the water that remains. Follow the included instructions to install the new valve seat and flapper. The Fluidmaster flapper we show includes a plastic cup that allows you to adjust the length of time the flapper stays open. It's for toilets that use 3.5 gallons or less for a flush. If your toilet uses more than this, remove the timing cup. Install the new flapper. Then adjust the length of the chain so it's just slightly slack when the flapper is down. Turn on the water and test the flush. You may have to fiddle with the length of the chain to get the flapper working correctly. When you're done, cut off the excess chain to keep it from getting stuck under the flapper.

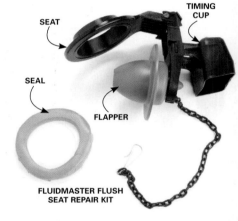

SEAT

TIMING CUP

SEAL

FLAPPER

FLUIDMASTER FLUSH SEAT REPAIR KIT

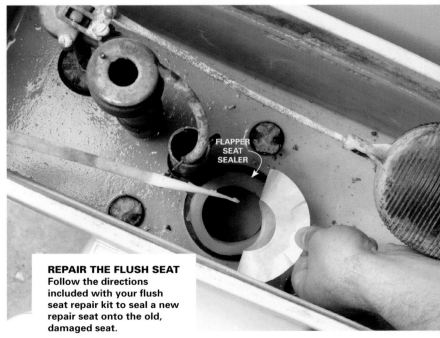

FLAPPER SEAT SEALER

REPAIR THE FLUSH SEAT
Follow the directions included with your flush seat repair kit to seal a new repair seat onto the old, damaged seat.

Stuck laundry hoses?

Rusted-on laundry hoses are nearly impossible to unscrew. If you need to remove or replace your laundry hose and just can't get it loose, here's the solution. Carefully cut through the hose end. Try to avoid cutting too deep, but don't worry if you nick the threads on the valve. The threads don't seal the connection. That's taken care of by the rubber washer. You can use a hacksaw to make the cuts, but a Dremel tool with an abrasive cutoff wheel works even better (Photo 1). Cut the hose end in two places, then try to unscrew the fitting with water pump pliers or a pipe wrench. If it's still stuck, break it off with pliers (Photo 2).

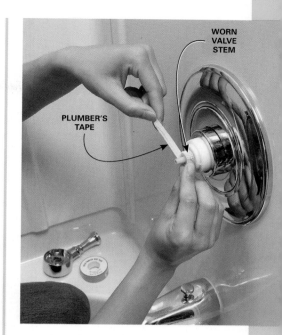

WORN VALVE STEM

PLUMBER'S TAPE

CUTTING WHEEL

HOSE END

1 **SLICE A CORRODED HOSE END WITH A DREMEL**
Cut through the hose end a little at a time until the slice extends through the metal. Don't forget your safety glasses. Make two slices on opposite sides of the hose end.

2 **PRY IT OFF**
If you still can't unscrew it, pry it loose with water pump pliers. After you've removed the hose, clean off any remaining rust and corrosion from the valve threads with a wire brush.

Tighten a floppy faucet handle

If you have a loose valve handle—on a shower, bathroom or kitchen faucet—tighten the screw that holds the handle in place. With some faucets, you'll have to pry off the metal button at the center of the handle. With others, you'll find a setscrew near the base of the handle. Setscrews usually require a hex (or "Allen") wrench. If tightening doesn't work, the stem inside the handle may be worn, especially if it's plastic. Here's a trick to tighten worn stems on most types of faucets: Wrap the stem tightly with Teflon pipe thread tape and slip the handle back over the stem. In most cases, a single wrap creates a snug fit.

Fix your dripping laundry faucet

Laundry faucets like this are easy and cheap to fix. If it's dripping from the spout, you need a new faucet washer. And if water is leaking around the handle, the rubber O-ring around the valve stem is bad. But since you have to take out the valve stem for either repair, and the fix is simple, we recommend replacing both the hot and cold washers and the O-rings while the faucet is apart. Remember to turn off the water and purge the pressure before you start. If you're lucky, there'll be a separate shutoff for the laundry room. Otherwise, you'll have to shut off the water to the whole house by closing the main valve.

Photos 1 and 2 show how to do the repair. After you've removed the valve stems, take them to the hardware store. You'll find drawers full of faucet washers and O-rings. Just find washers that will fit snugly in the recess, and matching O-rings. If you damaged the screw that holds the washer on when you removed it, buy new brass screws. Now simply reassemble everything in the reverse order. No more drips!

1 **UNSCREW THE VALVE**
Remove the handle. Then turn the valve counterclockwise with a wrench. Pull out the valve.

VALVE

FAUCET HANDLE

2 **REPLACE THE WASHER**
Remove the screw that holds the washer to the valve. Install the new washer and replace the screw.

VALVE

OLD FAUCET WASHER

NEW FAUCET WASHER

Great goofs

Indoor waterfall

My wife and I decided to refinish our aging kitchen cabinets instead of getting new ones. We masked off the counters and the walls and spanned the double sink with a piece of plywood so we'd have a place to kneel while working on the upper cabinets. I put on my hearing protection and dust mask and started sanding. After several minutes I felt a tug on my shirt. I looked down and saw my wife motioning for me to stop.

I set the sander on the counter, and as the dust cleared, I could see water everywhere on the floor! My knee had bumped the sink faucet, turning it on, and the water was running onto the plywood, down to the floor and then even into the basement. Luckily our floor survived the soaking. We did finish the sanding that day—after we turned off the faucet valves below the sink!

—Debra and Mark Pettijohn

Fix your well yourself

If you own a home with a well, you know that trouble can hit at the worst possible time, like at the start of a holiday weekend, and off-hours repairs can cost a small fortune.

We spoke with Steve McCullough, owner of Lauren McCullough Well Drilling, to get his advice on how DIYers can fix well problems. If you're comfortable replacing electrical and plumbing components, you can save a lot of money on the service call as well as the parts. All the parts that can be replaced by a DIYer are located inside the house. You'll need to call a pro for outside electrical, piping, pump and check-valve failures.

Most of the time you'll find the parts you need at home centers. But home centers may not carry the highest-quality parts. If you want to get long-lasting parts, shop at a plumbing supplier.

Three common problems

The most common symptoms of well trouble are no water at all, pulsing water pressure and a pump that runs constantly. If you experience any of these, there's a good chance you can solve the problem yourself. We show you how on the following pages.

Problem 1: No water at all

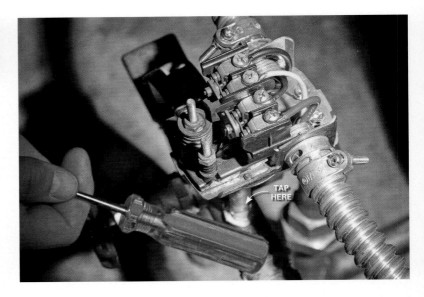

First, be sure the power is on

Start by checking that the well switch located near your pressure tank hasn't been switched off. Then check the well's double-pole circuit breaker to see that it hasn't tripped. If it has, reset it. A breaker that keeps tripping likely means a problem with the well pump, and you'll need to call a pro for that.

Then check the pressure switch

You'll find the pressure switch mounted on a 1/4-in. tube near the pressure tank. It's what senses when water pressure has dropped to the point where the pressure tank requires more water. The switch then powers up the well pump.

If the switch is bad, it won't start the pump and you won't have water, so testing the switch is your first step. Remove the cover and bang a screwdriver handle sharply against the tube below the switch to jar the electrical contacts. If you see a spark and the pump starts, the pressure switch is the problem. Replace it. A new switch is about $25. If there's still no spark, you'll have to replace the controller.

If the switch is bad, replace it

If you find the pressure switch is bad, test the pressure tank to make sure it isn't waterlogged (see "Problem: Pulsing Water," p. 104). To replace the switch, start by removing the wires to the old switch (be sure to label them) and unscrew the switch (photo right). Coat the tubing threads with pipe dope or Teflon tape and screw on the new switch so it sits in the same orientation. Then reconnect the wires.

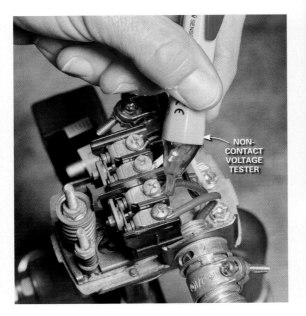

NON-CONTACT VOLTAGE TESTER

PRESSURE SWITCH

DRAIN OPEN

VALVE OFF

WARNING: Confirm the power is off!

Before you replace the pressure switch or file the contacts, turn off the power at the main panel and check the wires with a noncontact voltage tester.

Temporary quick fix

If banging on the tube under the pressure switch kicked on the pump, it means the contact surfaces of the electrical contacts are pitted or burned, causing a poor connection. You can temporarily restore the surfaces to keep it going until you can buy a replacement switch.

First, turn off the power and double-check with a voltage tester. Pull the contacts open and file off the burned and pitted areas using an ordinary nail file or emery board. Replace the pressure switch as soon as possible because this fix won't last long.

If all else fails, replace the controller

The pump controller houses a capacitor to help start the pump. Most pump controls are mounted in the house near the pressure tank, but others are mounted inside the well pump itself and the fix requires a pro. If you don't have the box shown below, this fix isn't for you.

There's no way to test the controller, so you either have to risk wasting money by replacing a good one, or throw in the towel and call a pro. Replacing the pump controller as shown here is easy, and it's your last, best shot at avoiding a service call. If you've replaced the pressure switch and the pump still won't start, we think it's worth the risk to replace the pump controller.

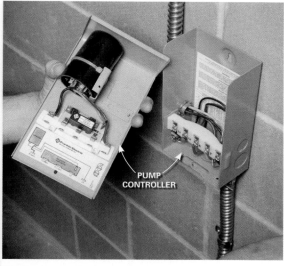

REPLACE THE PUMP CONTROLLER
Remove the screw at the bottom of the pump control cover and lift it off the box to disconnect it. Take it to the store and buy an exact replacement. Snap the new cover onto the old box (no need to rewire if you buy the same brand). Then start the pump.

Figure A
Anatomy of a well

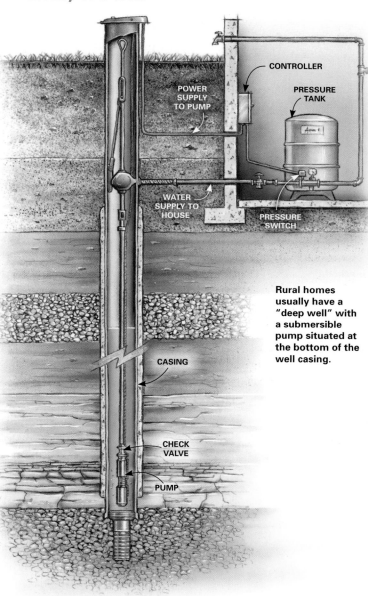

Rural homes usually have a "deep well" with a submersible pump situated at the bottom of the well casing.

Problem 2: Pulsing water

Check pressure tank

When water "pulses" at the spigot, it usually means you have a waterlogged tank. Replacement is your only option. A new tank costs about $200 and up. At right are two methods for diagnosing a bad tank: checking for water at the air valve and shaking the tank.

A typical pressure tank stores about 6 to 10 gallons of water inside a balloonlike bladder on the bottom half of the tank. The top portion is filled with air. As the pump fills the tank, the water compresses the air above the bladder. The compressed air is what powers water through your house when you open a faucet. When the bladder fails, water seeps into the top half, reducing the tank's ability to force out more than 2 or 3 gallons of water. The water also rusts the tank from the inside.

These are the symptoms of a bad pressure tank:

▶ Water pressure in one faucet drops dramatically when someone opens another faucet or flushes a toilet—because the tank has lost its capacity to store and pressurize water.

▶ Water pressure fluctuates while taking a shower or filling a tub—the tank can only pressurize a few gallons of water, forcing the pump to cycle on and off.

▶ Water leaks onto the floor around the tank, or water starts to look rusty.

▶ Your electrical bill jumps for no apparent reason—because the pump has to start so many times, and frequent starting takes more power than longer run-times.

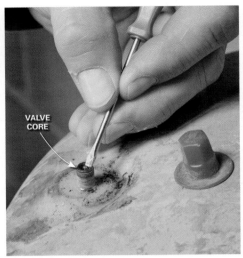

VALVE CORE

TEST FOR WATER AT THE AIR VALVE
Unscrew the plastic cover from the air valve on the top of the tank. Use a small screwdriver to depress the air valve to see if water comes out.

ROCK THE TANK
Push against the top of the tank to rock it slightly. If you can't rock it or it feels top heavy, it's bad. Drain it and replace it.

Tank replacement tips

▶ **Buy a larger pressure tank.** Frequent starts wear out well pumps, controllers and pressure switches much faster than longer run-times. The larger the pressure tank, the fewer times your well pump must start. Since well pumps are much more expensive, the longer pump life more than offsets the higher tank cost. This is particularly good advice if your home uses more water than average (for example, you run a business with high water needs, irrigate a large area or raise animals that require large amounts of water).

▶ **Don't buy a tank based on price alone.** Cheap tanks cost far more in the long run because of shorter bladder life and accelerated tank rust-out. Steve swears by the Well-X-Trol brand, but it may not be available at your local home center.

Problem 3: Pump runs nonstop

When a pump turns on, you'll hear the clicking of the pressure switch opening and closing. If you hear frequent clicking when no water is flowing, you have problems outside the house and you'll need to hire a pro. It could be a broken water line from the well to the house (usually you'll have a wet area between the well head and the house), a bad check valve just above the submersible pump at the bottom of the well, a bad connector leaving the well casing or even a broken water line inside the well casing. Each of those problems requires a pro.

Exploding toilet trick

Our toilet wouldn't stop running because the float wouldn't turn the water completely off. I'd fixed the same problem in our old toilet by bending the float arm down a little to increase the pressure on the shutoff valve in the tank. But since our new toilet had a plastic arm, I decided to apply a little heat to soften it so I could bend it.

First I sprayed silicone lube on everything in the tank to help things slide better. Then I leaned over the tank with my lighter, clicked it and...WHOOOOMPP! The aerosol silicone spray I had just shot into the tank exploded. Luckily, I escaped with only singed hair and eyelashes. But now my wife can't stop telling people about our exploding toilet.

—Ron Woodward

A flush to remember

After removing an old toilet, I did the classic handyman trick of stuffing a bunch of plastic bags into the sewer opening. This kept the stench from seeping into the bathroom while I installed the new toilet over the weekend.

After setting and hooking up the new commode, I did a test flush. It was very satisfying to watch the water swirl down and the bowl fill up — and up and up! The toilet gushed water all over the floor.

Turns out the other half of that trick is removing the bags from the sewer opening.

—Rob Kiesling

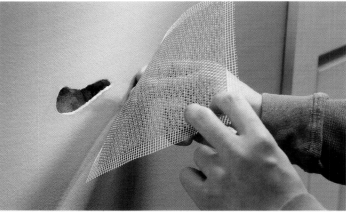

Chapter Three

INTERIOR MAINTENANCE & REPAIR

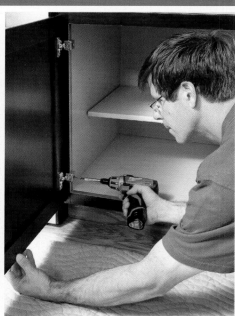

Fix sagging cabinet shelves

Stocked up on canned goods, did you? Now the shelves are sagging and you're looking for a quick fix.

If your cabinet has a center stile, check the back of the stile and the back of the cabinet to see if the manufacturer drilled shelf bracket holes to support the center (Figure A). They're hard to spot and often ignored by whoever installed the cabinets.

If you find predrilled holes, just buy some brackets at the hardware store and install them. That'll support the center of the shelf. If there are no holes, you have two choices: You can drill holes or you can make a "bridge" (Figures B and C).

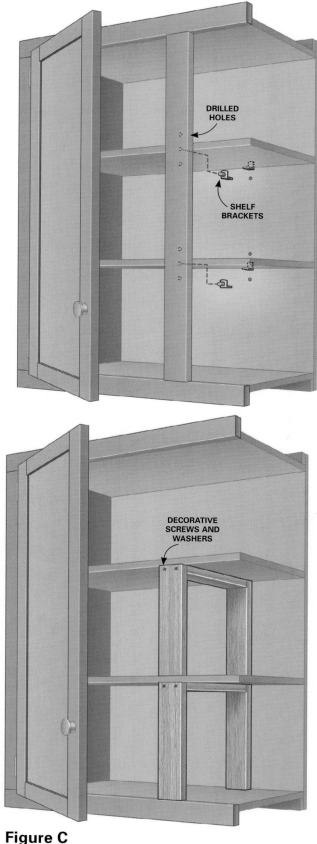

Figure A

Install brackets in predrilled holes or drill your own with a right angle drill.

DRILLED HOLES

SHELF BRACKETS

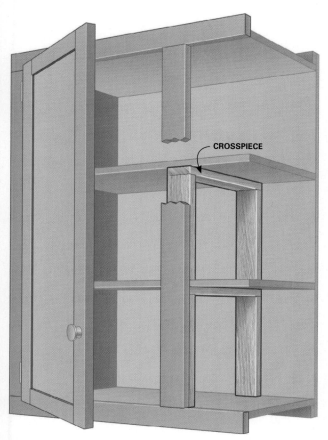

CROSSPIECE

Figure B

For cabinets with a center stile, build 1x2 bridges. Nail the crosspiece on top of the uprights. Then slide the bridge into place under the shelf.

DECORATIVE SCREWS AND WASHERS

Figure C

For cabinets with no center stile, position the crosspiece between the two uprights. Secure with decorative screws and washers.

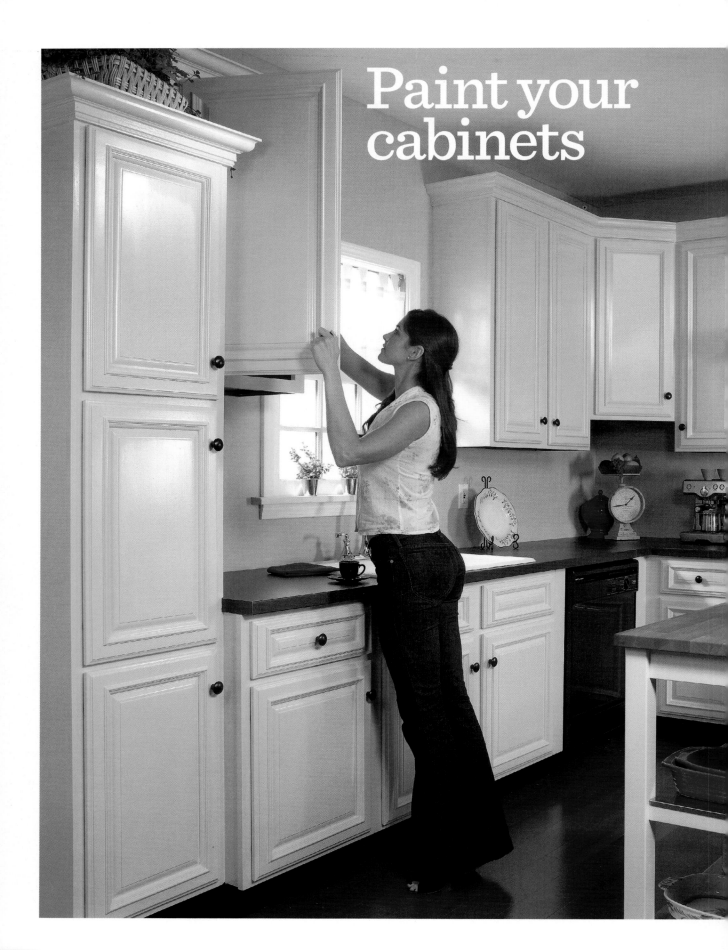

Paint your cabinets

It only takes two coats of paint!

You don't need to spend thousands of dollars on new cabinets to give your kitchen a stunning new look. If your cabinets are in good shape, you can give them a fresh face with paint. Everything you need to give your drab cabinets a silky smooth painted finish costs a tiny fraction of the cost of new cabinets.

Professional painters typically spray-paint doors because it produces an ultra-smooth finish. Here, we'll show you how to spray-paint your doors and drawers. There's just a short learning curve to use the sprayer effectively. You could also spray the cabinet frames, sides and trim, but masking off the cabinet openings (and the rest of the kitchen) takes a lot of time, so just use a brush for those areas.

Despite our enthusiasm, there are downsides to a painted finish. The paint isn't as tough as a factory finish, and even if you're careful, you can still end up with paint runs and have brush marks on your cabinet sides.

All the materials you need to paint your cabinets are available at home centers and paint stores. Plan to spend four or five days to complete the job—you'll have to let the paint dry overnight between coats, and you can only paint one side of the doors per day.

New-looking cabinets in 3 steps

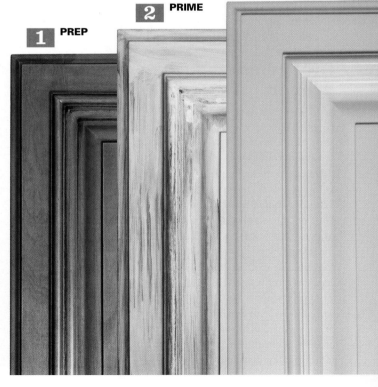

Is painting right for you?

Not all cabinets are worth painting. They must be structurally sound—paint obviously isn't a cure for doors that are falling apart or don't close properly. If your cabinets are oak or some other species with coarse grain and you want a smooth finish, you'll have to fill the grain on the door panels, cabinet frames and cabinet sides with spackling compound. That nearly doubles the length of this project because sanding the compound takes a long, long time (but if you don't mind a coarse finish, you can skip this step).

If you like the style of your cabinets and they're in good shape, and you're willing to invest the time to paint them, this project is for you.

Wash, rinse, tape, repeat

As with any successful painting project, preparation is the key—and the most time-consuming step. Start by removing the cabinet doors and drawers as well as all the hardware. Label the doors as you remove them so you'll know where to reinstall them. Writing a number in the hinge hole (for Euro hinges) or where the hinge attaches works great—it's the only part that's not painted.

Take the doors and drawers to the garage or another work area and spread them out on a work surface. It's surprising how much space doors and drawers eat up—even if you have a small kitchen. An extension ladder placed over sawhorses gives you a surface to set the doors on. Wash the front and the back of the doors and the drawer fronts to remove grease (Photo 1). Then stick tape in the hinge holes or where the hinges attach to keep out the paint.

Wash the grease off the cabinet frames in the kitchen, too. Then tape off everything that abuts the cabinet frames (Photo 2). Use plastic sheeting or brown masking paper to cover appliances. Use rosin paper for countertops—it's thick enough to resist tears and won't let small paint spills seep through.

Give cabinets a fresh start with primer

Some cabinets, like ours, have a catalyzed lacquer finish that's very hard. Primer won't form a good bond to this surface unless you scuff it up first. First, sand any damaged areas on the doors or cabinet frames with 320-grit sandpaper to remove burrs or ridges, then fill the areas with spackling compound (Photo 3).

Lightly sand the doors and cabinet frames, trim and sides with 320-grit sandpaper. Sand just enough to take off the shine—you don't need to sand off the finish. Vacuum the dust off the wood using a bristle attachment. Right before you're ready to apply the primer, wipe down the doors and frames with a tack cloth. Running the cloth over the surface is enough—you don't need to scrub to remove the fine dust particles.

Apply a stain-killing primer (Bulls Eye 1-2-3 and BIN are two brands) with a paintbrush (Photo 4). You can use a cheap brush—even a disposable one—for this. Don't worry about brushstrokes in the primer (you'll remove them later with sandpaper) or getting a uniform finish. The doors and frames

1 **WASH OFF YEARS OF KITCHEN GREASE** with warm water and dish detergent. Clean away all the grease or the primer and paint won't adhere. Rinse clean with water.

2 **TAPE OFF THE WALLS, CEILING AND FLOORING,** and cover the countertops with rosin paper. Wrap appliances and the vent hood with plastic sheeting or masking paper.

don't have to look pretty at this stage. But don't use a roller. It leaves a texture that will affect the finish. Besides, brushing is almost as fast as rolling, and you can use the bristles to work the primer into crevices.

Once the primer is dry (just one or two hours), lightly sand the doors and cabinets with 320-grit sandpaper to remove any brushstrokes (Photo 5). Sandpaper works better than a sanding sponge—you can feel the rough spots through the paper, and paper doesn't round over corners like sponges do.

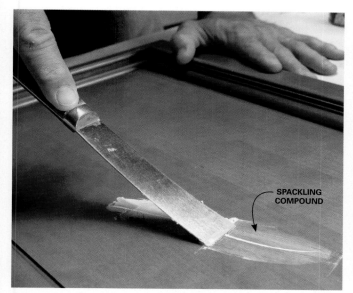

3 **FIX SCRATCHES, HOLES AND DINGS WITH SPACKLING COMPOUND.** Work the compound into damaged areas with a putty knife. Fill in holes from handles and hardware if you're replacing it and need holes in different places.

4 **PRIME THE DOORS AND CABINET FRAMES WITH STAIN-BLOCKING PRIMER.** The primer covers any stains and seals in cooking odors. Prime one side of all the doors, let them dry while you prime the cabinet face frames and sides, then prime the other side of the doors.

5 **SAND THE DOORS AND CABINETS WITH FINE-GRIT SANDPAPER.** Sand with the grain. Be careful not to round over corners. Wipe the surface clean with a tack cloth.

6 **START IN A CORNER TO PAINT THE CABINET FRAMES.** Use a high-quality paintbrush to paint an entire rail or stile, including the inside edge, before moving to an adjacent rail or stile.

Immaculate finish in 90 minutes

For this project, we used a Wagner Control Spray Double Duty spray gun. The high-volume, low-pressure (HVLP) sprayer gives the doors a thin, even coat of paint and makes quick work of painting. We sprayed our 18 doors and four drawers in less than 90 minutes per coat. The sprayer occasionally "spits" paint, but the Floetrol that you mix in levels out the finish. You can clean the sprayer in about 10 minutes.

The paint experts we talked to say you can get a nice-looking finish with non-HVLP sprayers too. But the advantages of an HVLP sprayer are that the low pressure produces little overspray, so most of your paint ends up where you want it—on the doors—and the spray is easy to control.

If you have doors with coarse wood grain (like oak) and want a smooth finish, fill in the grain with spackling compound (MH Ready Patch is one brand). Use a putty knife to skim-coat the door with compound, working it into the wood grain. Wait for it to dry, sand it with medium-grit sandpaper, then prime it again.

Complete the transformation with paint

Use a gloss or semigloss latex enamel paint for your cabinets. Its hard, shiny finish resists stains and fingerprints.

To get started, pour a gallon of the paint into a bucket and thin it with half a cup of water and half a quart of Floetrol paint additive. The water and the Floetrol level out the paint when it's applied and slow the drying process, which helps eliminate brush and lap marks. The thinner paint also provides a more even coat when you're spraying.

Paint the cabinets with a brush (Photo 6). Paint an entire rail, stile or trim piece before the paint dries, then move on to the next part of the cabinet. Paint any exposed sides of cabinets with a brush. Most light brush marks will disappear as the paint dries (thanks to the Floetrol).

Before spray painting the doors and drawer fronts, construct a makeshift booth to contain the airborne spray. Assemble a work surface (putting boards over sawhorses works great), then hang plastic sheeting around the work area. Make sure to ventilate the room—even if it's just a fan blowing out an open window.

Fill the spray container with the paint mixed with Floetrol and water. Wear a mask respirator when spray painting. Test the spray pattern on cardboard, keeping the nozzle 10 to 12 in. from the surface (Photo 7). Sweep your entire arm back and forth across the door panel; don't just use your wrist. Practice spraying on the cardboard to get a feel for the sprayer. When you're ready to paint, set a block of wood or a cardboard box on the work surface to elevate the doors. Place a lazy Susan turntable over the box, then set the door on top of it (Photo 8).

Spray the back of the doors first. This lets you get used to spraying before you paint the front. Start by spraying the edges. Rotate the door on the turntable to paint each edge so you won't have to change your body position. Move your arm across the entire edge of the door, starting the spray before the paint lands on door, and keep spraying past the end. Keep the nozzle 10 to 12 in. from the door. After painting all four edges, start at the top of the door and spray in a sweeping motion back and forth, moving down just enough each time to overlap the previous pass by 50 percent until you reach the door bottom.

Let the paint dry overnight. Then give the cabinet frames, sides and trim a second coat. Spray a first coat on the door fronts (Photo 9).

Cover the drawers with masking paper or plastic sheeting so only the paintable surface is visible. Set the drawer face down on the turntable and spray the back. Then place the drawer on its bottom and spray the front (Photo 10). Be careful not to overspray the drawer. It's easy to get runs in the paint on drawer fronts. Don't worry about areas that are lightly covered. You'll give everything a second coat.

7 **PRACTICE SPRAY PAINTING ON CARDBOARD.** Adjust the nozzle to get a vertical fan pattern. Adjust the flow rate so the paint covers the surface without running.

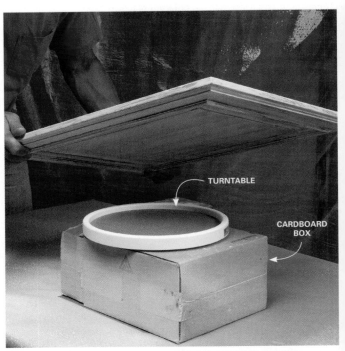

8 **SET THE DOORS ON A TURNTABLE WHEN SPRAY PAINTING.** Then you can stand in one spot and rotate the door to paint each side. Keep the nozzle 10 to 12 in. from the door and maintain a consistent angle while spraying.

If you catch paint runs while they're still wet, gently brush them out with a paintbrush (Photo 11).

Let the doors and drawers dry overnight, then give them a second coat. It's up to you if you want to give the back of the doors two coats. We gave ours just one.

When the doors are dry, install the hardware and hang the doors (Photo 12). If any paint seeped into the hinge holes, scrape it out so the hinges will fit snugly.

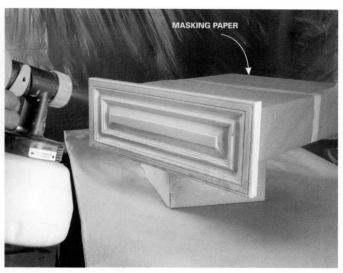

9 **PAINT THE EDGE AND DETAIL WORK ON ONE SIDE,** then turn the door to paint the adjacent edges and details. Start the spray before the door, and keep spraying past the edge. Don't worry if you missed a spot. You can catch it on the second coat.

10 **PAINT THE DRAWERS WITH THE SPRAYER AFTER WRAPPING THE INSIDE WITH PLASTIC OR PAPER.** Paint the backs first, then the edges and then the faces, starting at the top and working down. Start and stop the spray past the sides of the drawer.

11 **FIX PAINT RUNS WITH A PAINTBRUSH WHILE THE PAINT IS STILL WET.** If the paint is dry or tacky, wait until the next day, then sand out the run or imperfection and repaint.

12 **REINSTALL THE DOORS AND DRAWERS IN THE KITCHEN.** Attach the hinges to the doors first, then screw them to the cabinet frames.

Figure A
Painting Doors

Spray the door edges first. Then spray any detail work. Then spray the entire door, starting at the top and sweeping your arm back and forth until you reach the bottom. Keep the angle of the spray gun consistent as you spray.

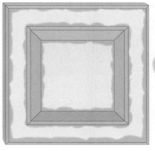

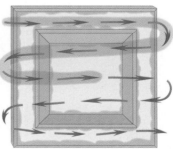

Cabinet refacing

*Get the look of new cabinets
in one weekend for one-third the cost!*

Cabinet refacing is a quick and easy way to change the look of your kitchen without the mess and expense of a complete remodeling. You simply cover the cabinet face frame with self-sticking wood veneer and the end panels with 1/4-in. plywood. Replace the old doors and drawer fronts with new ones. Refacing costs about one-third what new cabinets would cost, plus you can leave the countertop in place for even greater savings. And by doing the work yourself, you'll also save at least $1,000 in labor for a small kitchen, and a lot more if your kitchen is large.

Refacing does require attention to detail and some experience working with tools, but you don't have to be a master carpenter. If you can measure and cut accurately, you shouldn't have any trouble.

Voice of experience

Joel Bour is a remodeling contractor who specializes in kitchens and kitchen cabinet refacing. In addition to his other kitchen jobs, he completes about two dozen refacing projects a year.

Three simple steps to transform your kitchen cabinets

Refacing your cabinets is a quick and easy way to give your kitchen a new look with a minimum of mess and inconvenience. In a nutshell, here's what you'll do:

1 Remove the doors and drawers and cover the front edges of the cabinets with peel-and-stick wood veneer.

2 Hang the new doors with easy-to-adjust, easy-to-install cup hinges.

3 Attach new drawer fronts to your existing drawers. Finish up by replacing moldings and installing new hardware.

Special tools for working with veneer

Joel uses a Virutex laminate slitter to cut strips of veneer (Photo 3, p. 117). It's the perfect tool for this project, but if you don't want to spend the money, you can rent a laminate slitter from refacedepot.com. A table saw also works.

You'll need a veneer tool (Photo 6) to apply adequate pressure for a good bond. You can get a veneer scraper tool like the one shown at amazon.com or buy a similar tool, called a veneer smoothing blade, at rockler.com.

For cutting veneer strips to length, Joel uses a paper cutter he's modified slightly for more-accurate cuts. We found that even an inexpensive paper cutter like the Swingline ClassicCut Lite works great for cutting veneer.

How to order new doors and drawers

There are three standard types of cabinet doors: overlay, inset and 3/8-in. lip (Figure B, p. 119). Regardless of what type of doors you currently have, in most cases you can replace them with overlay

Before

After

doors that use modern, fully adjustable cup hinges. And that's the situation we're showing here.

To size the doors, you'll need to decide how much of the door you want to extend past the face frame opening. This is called the overlay distance and is determined by the hinges you install. To keep it simple, Joel gives his customers a choice between 1/2-in. overlay, which is the most common, or 1-1/4-in. overlay. Depending on the hinge, you can choose a different overlay if you like. The 1-1/4-in. overlay doors hide more of the face frame for a more contemporary look. But the extra door width can cause problems. You have to measure carefully at inside corners and between doors to make sure there's enough room. And remember, the new drawer fronts will be the same width, so check at inside corners to make sure there's clearance for the drawers to open without handle conflicts. Also, there's usually not enough space to add the extra 1-1/4 in. to the top and bottom of both doors and drawer fronts, so you may have to customize these overlay distances.

For this kitchen, Joel ordered doors that overlay the cabinet 1-1/4 in. on the sides and bottom, but reduced the top overlay to 3/4 in. Then he reduced the top and bottom overlay of the drawers to 3/4 in. to avoid conflict with a built-in breadboard. If you decide to order an overlay greater than 1/2 in., you can check the fit by applying tape to the face frame to represent the outside edges of the doors and drawers. This allows you to visualize the doors installed and alerts you to any problems.

The most critical part of the cabinet refacing job is measuring for and ordering the new doors and drawers. Start by making a sketch of each wall of cabinets showing the doors and drawers.

MEDIUM-GRIT SANDING SPONGE

1 PREPARE THE CABINETS
After removing the doors and drawer fronts, clean all the face frame and end panel surfaces with denatured alcohol. Then scuff the surfaces with a sanding sponge. Finally, clean again with denatured alcohol.

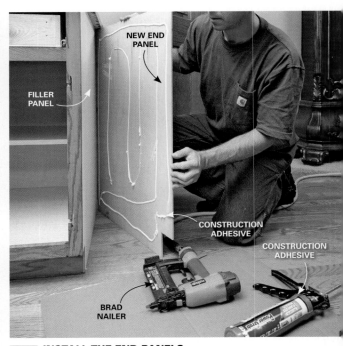

NEW END PANEL

FILLER PANEL

CONSTRUCTION ADHESIVE

CONSTRUCTION ADHESIVE

BRAD NAILER

2 INSTALL THE END PANELS
If the face frame protrudes past the side of the cabinet, add a filler panel to bring them flush. Then cut end panels to fit and attach them with construction adhesive and brads.

Then measure the openings and write down the measurements—width first, then height (Figure A). Double the overlay distance and add this to the opening size to get the size of the door or drawer. For example, if the opening is 18 x 20 in., the door size with a 1/2-in. overlay would be 19 x 21 in. If you want a pair of doors to cover one opening, add two times the overlay to the opening size as usual. Then subtract 1/4 in. for clearance and divide this number by two to get the size of each door.

Calculate drawer front sizes the same way. Add two times the overlay distance to the opening size to arrive at the drawer front size.

Inside corner cabinets with or without rotating shelves can be a little trickier. Joel finds he can replace most existing corner cabinet doors with a "scissors-hinged" door—that is, a pair of doors hinged together and hung from one pair of hinges (bottom-left photo, p. 120). Ask your cabinet door supplier for help figuring the size of corner cabinet doors.

Double-check all your measurements and calculations before you place the order.

Where to get your materials

In addition to new drawer and door fronts, a typical cabinet refacing job includes covering the face of the cabinet frames with veneer and the end panels with 1/4-in. plywood to match. While it's optional, most cabinet refacing projects also include a new cove molding at the top of the cabinets and a thin layer of matching plywood to cover the cabinet toe-kick.

Joel orders doors, drawer fronts, veneer, plywood and moldings prefinished from the manufacturer, but his supplier only sells to

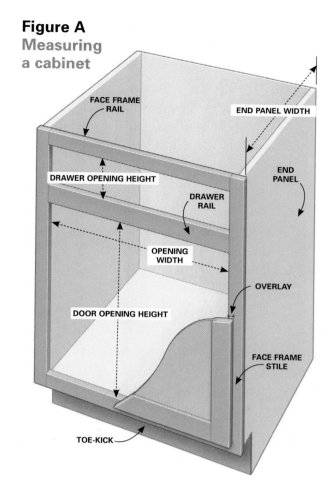

Figure A
Measuring a cabinet

FACE FRAME RAIL

END PANEL WIDTH

DRAWER OPENING HEIGHT

DRAWER RAIL

END PANEL

OPENING WIDTH

OVERLAY

DOOR OPENING HEIGHT

FACE FRAME STILE

TOE-KICK

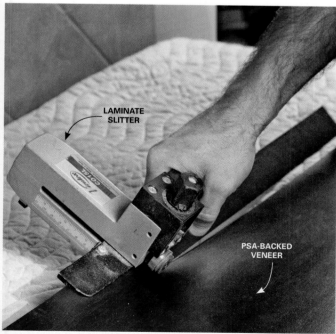

LAMINATE SLITTER

PSA-BACKED VENEER

3 **CUT VENEER INTO STRIPS**
Measure the width of the stiles and rails and cut strips of veneer to fit. Joel is using a laminate slitter in this photo, but you can also use a table saw (see p. 120).

PAPER CUTTER

4 **CUT THE VENEER TO LENGTH**
A paper cutter is the perfect tool for this. Measure the length of the stile and mark the strip of veneer. Line up the mark with the paper cutter blade and cut the strip to length.

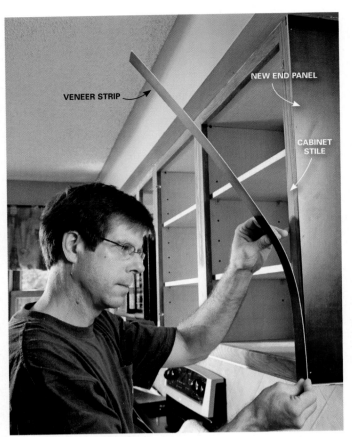

VENEER STRIP

NEW END PANEL

CABINET STILE

5 **APPLY THE VENEER**
Carefully align the veneer and press it lightly to the surface of the face frame. If you don't press too hard, you can still realign it.

professionals. You can search online for cabinet-refacing supplies to find companies that will provide all the parts prefinished, or you can buy unfinished parts and finish them yourself. One online source for prefinished doors and parts is refacedepot.com. A few sources for unfinished doors are distinctivedoordesigns.com and rawdoors.net. At rockler.com, you'll find doors and 2 x 8-ft. sheets of veneer with pressure-sensitive adhesive (PSA) on the back. Ask at your local lumberyard for 1/4-in. hardwood plywood and moldings.

Measure and make a list of the veneer strips you'll need to cover the face frames. From this list, figure out how many 24 x 96-in. sheets of PSA-backed veneer sheets you'll need. Allow extra material, though. There are a few inches on the outside edges of PSA veneer that are unusable. On average, one sheet will cover face frames for about 15 doors.

Then measure the end panels and make a list of the sizes you need. You can order the plywood cut to rough size from some online suppliers, or figure out how many 4 x 8-ft. sheets of 1/4-in. plywood to buy from the lumberyard. The face frames on most modern cabinets overhang the end panel slightly. Rather than cut off this overhang, which is messy and time-consuming, Joel creates a flush surface by gluing a filler panel to the end first (Photo 2, p. 116). Joel says most cabinets have either a 1/8-in. or a 1/4-in. overhang, so check yours and buy the appropriate thickness of plywood or hardboard to fill the space. Finally, make a list of the moldings you'll need, including the toe-kick cover.

You'll also need denatured alcohol, rags, medium-grit sanding sponge, construction adhesive (Joel prefers Loctite Power Grab), 3/4-in. brad nails and a stain pen and colored putty to match the new stain color.

VENEER TOOL

6 **PRESS THE VENEER**
Pull the veneer tool along the veneer to smooth and adhere it. Press down firmly to ensure a good bond.

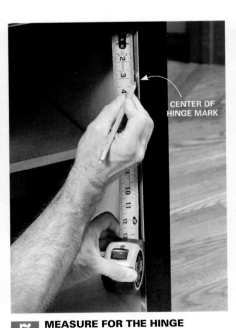

CENTER OF HINGE MARK

7 **MEASURE FOR THE HINGE LOCATION**
Mark the center of the hinge on the face frame stile. Calculate this distance by measuring from the top of your new door to the center of hinge and subtracting the overlay.

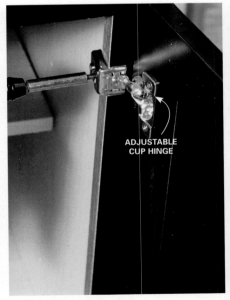

ADJUSTABLE CUP HINGE

8 **HANG THE DOOR**
Line up the center of the hinge with your mark and drill a pilot hole. Then drive a screw through the top hinge plate into the stile. Attach the bottom hinge the same way.

Prepare the cabinets

Since the sanding involved creates a little dust, Joel recommends emptying the cabinets before you start. Next, remove the doors by unscrewing the hinges from the face frame. Also remove or modify the drawer fronts. There are two types of drawers. On most new cabinets, the drawer front is a separate piece and can be taken off by removing the screws from inside the drawer. But some drawer fronts are attached to the drawer sides. If you have this type of drawer, you'll have to take the drawer out and remove the overhanging parts of the front by sawing them off. Then you'll screw through the old drawer fronts to attach the new ones.

Test the fit by placing the modified drawer back into the cabinet and pushing it in to make sure there's enough clearance behind the drawer for the drawer front to sit flush with the surface of the face frame. If the drawer protrudes, you'll have to order or build new drawers. In addition to removing doors and drawer fronts, pry off any moldings you plan to replace.

To ensure that the pressure-sensitive adhesive on the veneer and the construction adhesive for the end panels bond well, the face frames and end panels must be clean and scuffed up slightly. Start by cleaning the face frame and end panels with a rag dampened in denatured alcohol. Then scuff all the surfaces with a medium-grit sanding sponge (Photo 1). Don't use a power sander or sand to bare wood. The PSA-backed veneer won't stick well to bare wood. Finally, clean the surfaces again with denatured alcohol to remove the dust.

Joel doesn't bother to fill small screw holes or other small imperfections. The veneer is thick enough to span them without a problem. But he uses a two-part hardening-type wood filler to fill large dents and chips. Joel said he sometimes encounters a face frame stile at the end of cabinets that's rounded or beveled. He fills the bevel or round-over with the two-part wood filler after installing the new end panels but before applying the face frame veneer.

Figure B
Cabinet door types

If you have inset or lip doors, you can convert them to overlay doors for your refacing project just by using the correct overlay cup hinge.

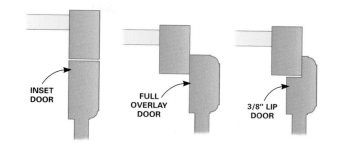

INSET DOOR FULL OVERLAY DOOR 3/8" LIP DOOR

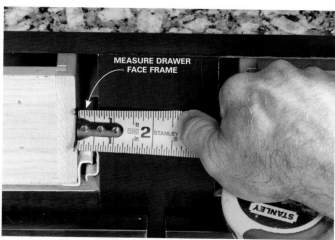

9 MEASURE FOR THE DRAWER FRONT PLACEMENT
Measure the distance from the drawer side to the face frame stile. Also measure from the drawer bottom to the face frame drawer rail. Add the overlay distance to these measurements to arrive at the dimension you'll mark on the back of the drawer front (Photo 10).

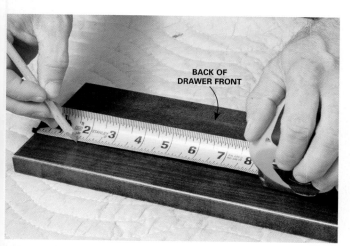

10 MARK THE DRAWER LOCATION
Use the dimensions you calculated (Photo 9) to mark the back of the drawer front.

11 ATTACH THE DRAWER FRONT
Align the drawer box with the marks and drive screws through the drawer into the drawer front. Double-check the screw length to make sure the screws won't go through the face of the new drawer front.

Cover the face frame and end panels

With the cabinets prepped and cleaned, it's time to start making the transformation. The first step is to install the end panels. If the face frame overhangs the existing end panel, add a filler to create a flush surface. Joel attaches plywood with construction adhesive and uses a few 3/4-in. brads to hold it in place. Next, measure and cut an end panel to size so its front edge is flush with the surface of the face frame. Hold the end panel in place and mark the notch for the toe-kick. Cut out the notch. Then install the panel with construction adhesive and a few brads (Photo 2). Cover all the end panels before starting on the face frame veneer.

There are two methods for applying veneer to a face frame. You can cut and install oversize strips and trim them in place with a sharp razor knife. But Joel prefers to cut the strips to the exact width and length needed before applying them. He does this easily with a special tool called a laminate slitter. The tool is intended to cut strips of plastic laminate, but it works great for veneer, too. To use it, you set the depth and width of the cut. Then simply slide the tool along the edge of the sheet to create a perfect-width strip. You can also use a table saw to cut strips of veneer.

Measure the width of the stiles and rails and cut strips from the sheet of PSA-backed veneer (Photo 3). Then measure the height of the end stiles and cut strips to length with a paper cutter (Photo 4). Start by applying veneer to the outermost stiles in a run of cabinets (Photo 5). Smooth and bond the veneer by pressing it with the veneer tool (Photo 6). Next, measure the distance between the stiles and cut strips of veneer to cover the long horizontal rails. Check the fit before you pull off the paper backing. Then apply these strips and press them down. Cover the remaining stiles, and on the lower cabinets finish by covering the drawer rails.

If you have any veneer that overhangs the face frame slightly, carefully sand it flush. Finally, use a matching stain pen to touch up the unstained edges of veneer and any other imperfections.

Hang the doors and install the drawer fronts

Start the door installation by mounting the cup hinges in the doors. Simply line up the hinge and press it into the large round recess. Then tighten the supplied screws to anchor the hinge. Prepare for hanging the doors by marking the center of the top hinge on the face frame stiles (Photo 7). You don't need to mark for the lower hinge. Hang the door from the top hinge (Photo 8). Then drill the pilot hole for the lower hinge screw and drive the screw to finish the job.

Photos 9 – 11 show how to attach the drawer fronts to the drawer boxes. The key is to measure the distance from the drawer box to the face frame and add the overlay distance. Then transfer these measurements to the back of the drawer front, align the drawer and attach it with four screws. To make the drawer front adjustable, drill oversize screw holes through the drawer and put washers under the screw heads. With this method, you can loosen the screws and move the drawer front slightly to align it perfectly.

When you're done with the door and drawer installation, adjust hinges to align doors with each other. Now you're ready to install your new cabinet door and drawer hardware. For great tips on installing door hardware, go to familyhandyman.com and search for "cabinet hardware."

Finish the project by installing cove molding along the top of the wall cabinets and covering the toe-kick with a thin strip of plywood finished to match the rest of the wood.

Another way to cut veneer

The slitter shown on p. 117 isn't the only tool you can use to cut veneer—you can use your table saw. For the best results, build a simple veneer-ripping jig. Cut a 3-in. strip from a 24 x 24-in. piece of particleboard or plywood and glue it to the edge of the remaining piece. Add 3/4 in. to the width of the veneer you wish to cut, and set the fence. Then send the jig through the saw, stopping about halfway through. Clamp the jig to the table saw fence and you're ready to cut veneer strips. The jig keeps the thin veneer from sliding under the fence, and the narrow slot left by the saw blade supports the veneer to help prevent splintering.

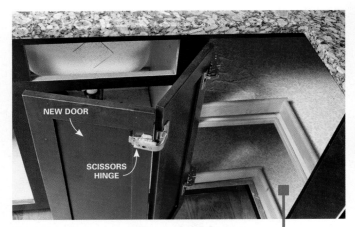

NEW DOOR

SCISSORS HINGE

Corner doors need special hinges

Talk to your door supplier if you need corner doors like these. They require special hinges. If your doors have a 1-1/4-in. overlay like these, you may have to cut 3/4-in.-deep notches in the face frame stile to mount the hinges.

Repair a cabinet hinge screw hole

Cabinets made from particleboard work great in utility and laundry rooms, and they're fairly inexpensive. But particleboard has a major weakness—it doesn't hold screw threads very well. So if you swing the door open too fast, the force can rip the hinge screw right out of the cabinet wall. Don't worry;

the fix is easy and cheap. Here's how to patch things up. You'll need a bottle of wood glue, a 1/2-in. drill bit and a package of 1/2-in.-diameter hardwood plugs (about $2 at a home center).

Start by removing the hinge screws on the cabinet and flipping the hinge out of your way. If the accident pulled out a large

chunk of the particleboard, glue it back into place and let the glue set up before proceeding with the rest of the repair. Drill out the stripped screw hole to accept the plug. Next, fill the hole with wood glue and install the plug (Photo 1). Then drill a pilot hole (Photo 2) and install the new screw—you're all set.

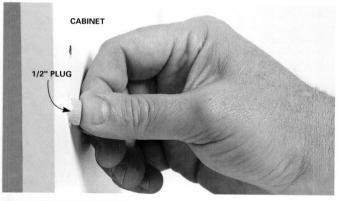

CABINET

1/2" PLUG

1 POP IN THE PLUG
Smear some glue onto the plug and embed it in the hole. Tap the plug with a hammer to fully seat it. Then wipe up any glue ooze with a wet rag.

2 DRILL A PILOT HOLE
Mark the location for the new screw hole. Then drill a pilot hole with a bit that's smaller than the screw's diameter.

Great goofs

Panel remover

While I was enjoying a Sunday nap, my overly ambitious girlfriend removed all the kitchen cabinet doors, took them out back and lined them up against the fence. I awoke to the sound of my 3,000-psi pressure washer's engine and reached the backyard just as she squeezed the trigger and almost instantly blasted the panels out of a few doors. I just laughed—hard! Those doors were ugly anyway.

—Larry Dullock

Fix a swollen sink base bottom

Let's face it—it's easy to get water on the floor of your sink base cabinet. We'll never understand why cabinetmakers use particleboard for the base, but they do. And once it starts swelling, your only option is to replace it. But you don't have to cut out the entire bottom. Here's an easier way to install a new sink base bottom.

Remove the drain lines (and garbage disposer, if there is one) to get maneuvering room. Then trace a cutting line about 3 in. in from all four edges. Then cut out the middle section of the swollen sink base with a jigsaw (Photo 1). Next, cut a piece of 1/2-in. plywood to the interior size of the sink base. Cut slots for the water supply tubes. Then seal the edges and face of the plywood with urethane varnish. Then install the new plywood floor and fasten it to the old floor (Photo 2). Caulk around the edges and pipes to prevent water from seeping under the new floor. Then reattach the P-trap and garbage disposer.

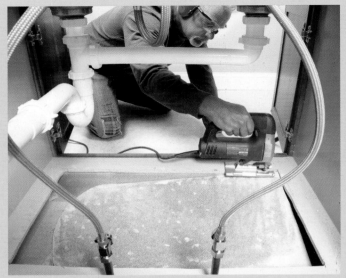

1 REMOVE THE MIDDLE SECTION
Drill a 3/4-in. hole in each corner of the traced cutout line. Then run your jigsaw along the line. Remove the old, swollen floor.

2 DROP IN THE NEW FLOOR AND SCREW IT INTO PLACE
Predrill holes around the perimeter using a countersink bit. Then install brass-colored drywall screws.

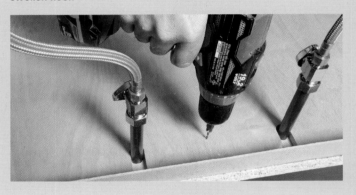

Great goofs

No spaghetti for you!

During a kitchen remodel, we decided to buy new pots and pans the day before our countertops arrived. We couldn't wait to put them away in our new cabinets, and since the countertops weren't on yet, we set the cookware in through the tops of the lower cabinets. A couple of days later after the countertops were installed, we went to grab the big spaghetti pot, but it wouldn't fit through the door opening. Maybe the next homeowners will be able to get it out if they remodel the kitchen.

—Sean Donley

Protect your floor during remodeling

Whenever you're remodeling, it's important to protect any uncarpeted floors from demolition debris and dropped tools. When canvas drop cloths aren't enough, use 4 x 8-ft. sheets of 1/8-in. tempered hardboard, commonly called Masonite.

Start by thoroughly vacuuming the floors so grit doesn't scratch the flooring under the hardboard. Then cut and lay down the hardboard and duct-tape the pieces together at the seams.

If you'll be running the HVAC system during the remodel, be sure you don't cover grilles or registers. Finally, seal around the perimeter with masking tape so grit can't get underneath the hardboard at the edges. A sheet of 1/8-in. hardboard costs about $5 at home centers.

First aid for carpets

After a carpet spill, doing the right thing—right now—can make the difference between a complete recovery and permanent damage. You can treat most food or drink spills with the steps shown here, whether it's wine, coffee or spaghetti sauce.

Use the wet/dry vacuum first

Getting as much of the liquid and solids out of the carpet as quickly as possible is the single most important part of removing a carpet stain. But blotting and scooping can actually drive the stain deep into the carpet backing and pad. Instead, reach for your wet/dry vacuum and vacuum up the spill. Convert your wet/dry vac to wet mode by removing the paper filter and installing a foam cover (if equipped) before sucking anything up (Photo 1).

Apply a cleaning solution

After sucking up as much of the spill as possible, resist the temptation to hit the stain with strong cleaners like vinegar and hydrogen peroxide right out of the gate. Those products can set the stain and even discolor your carpet. They can be used in some cases to remove a stubborn stain, but only as a last resort after you've used a milder cleaning solution.

If you keep a store-bought carpet stain removal product on hand, great. Use it. If not, you can make your own by mixing 1/4 teaspoon dish soap (clear is best) in 1 cup of water. Pour the homemade solution into a spray bottle and apply a generous amount to the soiled area, but don't saturate it. Let the cleaning solution soak into the fibers for a few minutes before moving on to the next step.

Blot from the outside in

Blot the stain with a clean white cloth (dyed fabric can transfer color to the carpet), working from the outside in (Photo 2). Your goal is to move the carpet fibers, spread the cleaner slightly, and soak up the stain. Avoid aggressive blotting, scrubbing and stomping on the blotter. That just drives the stain deeper into the pile, backing and padding, making stain removal even more difficult. After blotting, use your wet/dry vac again to remove as much cleaning solution as possible.

Rinse, rinse, rinse

Leaving cleaning solution in the carpet is a big mistake. The leftover cleaning chemicals attract dirt, causing the spot to get soiled faster than the rest of the carpet. Even if you remove the stain, you'll eventually have a dirty area at the exact spot of the stain. Plus, the rinsing step helps remove any leftover stain liquid. So rinse the stained area multiple times with clear water (Photo 3). Vacuum the rinse water between applications and continue vacuuming until you remove as much final rinse water as possible.

Leaving food or organic matter in your shop vacuum will turn it into a stinky science experiment in no time. So clean it right away (Photo 4).

WET VAC NOZZLE

1 SUCK UP THE MESS
Push the hose directly onto the carpet fibers and leave it in place for several seconds. Don't rub or drag the hose over the carpet. Move to an adjoining spot and repeat as many times as required to remove as much of the spill as possible.

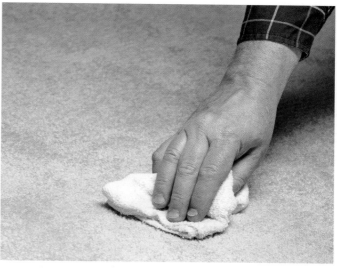

2 BLOT GENTLY
Fold a clean white cloth into a small square and dab the carpet, starting at the outside edge. Roll the cloth toward the center and refold the cloth to a clean section as you soak up more stain.

3 RINSE THE STAINED AREA
Dab or spray clean water onto the stained area. Never pour water directly onto the carpet—it'll push the cleaning solution and stain into the backing and padding and can cause mold.

4 CLEAN YOUR SHOP VACUUM THE EASY WAY
Dump some disinfecting cleaner into a bucket of warm water and drop your hose into it. Empty the tank and rinse both the hose and tank with clean water.

What to do next

Our techniques won't set the stain or damage your carpet, so if your stain is particularly stubborn, you can proceed to the next level and follow specific spot removal advice. Pet vomit, and fecal and urine stains, require additional neutralization and disinfection steps. Find advice for treating those stains by searching for "carpet pet" at familyhandyman.com.

Pull the wrinkles out of your carpet

Have you got carpet wrinkles? If you ignore them, they'll wear and become permanent eyesores—even if you stretch them later. The good news is, you don't have to hire a carpet layer—fix it yourself with rental tools and these instructions. Rent a power stretcher and knee kicker for less than $40 (for four hours) at an equipment rental store. Then buy a carpet knife (not a utility knife) for about $9 at any home center.

You'll be stretching from the center of the carpet and pulling it at an angle into a corner. So move any furniture that'll be in the path of the stretch. Loosen the carpet in the corner (Photo 1). Next, set up the power stretcher at an angle across the room. Set the tooth depth on the power stretcher based on the carpet pile depth (Photo 2).

Operate the power stretcher with the lever and capture the excess carpet in the tack strip as you stretch. Use the knee kicker on both sides of the locked power stretcher to help lock the carpet into the tacks. Once the wrinkles are out and the carpet is secure in the tack strip, cut off the excess (Photo 4).

TACK STRIP

1 **PULL THE CARPET FREE**
Grab the carpet right next to the baseboard and pull it straight up. Then loosen the rest of the carpet along the wall.

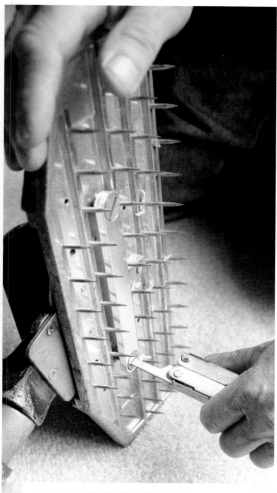

3 SINK AND STRETCH
Set the teeth into the carpet near the wall and push down on the stretcher handle. Then lock the stretched carpet into place by jamming it behind the tack strip with a putty or linoleum knife.

2 DIAL IN THE CORRECT TOOTH DEPTH
Adjust the tooth depth by loosening or tightening the screws on the spacer bar. Set the bar so the teeth grab just the carpet pile, not the jute backing or pad (the pad is stapled to the floor and shouldn't be stretched).

4 TRIM OFF EXCESS CARPET
Fold the excess carpet so the backing is facing up. Then cut it off with the carpet knife.

Smooth talk about wrinkles

Professional carpet installer Steve Hoover explained how carpet gets wrinkled. "Carpet has to acclimate to interior conditions before it's installed. That's especially important if the carpet has been in a cold truck or exposed to high humidity. If it's installed while it's still cold or humid, you're going to have wrinkling problems later on," he said.

Improper stretching during installation is another cause. "Some installers lay the pad and carpet and secure it with just the knee kicker. Since the carpet was never really stretched, it's going to wrinkle after it's seen some traffic," he added.

Steve's advice? Make sure the installers allow enough time for the carpet to acclimate and insist that they actually stretch it with a power stretcher during installation.

"If the carpet wasn't stretched during installation, it's going to wrinkle later."

Rescue your carpet from pet accidents

Many pet owners do exactly what they shouldn't do when they clean up pet messes. But if you learn how to clean up the mess right way, with the right products, you can prevent a permanent stain. Here are three tips that work with all pet messes. You'll get the best results if you have the right products and a carpet extractor on hand when you discover the accident.

Wet messes

Using paper towels to blot up urine and vomit soaks up the surface liquid but still leaves a lot in the carpet. And stomping on those paper towels only makes it worse. That forces the liquid deeper into the padding and then into the subflooring. Instead, invest in a handheld carpet extractor (shown is the Bissel SpotLifter 2X). Don't use a shop vacuum—the smell will linger in the filter and it's much harder to clean than a small extractor. Hit the carpet as soon as possible and vacuum like there's no tomorrow.

Solid messes

Scooping up the solids with paper towels or rags can actually force them into the carpet. Instead, use a puttyknife and dustpan to scrape them up, as shown.

Treating the carpet

To treat a urine stain, fresh or dried, use a urine-specific bio-enzymatic cleaner (one choice is Nature's Miracle Urine Destroyer). It neutralizes the urea and uric acid and eliminates proteins and starches. Ordinary carpet cleaners can't do that. In fact, using a carpet cleaner before a bio-enzymatic cleaner can set the stain permanently.

Liquid messes spread as they're absorbed into the carpet, so always treat a larger area than the original stain. For all solid messes, saturate the stain with an oxygenated bio-enzymatic cleaner. Let it sit for 45 minutes to separate additional solids from the carpet fibers. Then clean up those solids.

THE BEST TOOL FOR THE JOB
Buy a handheld extractor to suck liquids from the carpet. It works much better than trying to absorb a mess with paper towels or rags. An extractor is made for this task and, unlike a shop vacuum, is easy to clean.

USE A PUTTY KNIFE FOR SOLIDS
Sink the edge of the putty knife into the carpet at the edge of the mess. Then push it forward to scrape the solid waste up and into the dustpan.

Bio-enzymatic cleaners take a long time to work. Just let the treated area air-dry. Then vacuum to raise the nap.

Cleaning solutions

Home remedies that use vinegar and baking soda simply mask the odor for a short time and don't eliminate the cause. Instead, buy a product made for your particular type of pet mess.

Commercial pet cleaning products range in price from a few dollars to more than $20 per quart. The least expensive products usually contain a carpet detergent for the stain and an odor-masking chemical. Since they don't actually neutralize the substance, the smell usually returns on humid days.

Spend more to get a product with enzymes. These products are good for small surface stains. But if you're dealing with a large stain, one that has soaked deep into the carpet, or one that has already dried, spend more yet and use a product with bacteria, enzymes and an oxygen booster.

Cookie cutter carpet patch

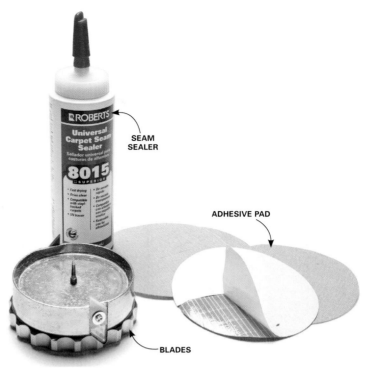

SEAM SEALER

ADHESIVE PAD

BLADES

Are you tired of looking at that wine stain your brother-in-law so graciously gifted you last Christmas? Before replacing the carpet in the entire room, first try a cookie cutter repair kit. They're available online (search for "cookie cutter carpet tool") and at flooring supply stores. The idea is to cut out the stain from the highly visible area and replace it with a patch from a remnant, a closet or from under the sofa.

An adhesive pad holds the new piece in place. Some adhesive pads require ironing. For a stronger bond, use carpet seam sealer around the perimeter to fuse the backing of the patch to the backing of the surrounding carpet. You can buy seam sealer.

The kit we tried came with thorough instructions, but here are a few things to keep in mind: You'll need to cut out the stained portion first so you can cut out a replacement piece with an identical pattern. Even if your carpet appears to have no pattern, it does. Before installing the new piece, examine the backing on the carpet. It should look like a grid of sorts (you may have to lift it up a bit). The orientation of the grid on the patch should line up with the surrounding carpet.

Try to clear a path for the cutting knives. The fewer carpet fibers you cut, the better. This is harder to do with looped-pile carpeting like Berber. If you're lucky enough to have a remnant, try a practice run on that. As with most seams in carpeting, it might take a while for the patch to blend in, but it will be less noticeable than the eye-grabbing merlot stain.

1 CUT OUT THE STAIN
Twist to slice out the damaged area. Do the same in a closet to cut a perfect patch.

ADHESIVE PAD

2 STICK IN THE PATCH
Lay in an adhesive-backed pad to secure the carpet patch. Make sure the nap direction of the patch matches the nap of the surrounding carpet.

Flawless floor sanding

26 tips for a smooth job

Sanding hardwood floors might seem like a pros-only project. It's a big job that creates big disruptions in your household. And then there's that big, scary sanding machine...

But it's really not that difficult. I've helped hundreds of homeowners—some of them complete DIY novices—successfully prep their floors for a new finish. Here are some of my most important tips for smooth sanding.

Our floor-sanding savant

Kadee Macey is owner of Pete's Hardwood Floors in St. Paul, MN. Despite a background in art history and English literature, she's spent 13 years sanding hardwood and teaching others to do it themselves.

Good-bye, base shoe

If a room has quarter-round molding (aka "base shoe") at the bottom of baseboards, I usually pry it off and reinstall it later. Here's why: Edge sanding slightly lowers the floor and leaves the baseboard standing on a little plateau. You think you won't notice this, but you will. Edge sanding also scuffs up base shoe, which means touch-up work later.

Removing the base shoe sidesteps both problems. Label the base shoe as you remove it to avoid confusion when you reinstall it. Exception: If the base shoe is bonded to the baseboard by decades of paint buildup, I leave it in place. If you have newer baseboards and no quarter-round, leave it in place, but expect lots of the aforementioned touch-ups.

Pet stains are forever

Water stains usually disappear after a couple of passes of the sander. But stains caused by pet urine often penetrate so deep into the wood that you just can't sand them out. Bleach formulated for wood floors may be worth a try, but in my experience the results are mediocre at best, and at worst, the wood is left pitted and blotched.

Often, the only solution is to replace the wood—or finish over the stain and think of it as a permanent memorial to a beloved pet.

How do you tell water from pee? Pet stains are darker (deep gray, almost black around the edges) and often look like a map of Indonesia, with big and small islands covering a large area. To see how to replace a section of wood floor, go to familyhandyman.com and search for "patch wood floor."

Prep the room

Some of the prep work is obvious, like removing all the furniture and covering doorways with plastic. Here are some steps DIYers often don't think of:

- ► Cover or plug air grilles to keep dust out of ducts. Turn off the HVAC system at the thermostat; less air movement means less dust traveling around your house.
- ► Remove all window coverings and any art on the walls (unless you want to clean them later).
- ► Remove doors that open into the room. You can't completely sand under doors, even by opening and closing them.
- ► Raise low-hanging light fixtures; just tie two links of the chain together with wire. Otherwise, you're guaranteed to bump your head. Repeatedly.
- ► Nail down any loose boards with finish nails.
- ► When you're sanding, nail heads will rip the sanding belt (which costs you money) or gouge the sanding drum (which costs you more money). So countersink all nails by at least 1/8 in.

Detect nails

Drag a metal snow shovel across the floor (upside down). When it hits a nail, you'll hear it.

Scrape out corners

When the sanding is done, use a paint scraper to attack spots that the machines can't reach. A sharp scraper will leave a super-smooth glazed surface that won't take finish the same as the surrounding wood. So rough up scraped areas with 80- or 100-grit paper.

Rental tips

You'll need two rental machines: a drum sander to sand most of the floor and an edger to sand along baseboards. Here are some tips:

▸ Rent from a flooring specialty shop rather than a general rental store. You'll get expertise at no extra expense.

▸ Measure the room. Knowing the square footage will help the crew at the rental store estimate how many sanding belts and discs you'll need.

▸ Prep before you rent. The prep work will take longer than you think. Don't waste money by picking up the sanders before you're ready to use them.

▸ Get a drum sander that uses a continuous belt or sleeve, not one that requires you to wrap a strip of abrasive around the drum. That's tedious and often leads to chatter marks on the floor.

▸ Think twice before you rent a flat-pad sander (aka "orbital" or "square-buff" sander). Sure, they're easier to use, but they're just not aggressive enough to bite into finishes or hardwoods.

"We don't rent flat-pad sanders. For most jobs, they just don't work."

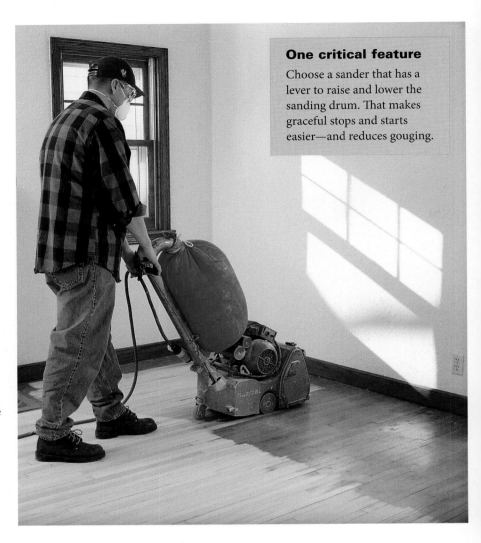

One critical feature

Choose a sander that has a lever to raise and lower the sanding drum. That makes graceful stops and starts easier—and reduces gouging.

Pick a starting grit

It takes coarse abrasive to cut through a finish and into hardwood. But determining just how coarse isn't easy for a DIYer. So I recommend a trial-and-error process: Start with 36-grit. If that doesn't completely remove the finish in one pass, step down to 24-grit. If 24-grit doesn't remove at least three-quarters of the finish in one pass, go to 16-grit. Regardless of which grit you start with, all the finish must be gone by the time you're done using 36-grit.

Nix the stripper

DIYers often think that paint stripper is a good way to get rid of the finish before sanding. But don't waste your time. Sanding is faster. And cheaper.

Edger education

The edger is basically a sanding disc mounted on a big, powerful motor. A simple tool, but not so simple to use. Here are some tips to help you master the edger and minimize the inevitable swirls left by the spinning disc:

▸ Follow up each phase of drum sanding with edging. After you've drum-sanded at 36-grit, for example, edge with 36-grit.

▸ Place a nylon pad under the sand-paper. This cushion minimizes gouges and deep swirls. Get pads at the rental store.

▸ Replace the sandpaper when it's dull. Dull paper won't remove swirls left by the previous grit.

▸ At the end of the job, lay a flashlight on the floor to highlight any leftover swirls. Then hand-sand them out with 80- or 100-grit paper.

▸ A warning to woodworkers: You'll be tempted to edge with your belt sander, but even the biggest belt sander can't cut half as fast as an edger. You'll also be tempted to polish out swirls with a

Change belts often

I sell sanding belts, so this might sound self-serving. But trust me. Using dull belts is a strategy you'll regret. Here's the problem: After the floor finish is gone, you can't see whether the sander is doing its job. So you keep sanding. The machine is raising dust and everything seems fine. But the dull paper isn't cutting deep enough to remove the scratches left by the previous grit. And you may not discover this until you put a finish on the floor. A dull edging disc is even worse, since it won't remove the ugly cross-grain scratches left by the previous disc.

Even if paper feels sharp, it may be beyond its prime. So the best way to judge is by square footage covered. The belts I sell cover about 250 sq. ft., and edger discs are spent after about 20 sq. ft. That varies, so ask at the rental store.

random orbit sander. But beware: That can overpolish the wood so it won't take finish the same as the surrounding wood. Hand-sanding is safer.

> *"Edging with a belt sander is like digging a ditch with a trowel. You can do it, but it will take forever."*

Don't skip grits

The initial coarse grits remove the finish and flatten the wood. But that's not enough. You need to progress through every grit to polish off the scratches left by the previous grit. On most of my jobs, the sequence is 24-36-60-80 for coarse-grained wood like oak. Scratches are more visible on fine-grained wood like birch or maple, so I go to 100-grit.

"The most common DIY mistake is timid sanding. If you don't sand deep enough, you'll end up with a dingy floor."

Screen the floor

After you've finished with the sanders, the floor will look so good that you'll be tempted to skip this step. But don't. "Screening" blends the edge-sanded perimeter with the drum-sanded field and polishes away sanding scratches. You can do it with a rented buffing machine or with a sanding pole (like the one used for sanding drywall). Either way, the abrasive to use is 120- or 150-grit sanding screen (again, just like the stuff used on drywall).

Clean up between grits

Sweep or vacuum the floor before you move up to the next grit. Even the best abrasives throw off a few granules while sanding. And a 36-grit granule caught under a 60-grit belt will leave an ugly gash in the floor. Wrap the vacuum nozzle with tape to avoid marring the floor.

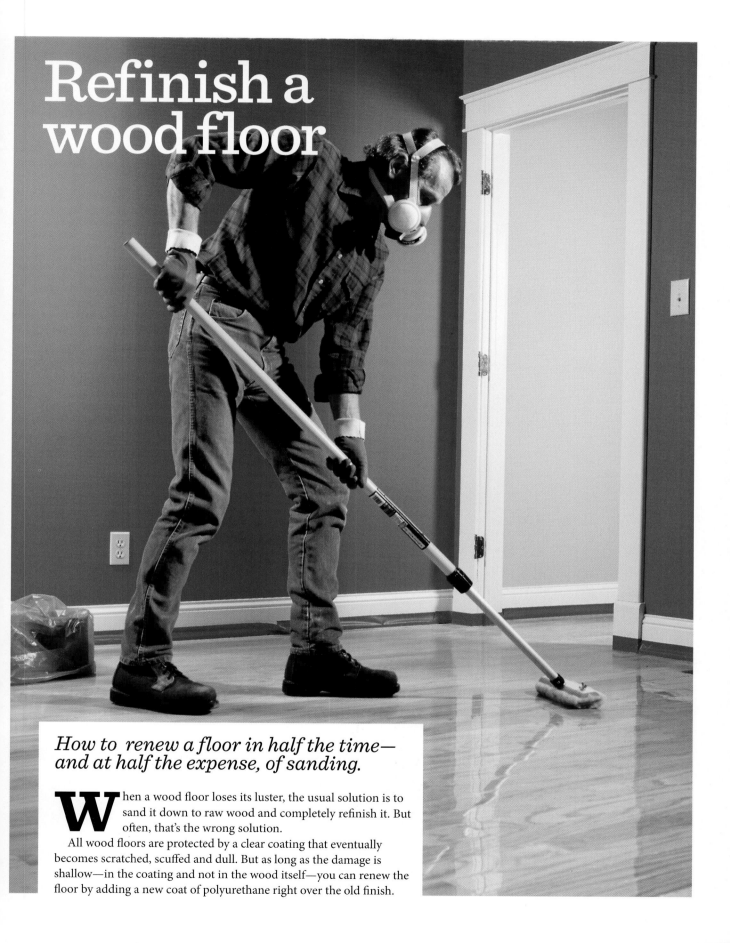

Refinish a wood floor

How to renew a floor in half the time—and at half the expense, of sanding.

When a wood floor loses its luster, the usual solution is to sand it down to raw wood and completely refinish it. But often, that's the wrong solution.

All wood floors are protected by a clear coating that eventually becomes scratched, scuffed and dull. But as long as the damage is shallow—in the coating and not in the wood itself—you can renew the floor by adding a new coat of polyurethane right over the old finish.

Test for adhesion

Pick at least two test areas on the floor: one in a high-traffic zone, the other along a wall or in a closet. Clean each area with a wood floor cleaner and roughen a 6 x 6-in. area with sanding screen. Then wipe away the sanding residue, mask around the test area, and give it a coat of polyurethane (Photo 1).

After 24 hours, take a look at the polyurethane. Aside from a few tiny "whiskers" caused by dust particles, it should be smooth. Then scrape the polyurethane with a coin. Press down firmly, but not too hard—even a sound finish might scrape off if you press as hard as you can (Photo 2).

If the polyurethane is smooth and doesn't scrape off with moderate pressure, your test is a success and you can recoat the floor.

But if the polyurethane flakes off as you scrape, or if the surface has a crackled or orange-peel texture (Photo 3), there's something on the old finish preventing the new finish from adhering properly. That "something" could be furniture polish, residue from window cleaner or a hundred other things. But whatever it is, there's only one solution: You have to sand down to bare wood and completely refinish the floor.

4 Clean the floor using a wood flooring cleaner. A dull putty knife is handy for scraping up petrified chewing gum and other gunk. For tough marks, use a scouring pad dampened with mineral spirits. If that fails, try sanding screen. As you clean, use pieces of masking tape to mark any deep scratches, ridges or areas where the finish has worn away. You'll have to give these trouble spots special attention later (see "Problem Areas," p. 138).

5 Roughen the existing finish along walls and in corners where the buffer can't reach. The purpose is only to scratch up the finish, not to wear it down—or worse, sand right through it. Three or four passes with the sanding screen are usually enough. Wear gloves to protect your hands from the abrasive screen.

As with any wood-finishing project, 90 percent of this job is preparation. You have to thoroughly clean the floor, touch up any deep scratches and roughen the existing finish so the new finish will adhere well. Expect to spend at least one full day on this prep work. The recoating itself usually takes less than an hour.

Recoating takes a lot less time, skill and money than full-scale sanding and refinishing. And although roughing up the existing finish creates plenty of dust, it's still much less messy than sanding down to bare wood. There's another advantage: Every time you sand a floor down to bare wood, you remove some of the wood. A solid wood floor can be sanded several times before that's a problem. But laminated floors (glue-down or floating floors) have only a thin layer of good-looking wood veneer over a plywood-like base. The veneer can be sanded once or twice—after that, sanding will expose the plywood core beneath.

Where recoating won't work

The type of flooring you have doesn't matter. Recoating works on solid wood, laminated wood and parquet floors alike. But a new coat of polyurethane may not stick to your existing finish.

If your floor's finish was applied before the 1970s, it's probably wax, old-fashioned varnish or shellac. No new finish will stick to a wax finish or any other finish that's ever had wax applied to it. Polyurethane might adhere to an old, unwaxed varnish or shellac finish. But these finishes do wear out, and since they're probably almost 50 years old, it's best to sand them off and start over.

In fact, if you have an old finish from the days before polyurethane, your only alternative to sanding is wax. If the floor is in fair condition, wax can restore the shine. A wood flooring dealer can recommend a suitable product. Wax is easy to use, but not very durable. You'll probably have to rewax every six months or so.

Even if the existing finish is polyurethane, good adhesion isn't a sure thing. Residue from all kinds of household chemicals, such as furniture polish, glass cleaner, insecticide and wallpaper paste, can interfere with adhesion. Since you can't know for certain all the potions that have landed on your floor, you must test for adhesion before you recoat your floor.

6 Set the buffer on the sanding screen. The screen isn't attached to the buffer at all, but stays put under the weight of the machine. The screen will wear out after 10 to 15 minutes of use. When it does, flip it over or start with a new screen. Check the screen for grit every few minutes and wipe away any large particles that might scratch the floor.

Note: Be sure to lock the buffer's adjustable handle in place before you begin buffing.

Problem areas

► As you're cleaning, you may find deep scratches that go through the finish and into the wood. You usually can't make these scratches disappear completely, but you can make them a lot less noticeable. If your floor is as light or lighter than the floor shown here, first wet the scratch with mineral spirits. A wet coat of mineral spirits produces approximately the same look as a coat of polyurethane. And on a light-colored floor, it might darken the scratch just enough to hide it.

► If that doesn't work, apply some wood stain to the scratch using a cotton swab. Because the scratch is rough and porous, it will absorb a lot of stain. So begin experimenting with a stain that's much lighter than the tone of your floor and wipe away the excess stain right after you apply it. For best results, use two stain colors to match the light and dark patterns in the wood grain (Photo 7).

If your floor has a high-traffic area where the clear finish is completely worn away, wet the area with mineral spirits to see what it will look like with a coat of polyurethane. If it looks good, clean the area thoroughly, apply a coat of polyurethane and give it at least two days to cure. Then you can buff and recoat the new polyurethane along with the rest of the floor.

► Look out for ridges. The buffer will eat right through the finish down to bare wood at high spots. And if your floor is colored with wood stain, you'll be left with light-colored strips where the stain has been rubbed off. Photo 8 shows how a solid-wood floor can buckle in high humidity. But smaller ridges, where the wood strips cup slightly or one plank sits a bit higher than the next, can cause just as much trouble.

If you can flatten a ridge by standing on it, fasten it down with a finishing nail or two. If you can't flatten the ridge, you'll have to roughen the area by hand using sanding screen. And remember to avoid that area with the buffer.

► Stains that have penetrated through the finish as well as the wood can only be removed by sanding. But there's no harm in recoating over them—if you can live with them.

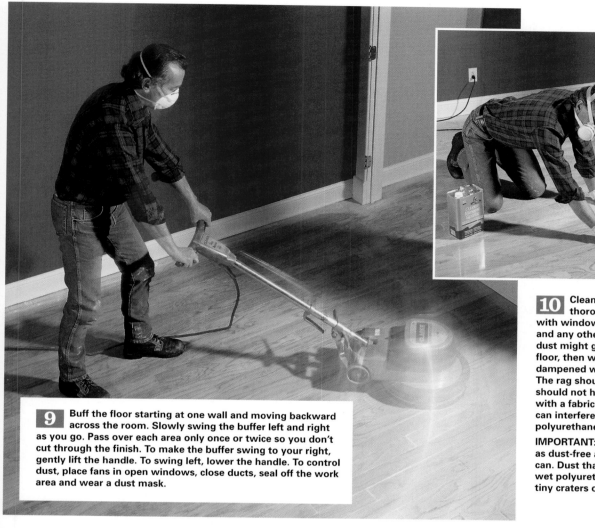

9 Buff the floor starting at one wall and moving backward across the room. Slowly swing the buffer left and right as you go. Pass over each area only once or twice so you don't cut through the finish. To make the buffer swing to your right, gently lift the handle. To swing left, lower the handle. To control dust, place fans in open windows, close ducts, seal off the work area and wear a dust mask.

10 Clean the room thoroughly, beginning with windowsills, moldings and any other surface where dust might gather. Vacuum the floor, then wipe it with a rag dampened with mineral spirits. The rag should be lint-free and should not have been washed with a fabric softener, which can interfere with the polyurethane's adhesion.

IMPORTANT: Make the room as dust-free as you possibly can. Dust that settles on the wet polyurethane will create tiny craters or bumps.

Money and materials

Recoating a typical floor (200 sq. ft. or so) usually costs less than $100. Most of that goes for tools and renting the buffer, so recoating floors in two rooms costs only a few bucks more than recoating one room.

All the tools and materials for this project are available at home centers. Wood flooring dealers also carry most of these products. Here's what you'll need:

▶ A liquid floor cleaner formulated specifically for wood floors.

▶ Scouring pads (a.k.a. "synthetic steel wool") to remove marks on the floor. Scotchbrite is one common brand. Regular steel wool will also work, but don't use steel wool if you plan to use a water-based finish; the tiny particles of steel left behind will cause rust stains.

▶ A 2- or 3-in. natural bristle brush made specifically for applying varnish and other clear coatings.

▶ A finish applicator pad designed to apply floor finishes (Photo 12). You can buy a long handle that screws into the applicator, but any push broom handle will work. Some applicators are made for oil-based finishes; others are made for water-based products. Check the label.

▶ A respirator that has organic vapor cartridges to filter out harmful fumes (Photo 10) while you're using mineral spirits and oil-based polyurethane. These respirators are pricey ($20 to $40), but absolutely necessary.

▶ A gallon of mineral spirits, 100-grit sanding screen and a dust mask.

▶ A buffer (Photo 9), which will cost you about $30 per day at a rental center or flooring store. You'll also need a buffing pad (made from synthetic mesh) and sanding screen discs (the same material used to roughen the floor by hand). The screens are available in several grits. Use 150- or 120-grit if available. They're less likely to cut through the finish into the wood than 100-grit. Get at least three screens for a typical room. You can return any you don't use.

Tip: The buffer is a heavy, powerful machine. Learn to control it by practicing on a smooth concrete floor, using only the pad.

11 Brush polyurethane along a wall that runs parallel to the wood strips. Then brush about 3 ft. along adjoining walls. This will give you a 3-ft. wide working area that runs the entire length of the room. Finish that area using the applicator pad (as in Photo 12), then brush along walls to prepare the next 3-ft. wide section. Even with oil-based polyurethane, you have to move fast so you can begin each section before the previous one starts to dry.

Buyer's guide

Organic vapor respirators are available at home centers and at paint and auto parts stores. Or you can get one by mail from the William Alden Co. (800-249-8665) for about $25. Ask for Item No. 539-387.

12 Apply polyurethane using an applicator pad attached to a long handle. When spreading the finish, you can dip the applicator into a paint tray filled with polyurethane, but a cardboard box lined with a plastic bag is less likely to tip over. To smooth the finish, first "unload" the pad by pressing it hard against a dry part of the floor. Then drag the applicator lightly across the floor from one end of the room to the other.

Choosing a finish

The best floor finish for a do-it-yourselfer is polyurethane. Other floor finishes are either less durable or much more difficult to work with. You'll find two types of polyurethane at home centers:

The oil-based polyurethanes (or "oil-modified urethanes") are easier to apply because they dry slowly, giving you more time to spread and smooth the finish. They have a yellowish hue and slowly darken with time, which may be good or bad depending on the look you want. The big drawback to oil-based products is the nasty vapor they give off. You must open windows and wear a respirator.

Water-based polyurethanes (or "waterborne urethanes") are generally a bit more durable than oil-based versions. They have a milky color when wet, but they dry crystal clear and remain clear. The milky color makes them easy to see, so you're less likely to miss spots. Still, water-based products are harder to apply because they dry fast.

Note: With either type of polyurethane, be sure it's recommended for wood floors before you buy.

Replace a laminate floor plank

You can fix minor chips and scratches in a laminate floor with filler products from the home center. But if the damage is severe, you have to replace the plank (you did save a few from the installation, right?). It's a job you can do yourself in about two hours. In addition to a spare plank, you'll need a circular saw, hammer and chisel, router or table saw, drill and wood glue.

Some flooring experts recommend removing the base molding and unsnapping and numbering every plank until you get to the damaged portion. That works if the damaged plank is close to the wall. But trust us, if the damaged section is more than a few rows out from the wall, it's actually faster to just cut it out. If your laminate floor is glued together, the unsnapping routine won't work at all. Start by drawing a cutting line 1-1/2 in. in from all four edges of the plank. Drill a 3/8-in. relief hole at each corner of the cutting line and again 1/4 in. from each corner of the plank.

Cut out the center section with a circular saw, cutting from hole to hole (Photo 1). Next, cut from the center section into each corner, stopping at the drilled hole (Photo 2). Finally, cut a relief cut from the center section out toward the seam of each plank. Tap a chisel into each relief cut to break out the uncut portion. Then remove all the cut pieces.

The new plank has a groove at one end and one side, as well as a tongue at the opposite end and side. But you can't install it until you cut off the bottom lip of both grooves and the side tongue. Use a utility knife to remove them (Photo 3). Here's a tip for cutting the groove: Stick the blade inside the groove and cut off the bottom from the inside (or use a table saw).

Apply a bead of wood glue to all four

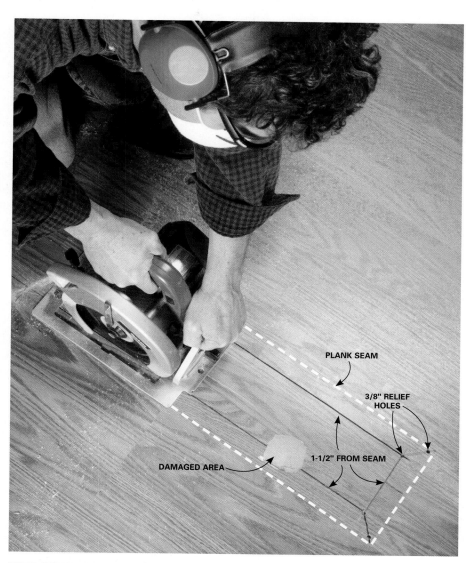

PLANK SEAM

3/8" RELIEF HOLES

DAMAGED AREA

1-1/2" FROM SEAM

1 REMOVE THE CENTER SECTION
Set the depth of your circular saw a tad deeper than the floor thickness. Then lift the blade guard and dip the blade into the cutting line.

edges of the new plank. Insert the glued tongue of the new plank into the groove on the existing flooring and drop the plank into place. Wipe off any excess glue and load books on the plank until it's dry.

2 **CUT TO THE CORNERS**
Cut from the center section to the drilled hole in each corner—but no farther! Break out the remainder with a chisel.

RELIEF CUT

CORNER CUT

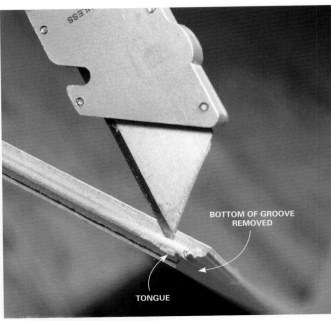

BOTTOM OF GROOVE REMOVED

TONGUE

3 **REMOVE THE BOTTOM LIP**
Score the tongue several times with a utility knife. Then snap it off with pliers. Shave off any remaining scraps with your knife.

Patch a chip in laminate flooring

D rop a knife or other sharp-edged item and you'll get an instant chip in your laminate floor. But you don't need to call in a pro, because this repair is strictly DIY. If you have the chip or an extra plank, take it to a home center and match it up with a tube of laminate floor patching material (SeamFil is one brand; about $7 per tube). You may have to buy the two closest colors and mix them to match. While you're there, buy a matching brand of cleaning solvent.

Clean the flooring with the solvent and let it dry. Next, squeeze a dollop of filler onto a scrap piece of flooring or a mixing board and mix it (Photo 1). Then press a shallow layer into the chip. Don't try to fill the entire chip in one application. Clean off any excess with solvent. Let the first coat set for one hour before applying the next.

After the filler hardens, use a knife and markers to add grain pattern (Photo 2).

1 **WORK THE FILLER UNTIL IT STIFFENS, THEN APPLY**
Blend two colors together or knead a single color with a putty knife until it begins to stiffen.

2 **ADD GRAIN TEXTURE**
Duplicate the grain pattern by making small cuts with a knife. Darken the cuts with furniture touch-up markers.

Fix a loose seam in a vinyl floor

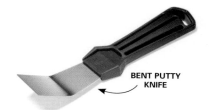

BENT PUTTY KNIFE

1 Protect the floor with masking tape and apply an even coat of adhesive. Then lay wax paper over the seam and press it down with a board and weights overnight.

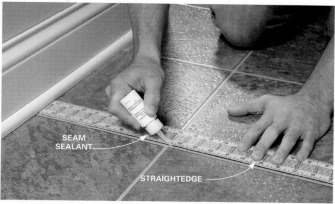

SEAM SEALANT

STRAIGHTEDGE

2 Apply a bead of seam sealant over the seam. Hold a straightedge about 1/4 in. away from the seam to guide the applicator nozzle, but don't get sealant on the straightedge.

If you have an open seam in your vinyl floor, don't procrastinate. Foot traffic can wreck the vinyl's exposed edges, making a good-looking repair impossible. Worse, water can seep into the opening, leading to subfloor damage. Start by inspecting the seam. Press the loose edges down to make sure they'll still join to form a tight seam.

If the seam closes neatly, you can make a nearly invisible repair using "multipurpose" vinyl adhesive and a seam sealing kit. Vacuum out any grit under the vinyl—even a tiny grain of sand can create a pimple on the vinyl's surface. Curl the vinyl back as you vacuum, but be careful not to kink or crack it. If the vinyl is too stiff to bend, soften it with heat from a hair dryer. You can leave most of the old adhesive alone, but scrape away loose spots. A putty knife bent in a vise makes a good scraper. It's also a handy adhesive applicator (Photo 1). After you spread the adhesive, rub down the seam with a block of wood. Use a wet rag to wipe away any adhesive that squeezes out of the joint. Then lay wax paper over the seam, followed by a scrap of plywood. Weigh down the plywood with stacks of books or buckets of water. Leave the weights in

TRANSITION STRIP

DAMAGED SEAM

3 Use a metal transition strip to cover a seam that has damaged edges. Cut the strip to length with a hacksaw, then nail or screw it into place.

place for at least 10 hours. Then apply the seam sealant (Photo 2). Sealant is available in gloss and satin versions to match your floor's sheen.

If the edges are damaged or the seam won't close neatly, the best repair is a metal transition strip (Photo 3) that completely hides the seam. Transition strips are available at home centers and hardware stores in various styles, lengths and finishes.

BRIDGING

EXISTING
BRIDGING

ONE-THIRD OF
JOIST SPAN

Metal bridging stiffens a bouncy floor

If the china cabinet in the next room rattles as you walk across the floor, try stiffening that floor fast with inexpensive metal braces called "bridging." Bridging allows each joist to share weight with its neighbors and can cut "deflection"—how much the joists flex—by half. Even if your floor already has a row of bridging running down the center, you can stiffen it substantially by adding two more rows. The catch, of course, is that the bouncy floor joists must be accessible from below.

Start by making sure the original bridging is tightly fastened; add nails or screws if necessary. Then measure the span of the joists (the distance between walls or beams that support the joists). Divide the span by three and add rows of bridging at both of the one-third points. The joists shown here, for example, span 12 ft., so we added rows of bridging 4 ft. from both ends of the span.

Various types of metal bridging are available at home centers and lumber-yards. To install the type shown here, drive the toothed end into the joist and nail the other end. Adding two rows of bridging costs less than $2.00 per joist. Other versions are just as easy to install and inexpensive. Measure the joist spacing before you go shopping; bridging is sized for joists centered 16 in. or 24 in. apart. Don't add bridging to manufactured lumber like I-joists or truss joists until you consult an engineer or building inspector.

Great goofs

This end up

When we moved into our first house, the number one priority was to replace the kitchen's vinyl sheet flooring. When the new flooring arrived, I unrolled it onto the lawn to make the cuts. Just to make sure I cut the piece correctly, I made a template of the floor by taping together sheets of old newspapers and brought this pattern outside to place it over the flooring. I carefully marked every detail and cut the flooring. When I brought it into the house, I turned it every which way, but it didn't fit. After a few minutes of scratching my head, I realized that I'd flipped the pattern upside down. I couldn't bear doing the project again, so we made do with patching the old floor.

—Bob Weir

Polka dots, no extra charge

When we decided to put in a new kitchen/laundry room floor, we went top quality all the way. The subfloor was in fine condition, but to get a perfectly clean and level surface, I installed a 1/4-in. layer of plywood. On the recommendations of a contractor buddy, I used cement-coated nails in the subfloor to prevent nail movement. We installed top-of-the-line perimeter glue-down vinyl, no seams. It looked beautiful. About three months later, however, a small yellow dot appeared in the floor. The manufacturer's representative immediately recognized that the cement coating on the nails was bleeding through the vinyl and causing a stain. The nails were incompatible with this floor, which voided the warranty. Soon we had hundreds of yellow dots, one for every nail.

—Gary Hesterberg

Floor-sander stampede

After giving our living room a fresh coat of paint, I decided to try my hand at refinishing the hardwood floors. So I rented a floor sander, an 80-lb. beast of a machine with a large rotating drum that sands the floor while you walk behind. I loaded a coarse-grit sandpaper, as recommended, and plugged in the machine. After sanding a few feet, the machine stopped. I noticed that the heavy plug had partially slipped out, so I walked over and wiggled it back in the outlet.

I quickly discovered that the sander's switch was still on. The thing started up and shot across the room like the rabbit at a dog race, with me chasing it. It crashed through the wall I had just painted, leaving a hole about the size of . . . well, a floor sander. Even worse, my wife and daughter had been watching. They quietly left the room. I also left the room . . . to get my drywall tools.

—Bob Berberich

Patch large holes

Don't melt down if a doorknob, misguided chair or an impromptu hockey game knocks a big hole in your wall. With a little patience, even a novice can complete a near-invisible repair. While the total time commitment isn't great, the process stretches over three to four days to allow coats of drywall compound and paint to dry.

Before cutting out the damaged area, check the wall for obstructions. Often you'll find a wire, pipe or duct (Photo 1). If so, work carefully around them with a drywall or keyhole saw. Or make a shallow cut by repeatedly scoring the line with a sharp utility knife.

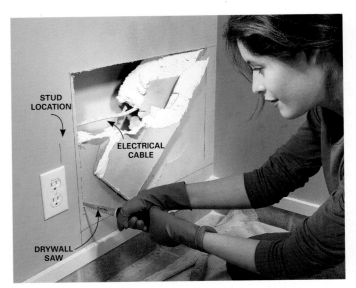

1 Draw a rectangle around the break with a straightedge or square. Look, or put your hand through the break to feel, for wires or other obstructions. Then cut out the section with a drywall saw or utility knife.

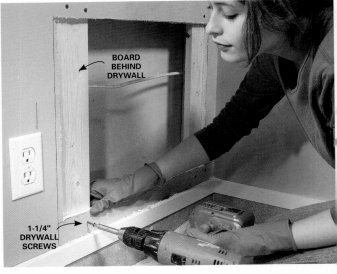

2 Insert 1x4 backer boards at each end of the hole and drive a pair of 1-1/4 in. drywall screws through the drywall into the boards to anchor them. Fit and screw a drywall patch to the boards.

6" TAPING KNIFE

3 Lay a 1/8-in.-thick bed of drywall compound over the joints and press paper tape into the compound with a flexible 6-in. knife. Immediately apply a thin layer of compound on top of the tape. Allow to dry.

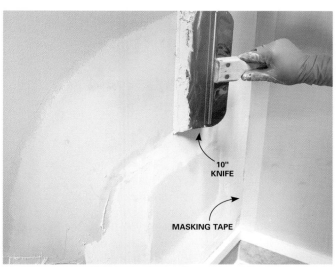

10" KNIFE

MASKING TAPE

4 Apply a second coat of compound, drawing it at least 6 in. beyond the edge of the first coat to taper the edges of the repair. Let dry, then add a third coat to smooth any remaining uneven areas.

100-GRIT SANDPAPER

5 Sand the dry compound lightly with 100-grit sandpaper to remove ridges and blend edges. Prime and paint.

Setting compound for fast fixes

Setting-type joint compound is a great product for filling deep holes and gaps and for your first taping coat because, unlike regular joint compound, it hardens quickly without shrinking. That means less time spent filling. And you can apply a second coat of compound as soon as the first hardens. You don't have to wait for it to dry completely.

For most repairs, buy the lightweight type that hardens in 20 minutes. It comes as a powder in sacks. Mix only what you can use in about 10 minutes. It hardens quickly, often in your pan if you're too slow! Completely clean your pan and knife before mixing a new batch. Otherwise it'll harden even faster! To avoid clogging the sink drain, throw leftover compound into the trash.

It's easier to add backer board than to try to cut the drywall over studs (Photo 2). Cut the backer boards about 4 in. longer than the height of the hole. Pine or other soft wood works well. Hold them tight to the back side of the drywall when fastening them. Hold the boards carefully so the screw points won't prick your fingers if they pop out of the back side. The drywall screws will draw the boards in tight. Sink the screwheads slightly below the drywall surface.

Measure the thickness of the drywall (most likely 1/2 in.), and look for a large enough scrap from a damaged piece at a home center, rather than buy a full 4 x 8-ft. sheet. Cut it to size and screw it into place, spacing the screws every 6 in.

Taping the edges of the patch to make it invisible is the trickiest part of the job (Photos 3 and 4). Buy a gallon tub of drywall compound and a roll of paper tape. You can use mesh tape, but it isn't as strong. If you have a lot of repairs, also buy a sack of 20-minute setting compound. It hardens quickly and doesn't shrink, so it's ideal for filling cracks and gaps before applying the joint tape. For smoothest results, also pick up flexible 6- and 10-in. taping knives.

Apply a coat of compound and tape to each joint (Photo 3). Thin the compound a bit with water to help embed the tape. Smooth the tape with the 6-in. knife, pulling out from the center toward each end. Squeeze some, but not all, of the compound out from under the tape so you don't create a big hump on the wall. Immediately apply a light coating to the top side of the tape, tapering it out onto the wall.

The second and third coats are to blend and smooth the taped joints so they'll be invisible when painted. After each coat is dry, set a straightedge against the wall to check for obvious dips and bumps. Knock off bumps and ridges with your taping knife. Add more coats as needed. Then sand, prime and paint.

Pro tip

When cutting out damage, leave a few inches of drywall at corners so you won't have to spread taping compound onto adjacent walls or ceilings and repaint them as well!

Fix small holes and nail pops

Small holes caused by screws or hooks, wall fasteners or drywall fasteners that pop up are simple to repair, but again time consuming because you almost always have to repaint the walls. Nail pops are common and particularly irritating, because you're likely to have more than one. But drywall screws sometimes pop up too, as a result of damp framing that dries out and shrinks during the first year or two in new construction.

The first step of the fix is to drive nails back down using a nail set (Photo 1). If you have screws, dig the drywall compound from their heads with a utility knife and turn them in tight with a screwdriver.

Then dimple the hole slightly concave with a hammer to indent any raised edges. But take care not to crush the drywall core. In addition, cut away any paper tears with a sharp utility knife. This is a good technique to use with old wall fasteners as well. It's usually easier to tap them into the wall slightly rather than pull them out.

Two coats of drywall compound, applied with two swipes of the knife in a "+" pattern, should fill the holes (Photo 3). The first

1 Drive a popped nail below the surface of the drywall with a hammer and a nail set. Cut away loose joint compound and paper shreds.

coat will shrink a bit, leaving a slightly smaller dent to be filled by the second coat. Scrape the excess off the surrounding wall so you don't build up a hump. Sand lightly to blend with the surrounding wall.

Be sure to prime the spot. Otherwise the topcoat will absorb into the patch and make the area look different from the surrounding paint. And use a roller when priming to help raise the surface texture to match the surrounding wall.

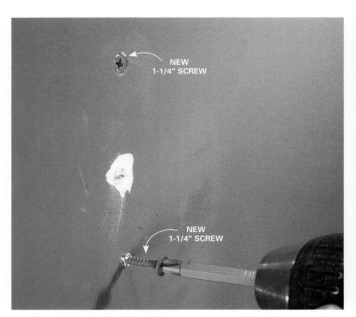

2 Drive drywall screws about 1-1/2 in. above and below the popped nail. Sink the screwhead just below the surface of the drywall.

3 Fill the holes with joint compound, swiping first across the holes, then down. Let dry, apply a second coat, then sand, prime and paint.

Repair cracked corners

Every home settles unevenly as it ages. This sometimes causes inside corners to crack or ripple. Often the crack will run from floor to ceiling. Once you spot this problem, watch it for two to three months for continued movement and fix it after all movement stops.

The key to renewing the strength of the corner is to remove all loose tape and drywall compound (Photo 1). If the drywall below has crumbled, cut it away with your utility knife and fill the gap with setting compound.

Retape the joint. Crease the paper tape down the middle so it fits into the corner easily (Photo 2).

It's difficult to spread compound smoothly on one side of the corner without marring the other side. The trick is to apply compound for the second and third coats only on one side at a time. Let the one side dry, then do the other side.

Finally, buy a fine-grit sanding sponge to smooth the corners (Photo 4). It'll do a nice job without gouging.

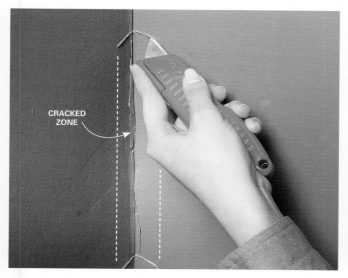

1 Cut through the tape at the ends of the cracked area and slice, scrape and tear away all loose tape and compound.

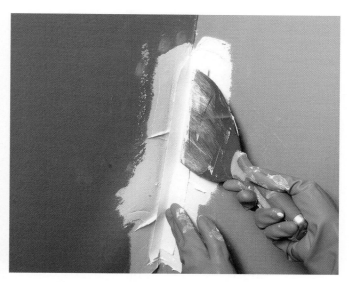

2 Apply a 1/8-in. layer of joint compound, then fold and press paper tape into it. Stroke the length of the tape, squeezing compound out on both sides. Let dry.

3 Apply second and third coats to smooth the joint, tapering the compound about 6 in. out. Let one side dry before applying compound to the other side.

4 Lightly sand the finished repair using a fine-grit sanding sponge to make a crisp corner. Prime and paint to match the existing wall.

Patch drywall fast

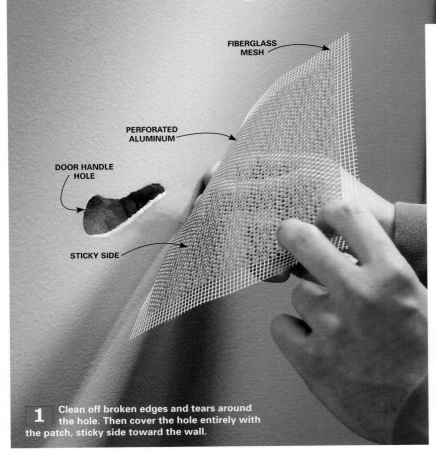

FIBERGLASS MESH

PERFORATED ALUMINUM

DOOR HANDLE HOLE

STICKY SIDE

1 Clean off broken edges and tears around the hole. Then cover the hole entirely with the patch, sticky side toward the wall.

The traditional method of repairing holes in walls is to square the hole, put wood backing behind it, cut and screw on a drywall patch, and then tape the edges. Aluminum patches, available at home centers and paint and hardware stores, give the same results with much less work. The patches, which come in various sizes, are stiff enough to span holes and thin enough to disappear after taping and painting.

Select a patch large enough to overlap the hole on all sides by an inch, then stick the patch on (Photo 1). Patches can be cut or overlapped as needed.

Trowel on the first coat of joint compound over the patch, spreading the compound flat enough to see the outline of the mesh through it (Photo 2).

Allow the compound to dry overnight, then apply a wider second coat (Photo 3), followed by a final, third coat after the second coat dries. Spread the compound in thin coats extending 8 to 12 in. beyond the patch in all directions.

After the final coat has dried, sand, prime and paint.

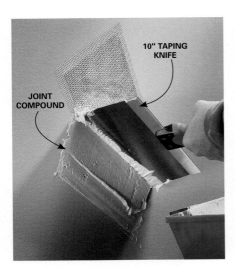

JOINT COMPOUND

10" TAPING KNIFE

2 Spread the first coat of joint compound over the patch with a wide taping knife. Let it dry overnight.

3 When it's dry, recoat the patch and then feather out the compound on all sides to make the patch blend in.

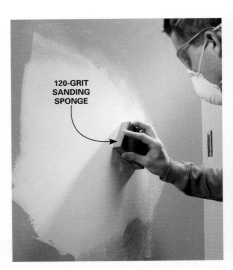

120-GRIT SANDING SPONGE

4 Sand the patched area with a sanding sponge until it feels smooth and even.

Repair a drywall crack

As homes settle, cracks may radiate from the corners of doors and windows. Whether your walls are made of plaster or drywall, you can repair the cracks in two steps over a day or two—and get the area ready to sand and paint. Use paper tape; it's stronger than fiberglass tape for wall repairs. For cracks more than 1/4 in. deep, clean out the loose material and use a quick-setting crack filler like Durabond to build up the area level with the wall. Then use the steps shown in Photos 2 and 3 to fix it.

1 Cut a V-notch through the full length of the crack, 1/8 to 1/4 in. deep, removing all loose wall material. Protect woodwork with masking tape.

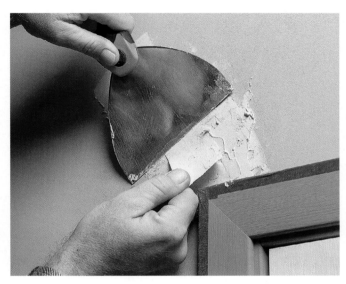

2 Embed paper tape in joint compound using a 6-in. taping blade. To avoid trapping air bubbles under the tape, moisten the paper tape with water, lay it over the crack and squeeze excess compound and air from underneath with the blade. Apply an additional thin layer of compound and feather it off 2 in. on both sides of the tape. Let dry.

3 Apply a second (and third, if necessary) coat of compound, smoothing it out 6 to 7 in. on both sides of the joint. Smooth the compound to a thin, even coat using long, continuous strokes with a 12-in. taping blade. Allow the repair to dry thoroughly, sand it smooth (avoid exposing the tape) and paint it.

Dust catcher

Minimize the mess when you're cutting or drilling a hole in drywall. Tape a bag below the work zone to catch the dust. Use an easy-release tape to avoid wall damage.

Counterattack closet mildew

For mildew, a dark, damp closet is paradise. Closet doors keep out light and block ventilation. That lack of air movement keeps closets from drying out after damp spells. In closets that adjoin exterior walls, heated air can't flow in, so wall surfaces stay cold and moisture condenses on them. Whatever the cause, here's how to deal with mildew:

1 Kill mildew with a mix of one part bleach to three parts warm water. Scrub with a sponge, but don't worry if you can't completely remove the dark stains. Let the surface dry completely before priming.

2 Cover the area with a stain-blocking primer. If you don't use a stain blocker, mildew stains can "bleed" through the paint. Use a primer that resists mildew (check the label).

Preventive measures keep mildew from coming back

Mildew is a tough enemy, but these strategies can discourage or even defeat it permanently:

► Add mildewcide to paint, or use paint that already contains mildewcide (check the label).

► Cut closet humidity with a chemical dehumidifier (available at home centers). These nontoxic products absorb moisture from the air. All you have to do is place the open container in your closet. Depending on humidity, the chemical will work for two to four weeks before you have to replace it.

► Leave closet doors open to improve ventilation. Better yet, replace solid doors with louvered doors that allow airflow even when closed.

CHEMICAL DEHUMIDIFIER

PAINT WITH MILDEWCIDE

MILDEWCIDE ADDITIVE

Cover a popcorn ceiling with drywall

The ultimate solution for an ugly ceiling

Covering an old ceiling with new drywall is a big job—heavy lifting, a serious time commitment and a major mess. But in some cases, it's the smartest way to go. We talked to a dozen remodelers, and every one of them made the same point: Sometimes, covering up an old ceiling saves time, money and headaches in the long run.

In the following pages, we'll focus on the details that make this job different from other drywall projects. For everything else you need to know about hanging and finishing drywall, go to familyhandyman.com and search for "drywall."

Money, time and materials

For a 12 x 12-ft. room, the total materials bill will fall in the neighborhood of $200, including drywall, joint compound, paint and drywall lift rental. With a helper or two, you can cover an average-size ceiling in one day. Finishing, or taping, all the joints is much more time-consuming and requires drying time between coats. Then comes sanding and painting. Even if you can devote a few hours every evening to this project, expect it to span at least a week.

We recommend 1/2-in.-thick "light-weight" drywall for this project. It's not only lighter than standard drywall but also stronger, so you can hang it from joists centered 24 in. apart. UltraLight, High Strength Lite and ToughRock are some brand names you'll find at home centers. If possible, get sheets that are long enough to span the room. Shorter sheets are easier to handle, of course, but you'll pay dearly for that convenience when it's time to finish the butt joints where ends of sheets meet. Unlike the tapered joints along the long edges of drywall, butt joints are tough to finish. Avoid them if you can.

Is this the solution for your problem?

Damaged drywall

The ceiling shown in this article had flaking texture, plus stains and holes, so covering it all with a new layer of drywall was actually faster and easier than repairing it. If you have only a few holes or stains, repairing them probably makes more sense. For articles and videos on those fixes, go to familyhandyman.com and search for "ceiling repair."

Popcorn ceiling

If you have a heavily textured ceiling and just don't like the look, you have a few options. With unpainted texture, the most common approach is to mist it with a spray bottle and scrape off the softened texture. That makes a big, sloppy mess

and almost always leaves you with repairs to do afterward.

With painted texture, some pros scrape as best they can and then "skim coat" the entire ceiling with a thin layer of joint compound. Scraping dry texture is a dusty mess, and skim coating requires some practice. And if your home was built before 1979, the texture might contain asbestos, which can do serious damage to your lungs. So before removing texture, it must be tested (you'll find lots of labs and instructions online). You can remove texture that contains asbestos yourself as long as you carefully follow safe procedures. For all of these reasons—mess, time, skill level, asbestos—covering a ceiling is often easier than removing texture.

Cracked plaster

If you have a plaster and lath ceiling with a few short, tight cracks, repairing them is probably smarter than covering the ceiling. But if cracks span the entire ceiling or the plaster alongside the cracks feels loose when you press on it, making lasting repairs is tough. Plaster cracks often come back, even after careful repairs. That's why several pros told us they routinely cover plaster ceilings: it's the best way to be sure that they won't have to come back and repair the ceiling again in a year or two. Remove any loose or sagging plaster before covering the ceiling.

JOIST

SPACER

1 SHIM OUT EXPOSED JOISTS
If you have a hole in the ceiling, hold a straightedge across it, measure to the framing and cut spacers to that thickness. Screw a spacer to the joist or truss to create a flush surface for the new drywall.

CENTER OF JOISTS

2 MARK THE JOISTS
Locate joists with an electronic stud finder, or just probe for joists by driving a nail through the drywall. All the joists should be centered either 16 or 24 in. apart, but double-check with a nail. Mark each joist location with a chalk line on the ceiling and with tape on the wall.

3 **EXTEND ELECTRICAL BOXES**
Screw a 1/2-in. "mud ring" to any junction boxes in the ceiling. This extends the box so that it will be flush with the new drywall.

This could be an opportunity

One of the best things about a ceiling cover-up job is that you can cut holes in the ceiling without fussy repairs later. So it's the perfect time to add or move light fixtures. If there's living space above the ceiling, you can even fix floor squeaks or run new plumbing for a future bathroom remodel.

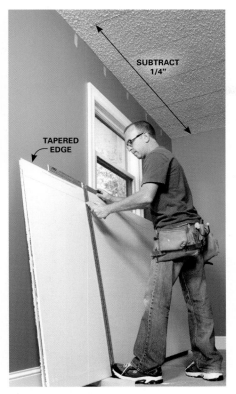

4 **MEASURE TO JOISTS AND CUT THE DRYWALL**
Cut sheets so that the ends fall on the centers of joists. Measure from the wall to the chalk line and subtract 1/4 in. to allow for a gap along the wall. Also cut off the tapered edge that will run along the wall.

Most home centers carry 8- and 12-ft. sheets. Specialty drywall suppliers usually carry those lengths, plus 10-, 14- or even 16-ft. sheets. Just be sure you can get long sheets into the room before you buy; sometimes 8-ft. sheets are the only option. Everything else you'll need is available at home centers: 2-in. screws, 10-ft. lengths of 1/2-in. tear-away bead, mud rings for junction boxes, joint tape and compound, primer and paint.

Hanging the drywall

This project is a lot like any other drywall job. But there are a few differences. For starters, you'll have to "fur down" joists at holes in the drywall (Photo 1). Don't try to simply span holes larger than 6 in. with drywall; your screws will pop right through the hollow space above the drywall. Also, shut off the power and remove any light fixtures in the ceiling. Next, take your time to carefully locate and mark the centers of joists (Photo 2). The rest of the project will go a lot smoother if your marks are accurate. The final prep

Figure A Drywall perpendicular to joists

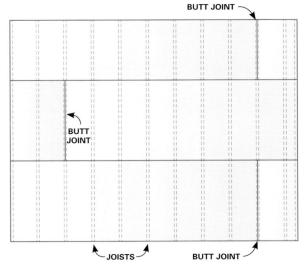

Figure B Drywall parallel to joists

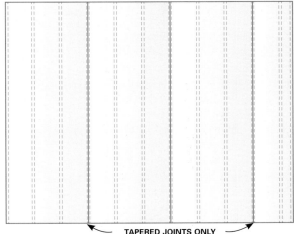

Joist direction matters

Drywall is normally hung perpendicular to the joists. But sometimes it's smart to break that rule. Let's say you have an 11 x 14-ft. room with joists spanning the 11-ft. length (as shown here) and that you can't get sheets longer than 12 ft. into the room. You could run sheets across the joists as usual, creating three hard-to-finish butt joints (Figure A). Or you could run the sheets parallel to the joists (Figure B) and eliminate butt joints completely.

step is to extend junction boxes with mud rings (Photo 3). If you have recessed lighting in the ceiling, you'll have to lower the cans by loosening screws inside the housings, but it's best to do that after the new drywall is up.

Now you're ready to head for the rental center to pick up a drywall lift ($40 per day) and hang the drywall. You can hang drywall without a lift, of course, but a lift makes the job faster, easier and better. When you cut the rock to length (Photo 4), remember to subtract 1/4 in. for the gap along walls. But you don't have to be exact about this: As long as the gap is between 1/8 in. and 1/4 in., you'll

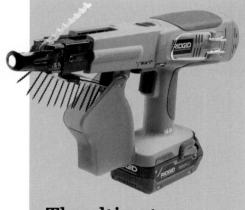

The ultimate screw gun

I love self-feed screw guns because they're fast: You just pull the trigger and push to automatically load and drive screws. Plus, the gun itself is long, so you can reach an 8-ft. ceiling without a ladder. Aside from drywall, I've used my gun for screwing down subfloors and decking too. The only thing I don't like about it is that it's usually missing from my toolbox, on loan to friends. You can get a corded version at any home center for about $100. A cordless one costs about $150.
—Travis Larson, Senior Editor

A drywall lift doesn't just make the job easier; it helps you do the job better. When you're raising sheets by hand, you're just dying to drive a few screws so you can put your arms down. With a lift, you can take your time, trim the sheet if necessary and get everything just right.

—Myron Ferguson, Veteran drywall contractor

5 RAISE ROCK THE EASY WAY
Hoist each sheet with a rented drywall lift. Be sure to leave gaps between the sheet and the wall. Those gaps allow you to slip tear-away bead behind the edges of the drywall bead later.

I've sheeted over dozens of ceilings and always finish up with a knockdown texture. Ceilings show every little flaw in the taping job, and knockdown is the easiest way to hide them.

—Tom Dvorak, Field Editor

To see how Tom applies knockdown texture, go to familyhandyman.com and search "knockdown texture."

6 SCREW TO THE JOISTS
Screw each sheet along the tapered edges, then add a couple near the center. That will be enough to hold it in place. Later, when all the sheets are up, snap chalk lines and drive the remaining screws.

have no trouble installing the tear-away bead. Here's another critical thing to remember: Along walls, cut the tapered edge off the sheet. Because tapered edges are thinner than the rest of the sheet, they'll cause trouble when you mud the tear-away bead later.

Raise and position each sheet (Photo 5). Take your time. Make sure it's aligned with the chalk line that marks the center of the joist. There's no need to completely fasten the sheets before removing the lift. Just drive enough screws to safely hold the sheet (Photo 6). When all the sheets are up, snap a fresh set of chalk lines and add the remaining screws.

Terrific tear-away bead

The usual way to finish the joint where walls meet the ceiling is to apply coats of joint compound. Making it all smooth, straight and square takes patience and practice. Plastic tear-away bead lets you skip all that. Tear-away bead is typically used where drywall meets a different material like brick, a shower surround or paneling. But for this job, it's an even bigger time-saver because it makes taping much easier—and you may not even have to paint the walls when you're done.

The bead is easy to cut using metal shears. Make miter cuts at corners (some installers simply overlap the beads, but that leaves an uneven guide for your knife). The same goes for splices along a wall: Butt the two sections together neatly; don't overlap them. Staple the bead to the drywall every 8 in. (Photo 7). Take your time and make sure the bead is tight against the wall. Gaps will look bad and possibly cause you more work later. When the tear-away bead is up, you're ready to skim on the joint compound (Photo 8).

Paint the ceiling before you pull off the tear-away bead's flange. The flange will keep ceiling paint off the wall. For extra protection, run a strip of painter's tape below the bead (we skipped this step—and regretted it). When the paint is dry, run your utility knife along the bead at the point where the flange will tear off. Press lightly; the purpose is to slice through the paint so the paint film doesn't tear when you pull off the flange. A needle-nose pliers helps you get a grip on the flange as you begin to tear it off. Then simply pull down to remove the bead (Photo 9) and check out the result.

It won't look exactly like a standard wall-to-ceiling joint. Instead, you'll see a tiny crack between the wall and the ceiling. If your walls are a deep color, that crack will be almost invisible. With white walls, the crack is visible, but only if you're looking for it. If you're especially fussy—or if you didn't fasten the bead tightly along the wall—you can caulk the crack. Even with caulking and paint touch-up, tear-away bead saves hours of time and effort.

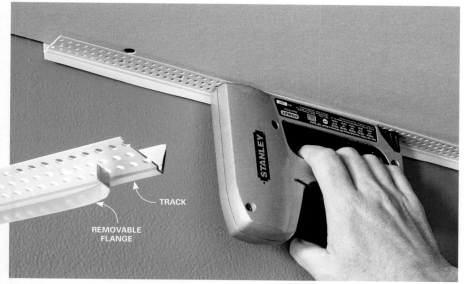

TRACK

REMOVABLE FLANGE

7 INSTALL TEAR-AWAY BEAD
Staple the bead to the drywall every 8 in. Be sure to hold the bead tight against the wall before you fasten it.

MESH TAPE

TRACK

8 MUG THE BEAD
Skim joint compound over the bead, using the track to guide your knife. Mesh tape isn't essential, but it's cheap insurance against cracks.

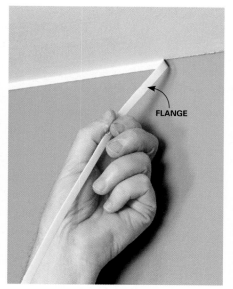

FLANGE

9 TEAR OFF THE FLANGE
After sanding and painting, rip the protective flange off the bead. To avoid scraping off the fresh paint, pull the flange downward along the wall, not outward along the ceiling.

Special Section

MAINTAIN YOUR HVAC SYSTEM

Spring central AC tuneup

Chances are that if you neglect a spring checkup, your air conditioner won't cool nearly as well as it could. A year's worth of dirt and debris clogging the cooling fins, a low coolant level, a dirty blower fan filter and a number of other simple problems can significantly reduce the efficiency of your air conditioner and wear it out faster.

You can't do everything; only a pro can check the coolant level. But you can easily handle most of the routine cleaning chores and save the cost to have a pro do them.

Here you'll see how to clean the outdoor unit (called the condenser) and the accessible parts of the indoor unit (called the evaporator). All the steps are simple and straightforward and will take you only a few hours total. You don't need any special skills, tools or experience. If you aren't familiar with air conditioners and furnaces/blowers, don't worry. See Figure A on p. 161 to become familiar with how an air conditioner works and the parts of the system.

You may have a different type of central air conditioner than we show here—a heat pump system, for example, or a unit mounted horizontally. However, you can still carry out most maintenance procedures because each system will have a condenser outside and an evaporator inside. Use the owner's manual for your particular model to help navigate any differences from the one shown in our photos. Call in a pro every two or three years to check electrical parts and the coolant level.

Cleaning the condenser

Clean your outdoor unit on a day that's at least 60 degrees F. That's about the minimum temperature at which you can test your air conditioner to make sure it's working. The condenser usually sits in an inconspicuous spot next to your house. You'll see two copper tubes running to it, one bare and the other encased in a foam sleeve. If you have a heat pump, both tubes will be covered by foam sleeves.

SPECIAL SECTION: MAINTAIN YOUR HVAC SYSTEM

1 Turn off the electrical power to the condenser unit at the outdoor shutoff. Either pull out a block or move a switch to the "Off" position. If uncertain, turn off the power to the AC at the main electrical panel.

BLOCK SHUTOFF

2 Vacuum grass clippings, leaves and other debris from the exterior fins with a soft brush attachment. Clear away all bushes, weeds and grass within 2 ft. of condenser.

3 Realign bent or crushed fins with gentle pressure from a dinner knife. Don't insert the knife more than 1/2 in.

4 Unscrew the top grille. Lift out fan and carefully set aside without stressing the electrical wires. Pull out leaves and wipe the interior surfaces clean with a damp cloth.

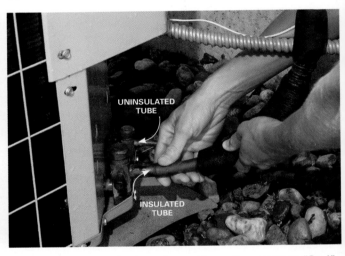

5 Spray the fins using moderate water pressure from a hose nozzle. Direct the spray from the inside out. Reinstall the fan.

6 Turn the power back on, then set house thermostat to "Cool" so the compressor comes on. After 10 minutes, feel the insulated tube. It should feel cool. The uninsulated tube should feel warm.

Your primary job here is to clean the condenser fins, which are fine metallic blades that surround the unit. They get dirty because a central fan sucks air through them, pulling in dust, dead leaves, dead grass and the worst culprit—floating "cotton" from cottonwood trees and dandelions. The debris blocks the airflow and reduces the unit's cooling ability.

Always begin by shutting off the electrical power to the unit. Normally you'll find a shutoff nearby. It may be a switch in a box, a pull lever or a fuse block that you pull out (Photo 1). Look for the "On-Off" markings.

Vacuum the fins clean with a soft brush (Photo 2); they're fragile and easily bent or crushed. On many units you'll have to unscrew and lift off a metal box to get at them. Check your owner's manual for directions and lift off the box carefully to avoid bumping the fins. Occasionally you'll find fins that have been bent. You can buy a special set of fin combs to straighten them at an appliance parts store. Minor straightening can be done with a blunt dinner knife (Photo 3). If large areas of fins

are crushed, have a pro straighten them during a routine service call.

Unscrew the fan to gain access to the interior of the condenser. You can't completely remove it because its wiring is connected to the unit. Depending on how much play the wires give you, you might need a helper to hold it while you vacuum debris from the inside. (Sometimes mice like to overwinter there!)

After you hose off the fins (Photo 5), check the fan motor for lubrication ports. Most newer motors have sealed bearings (the one shown does) and can't be lubricated. Check your owner's manual to be sure. If you find ports, add five drops of electric motor oil (at hardware stores or appliance parts stores). Don't use penetrating oil or all-purpose oil. They're not designed for long-term lubrication and can actually harm the bearings.

If you have an old air conditioner, you might have a belt-driven compressor in the bottom of the unit. Look for lubrication ports on this as well. The compressors on newer air conditioners are completely enclosed and won't need lubrication.

Pro tip

Call for service before the first heat wave, when the pros become swamped with repair calls!

Figure A
Parts of a central air conditioner

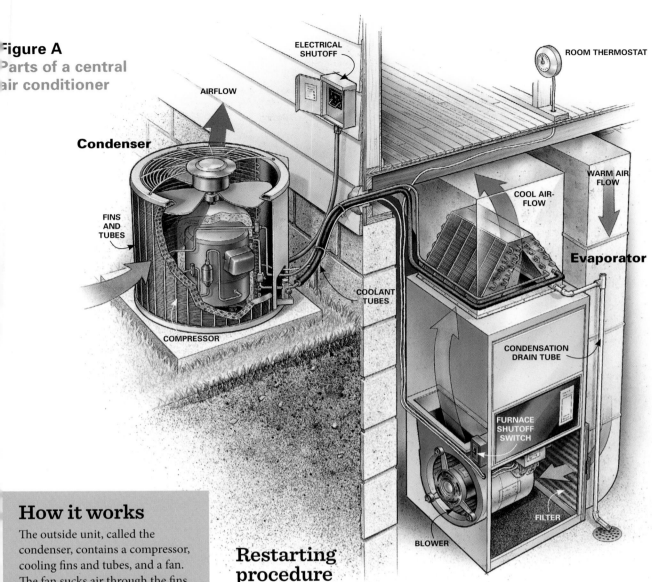

ELECTRICAL SHUTOFF

ROOM THERMOSTAT

AIRFLOW

Condenser

WARM AIR FLOW

COOL AIR-FLOW

FINS AND TUBES

Evaporator

COOLANT TUBES

COMPRESSOR

CONDENSATION DRAIN TUBE

FURNACE SHUTOFF SWITCH

FILTER

BLOWER

How it works

The outside unit, called the condenser, contains a compressor, cooling fins and tubes, and a fan. The fan sucks air through the fins and cools a special coolant, which the compressor then pumps into the house to the evaporator through a copper tube. The coolant chills the fins and tubes of the evaporator. Warm air drawn from the house by the blower passes through the evaporator and is cooled and blown through ducts to the rooms in the house. The evaporator dehumidifies the air as it cools it, and the resulting condensation drains off to a floor drain through a tube. The blower unit and ducting system vary considerably depending on whether you have a furnace (shown), a heat pump or some other arrangement. It may be located in the basement, garage, furnace room or attic.

Restarting procedure

In most cases, you can simply restore power to the outside unit and move inside to finish the maintenance.
However, the compressors are surprisingly fragile and some require special start-up procedures under two conditions. (Others have built-in electronic controls that handle the start-up, but unless you know that yours has these controls, follow these procedures.)

1. If the power to your unit has been off for more than four hours:
- ► Move the switch from "Cool" to "Off" at your inside thermostat.
- ► Turn the power back on and let the unit sit for 24 hours.
  (The compressor has a heating element that warms the internal lubricant.)
- ► Switch the thermostat back to "Cool."

2. If you switched the unit off while the compressor was running:
- ► Wait at least five minutes before switching it back on.
  (The compressor needs to decompress before restarting.)

With the air conditioner running, make sure it's actually working by touching the coolant tubes (Photo 6). This is a crude test. Only a pro with proper instruments can tell if the coolant is at the level for peak efficiency. But keep a sharp eye out for dark drip marks on the bottom of the case and beneath the tube joints. This indicates an oil leak and a potential coolant leak as well. Call in a pro if you spot this problem. Don't tighten a joint to try to stop a leak yourself. Overtightening can make the problem worse.

7 Turn off the power to the furnace at a nearby switch or at the main panel. Then pull out the furnace filter and check it for dirt buildup. Change it if necessary.

8 Open the blower compartment and vacuum up the dust. Check the motor for lubrication ports. If it has them, squeeze five drops of electric motor oil into each.

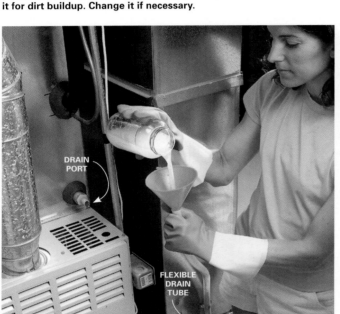

9 Pull off the plastic condensation drain tube and check it for algae growth. Clean it by pouring a bleach/water solution (1:16 ratio) through the tube to flush the line. Or simply replace the tube.

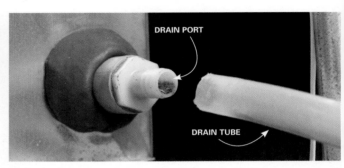

10 Poke a pipe cleaner into the drain port and clean out any debris. Reinstall the drain tube and turn the power back on.

Clean the indoor unit

The evaporator usually sits in an inaccessible spot inside a metal duct downstream from the blower (Figure A). If you can get to it, gently vacuum its fins (from the blower side) with a soft brush as you did with the condenser.

However, the best way to keep it clean is to keep the air-stream from the blower clean. This means annually vacuuming out the blower compartment and changing the filter whenever it's dirty (Photos 7 and 8).

Begin by turning off the power to the furnace or blower. Usually you'll find a simple toggle switch nearby in a metal box (Photo 7); otherwise turn the power off at the main panel. If you have trouble opening the blower unit or finding the filter, check your owner's manual for help. The manual will also list the filter type, but if it's your first time, take the old one with you when buying a new one to make sure you get the right size. Be sure to keep the power to the blower off whenever you remove the filter. Otherwise you'll blow dust into the evaporator fins.

The manual will also tell you where to find the oil ports on the blower, if it has any. The blower compartments on newer furnaces and heat pumps are so tight that you often can't lubricate the blower without removing it. If that's the case, have a pro do it during a routine maintenance checkup.

The evaporator fins dehumidify the air as they cool it, so you'll find a tube to drain the condensation. The water collects in a pan and drains out the side (Figure A). Most tubes are flexible plastic and are easy to pull off and clean (Photos 9 and 10). But if they're rigid plastic, you'll probably have to unscrew or cut off with a saw to check. Reglue rigid tubes using a coupling, or replace them with flexible plastic tubes.

Window AC care

Most people assume warm air from their A/C unit means it's low on refrigerant. That's not always the cause. Many times, window and through-the-wall A/C units can't blow cold air because the evaporator and condenser coils or cooling fins are clogged. You can clean a window unit yourself in about an hour. The supplies are inexpensive. If cleaning doesn't do the trick, you can always call in a pro (or buy a newer, more efficient unit). Here's how to clean your window A/C unit.

First remove the plastic filter holder/trim panel. It usually snaps off. Then remove it from the window or slide it out of the wall (get help—it's heavy).

If you're working on a window unit, remove the mounting frame and the case. The case screws are usually located along the bottom edge. Note the location of any odd-length screws since they have to go back in the same spots upon reassembly.

FIN COMB

Then straighten the bent cooling fins with a fin comb (Photo 1). The Frigidaire fin comb kit shown here is cheap and fits most brands of air conditioners (No. 5304464988; from frigidare.com).

Buy two cans of A/C coil cleaner (one brand is AC-Safe No. AC-921; from homedepot.com). Vacuum all visible buildup from both coils (Photo 2). Then spray both coils with the cleaner (Photo 3). While the foam works, clean the fan blades with household cleaner and a rag. If the fan motor has plastic- or rubber-capped oiling ports, pop them and squeeze in a few drops of electric motor oil (pros use the Zoomspout oiler).

Wash (or replace) the air filter and reinstall the unit.

1 COMB OUT THE MATS. Match the correct end of the fin comb to the fin spacing on your coils. Then insert the comb and pull up to straighten the fins. Wear leather gloves to prevent nasty cuts.

2 CLEAN OUT THE CRUD. Suck up all the spider webs, leaves, dust and dirt before you spray the coils.

3 APPLY A FOAM CLEANER. Shoot the spray over the entire surface of both coils and let the foam do the work for you. If the buildup is heavy, brush in the direction of the fins with a nylon-bristle brush.

4 SERVICE THE FAN MOTOR. Pop off the plastic or rubber caps on the motor's oiling ports. Then squeeze a few drops into each port and recap.

SPECIAL SECTION: MAINTAIN YOUR HVAC SYSTEM

Know your furnace

A little knowledge can save you big bucks!

Furnaces might seem complicated, but the basics are surprisingly easy to understand. Once you know them, you'll be able to avoid breakdowns and solve simple problems yourself. Plus, you'll understand what the heck a repair technician is saying, make smarter decisions and avoid rip-offs. That can add up to huge savings over the life of your furnace.

Anatomy of a conventional furnace

HUMIDIFIER
On some furnaces, a humidifier is mounted on the supply-air plenum to add moisture to dry air. When it stops working, it's usually because of a clogged or burned-out solenoid (electric water valve) or bad drum motor—all fairly easy to fix. For information on repairing an existing humidifier or installing a new one, visit familyhandyman.com and search for "humidifier."

SUPPLY-AIR PLENUM
The supply-air plenum is a large sheet metal box on top of the furnace. It distributes warmed (or cooled) air to the ducts.

COOLING COIL
If you have central air conditioning, a cooling coil cools air on its way up the supply-air plenum. Copper tubing connects the cooling coil to the compressor unit outside your home (that's the big box with the fan in it).

FLUE PIPE
All furnaces have a pipe that carries deadly exhaust outside by way of a chimney or through an exterior wall. Flues routed through walls can get blocked by shrubs, snow or small animals, causing the furnace to shut down.

HEAT EXCHANGER
A heat exchanger is the part of the furnace that heats the air. Flames warm the inside of the heat exchanger, while air passing across the outside of it gets warmed. Sometimes—due to age or lack of maintenance—heat exchangers can crack and leak deadly carbon monoxide into your house and kill you (see "Get a Carbon Monoxide Detector" on p. 168). Sometimes heat exchangers can be replaced. However, depending on how old your furnace is, replacing the entire furnace might be smarter.

RETURN-AIR PLENUM
Return ducts and the large return-air plenum carry air from rooms back to the furnace to be heated or cooled.

BLOWER
A blower is turned by a motor and forces warmed air through supply ducts. Motor bearings are usually sealed and don't require lubrication, but even sealed bearings can fail over time and cause the motor to overheat.

BURNER
The burner warms the inside of a heat exchanger, which heats the air for the house.

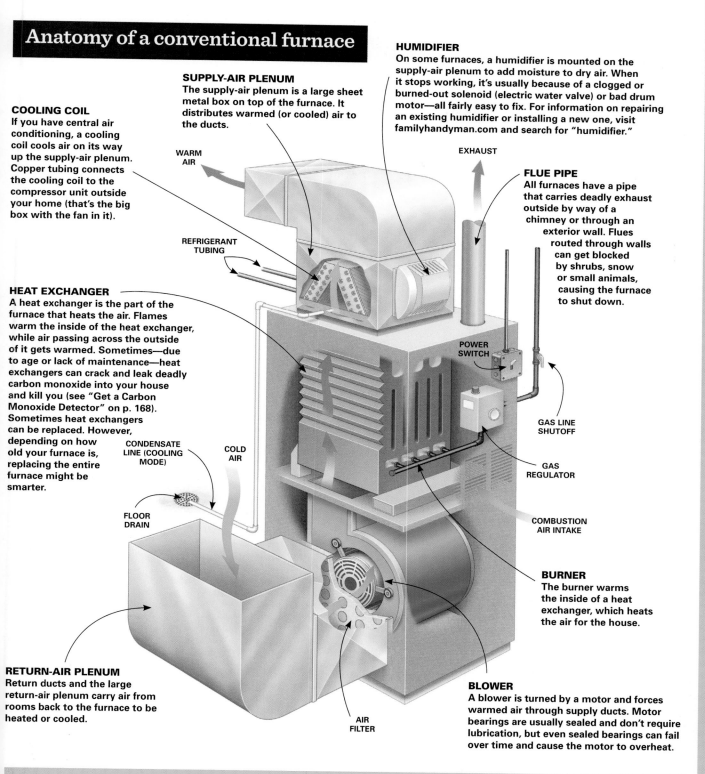

WARM AIR

EXHAUST

REFRIGERANT TUBING

POWER SWITCH

GAS LINE SHUTOFF

GAS REGULATOR

COMBUSTION AIR INTAKE

COLD AIR

CONDENSATE LINE (COOLING MODE)

FLOOR DRAIN

AIR FILTER

How it heats

A conventional "forced-air" furnace is a pretty simple system. A thermostat calls for heat, which triggers the furnace to burn fuel, which warms a heat exchanger. A motor spins a blower wheel, which moves cool air past the heat exchanger and pushes the newly warmed air through supply ducts and into the rooms of your house. Meanwhile, cooler air in each of the rooms gets pulled back toward the furnace through cold-air return ducts. You'll usually see return grilles mounted in the floor or low on a wall.

Anatomy of a "high-efficiency" furnace

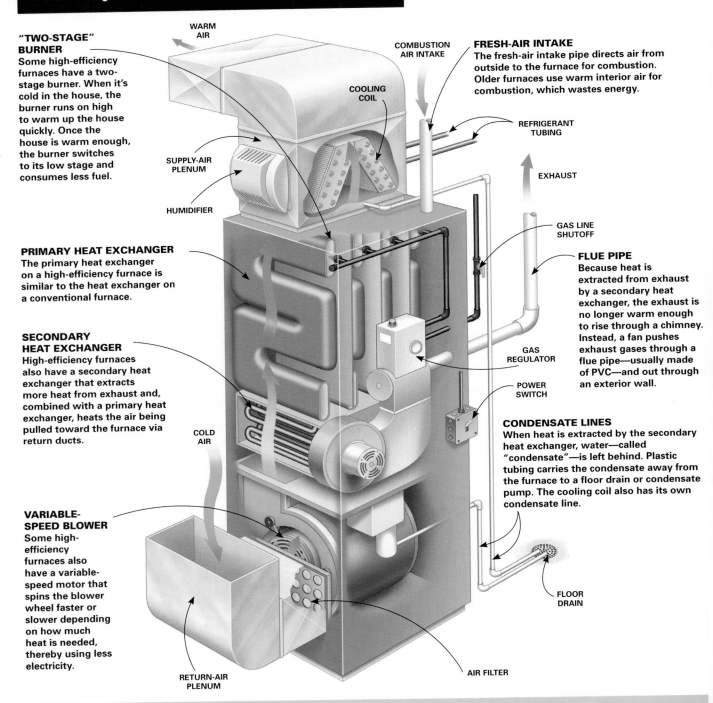

WARM AIR

COMBUSTION AIR INTAKE

COOLING COIL

FRESH-AIR INTAKE
The fresh-air intake pipe directs air from outside to the furnace for combustion. Older furnaces use warm interior air for combustion, which wastes energy.

REFRIGERANT TUBING

EXHAUST

"TWO-STAGE" BURNER
Some high-efficiency furnaces have a two-stage burner. When it's cold in the house, the burner runs on high to warm up the house quickly. Once the house is warm enough, the burner switches to its low stage and consumes less fuel.

SUPPLY-AIR PLENUM

HUMIDIFIER

GAS LINE SHUTOFF

PRIMARY HEAT EXCHANGER
The primary heat exchanger on a high-efficiency furnace is similar to the heat exchanger on a conventional furnace.

FLUE PIPE
Because heat is extracted from exhaust by a secondary heat exchanger, the exhaust is no longer warm enough to rise through a chimney. Instead, a fan pushes exhaust gases through a flue pipe—usually made of PVC—and out through an exterior wall.

SECONDARY HEAT EXCHANGER
High-efficiency furnaces also have a secondary heat exchanger that extracts more heat from exhaust and, combined with a primary heat exchanger, heats the air being pulled toward the furnace via return ducts.

GAS REGULATOR

POWER SWITCH

COLD AIR

CONDENSATE LINES
When heat is extracted by the secondary heat exchanger, water—called "condensate"—is left behind. Plastic tubing carries the condensate away from the furnace to a floor drain or condensate pump. The cooling coil also has its own condensate line.

VARIABLE-SPEED BLOWER
Some high-efficiency furnaces also have a variable-speed motor that spins the blower wheel faster or slower depending on how much heat is needed, thereby using less electricity.

FLOOR DRAIN

RETURN-AIR PLENUM

AIR FILTER

How it heats

Like conventional furnaces, high-efficiency models use a heat exchanger to warm the air. In fact, they have two heat exchangers—a primary one and a secondary one.

The secondary heat exchanger extracts heat from exhaust—heat that would otherwise go out the flue—and uses it, combined with heat from the primary heat exchanger, to warm the air in your home. Because heat is removed from the exhaust, it's not warm enough to rise, so it can't be vented up through a chimney. A small PVC exhaust pipe run through an exterior wall is all that's needed. These units also require a second PVC pipe—usually located close to the exhaust pipe—to deliver fresh outside air to the furnace for combustion.

Before you call for repairs...
7 things you must check

1 **AIR FILTER**
A badly clogged air filter can cause the furnace to overheat and shut off, so replace it if it's dirty. It can be hard to tell with some filters, so consider installing an air filter gauge that lets you know when it's time to replace the filter (see p. 169).

2 **POWER**
Make sure the power is on! The power switch for your furnace looks like a regular light switch and can get bumped and turned off accidentally. If the switch is off, just flip it back on.

POWER SWITCH

3 **THERMOSTAT**
Be sure your thermostat is set to "heat" and at a temperature higher than the temperature inside the house.

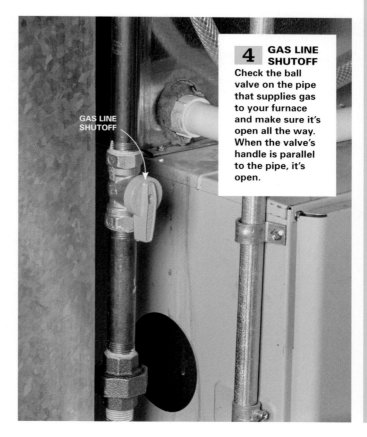

GAS LINE SHUTOFF

4 **GAS LINE SHUTOFF**
Check the ball valve on the pipe that supplies gas to your furnace and make sure it's open all the way. When the valve's handle is parallel to the pipe, it's open.

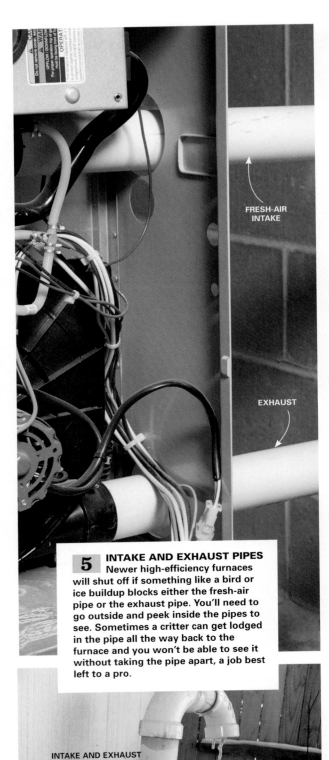

FRESH-AIR INTAKE

EXHAUST

6 DOOR SWITCH
Check the door switch. Whenever you remove the access door on the furnace, a little safety switch shuts everything off. Sometimes this switch will stay turned off if the door isn't completely closed.

DOOR SWITCH

5 INTAKE AND EXHAUST PIPES
Newer high-efficiency furnaces will shut off if something like a bird or ice buildup blocks either the fresh-air pipe or the exhaust pipe. You'll need to go outside and peek inside the pipes to see. Sometimes a critter can get lodged in the pipe all the way back to the furnace and you won't be able to see it without taking the pipe apart, a job best left to a pro.

INTAKE AND EXHAUST PIPES CLOGGED WITH ICE

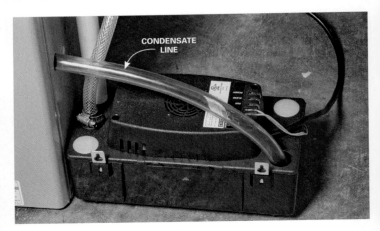

CONDENSATE LINE

7 CONDENSATE LINE
High-efficiency furnaces produce water called "condensate." If the drain tubing for the condensate gets clogged, the furnace shuts off. Check the tubing and clear any clogs. Or, better yet, just replace the tubing.

Get a carbon monoxide detector

When heat exchangers crack or there's a leak in the exhaust pipe, deadly carbon monoxide can seep into your home's living space. That's why it's critical that you have a working carbon monoxide detector. You can buy two-in-one carbon monoxide and smoke detectors, or stand-alone units that you just plug into a wall (with backup batteries) for $20 to $40 at home centers.

Got a cold room?

BLOCKED RETURN GRILLE

1 CHECK THE COLD-AIR RETURNS
If you have some rooms that are warmer or colder than others, the problem might be a blocked air return. They're usually located in the floor or low on an interior wall (see photo). When blocked, cold room air can't "return" to the furnace to be reheated.

WINTER
SUMMER
DAMPER HANDLE

2 ADJUST THE DAMPERS
Check dampers to make sure they're not restricting airflow to the rooms that need it. Some need to be adjusted differently for winter and summer. You'll usually find them near the supply-air plenum on the large ducts that feed the rooms in your house.

16x20x1
12x24x1
14x25x1
20x20x1

The best furnace advice: Change the filter

Clogged air filters are usually to blame when a furnace stops working. Dirty air filters are also hard on blower motors and heat exchangers, so it's a good idea to replace your air filter before there's a problem. It can be hard to remember to check it regularly. That's where an air filter gauge can help; it eliminates guesswork by measuring airflow and telling you exactly when it's time to change your air filter.

What "efficiency" means

An AFUE (annual fuel utilization efficiency) rating on a furnace tells you how efficiently the furnace turns fossil fuel into usable heat. An older-style furnace will have an efficiency rating of 56 to 83 percent, while a modern "high-efficiency" furnace will have a rating of 90 percent or higher. That means 90 percent of the furnace's fuel becomes usable heat for your home, while the other 10 percent is lost, with the exhaust, up the chimney.

Repair or replace a condensate pump

In the summer, central air conditioning units remove moisture from the air. And in the winter, condensing gas furnaces generate an enormous amount of wastewater. Plus, if your furnace has a humidifier, it also drains off extra water. All that water has to go somewhere. In newer homes, it goes right into a nearby floor drain.

But many older homes don't have a floor drain next to the furnace. So furnace installers mount a condensate pump right on the furnace and route the drain line to a far-off sink or floor drain. If that pump fails, the water overflows the pump and spills onto the floor. That doesn't necessarily mean the pump is bad; the problem could be just algae buildup in the pump's check valve.

So start your diagnosis by unplugging the pump. Disconnect the drain line and empty the water into a bucket. Then remove the check valve and plug in the pump (Photo 1). If the pump doesn't work, buy a new one (from a home center or online HVAC store) and swap out the old one. However, if the pump works, you've got a stuck check valve.

Try cleaning the valve by soaking it in warm, soapy water. Then flush it. Clean out any remaining crud with compressed air and test it (Photo 2). If you can't remove all the crud or the valve is still stuck, replace it with a new valve (try from the pump manufacturer's parts department). The furnace or A/C will continue to drain while you're waiting for the new part to arrive, so jury-rig a bucket system (Photo 3). Clean any algae buildup from inside the pump with soapy water and a brush before installing the new valve. Then install the new valve and test. To prevent algae clogs, place algae reduction tablets (such as Pan Tablets No. AC-912) in the pump reservoir.

1 TEST THE PUMP
Hold a bowl over the pump outlet to direct water into a bucket. Then slowly pour water into the pump reservoir until the pump kicks in. If water shoots from the outlet, the pump is good.

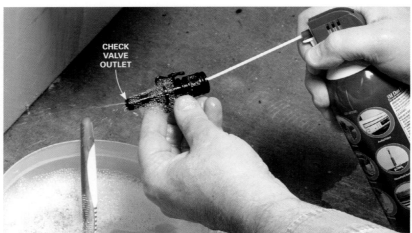

2 CLEAN THE CHECK VALVE
Soak the check valve in warm, soapy water. Then scrub with an old toothbrush. Rinse. Then blow it out with compressed air before testing.

CHECK VALVE

3 CATCH THE WATER WHILE YOU WAIT FOR PARTS
Remove the pump and aim the drain tubes into a bucket. Empty often to prevent overflowing. Then reinstall the pump with the new check valve when it arrives.

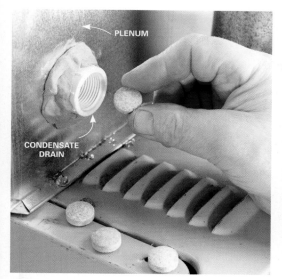

PLENUM

CONDENSATE
DRAIN

1 **TREAT THE PAN WITH TABLETS**
Shove the tablets into the drain pan opening and push them in farther using a dowel or long screwdriver. Add new tablets monthly during air-conditioning season, or less often if you rarely use your A/C.

2 **INSTALL NEW TUBING**
Screw the new fitting into the drain pan and slide on the tubing. Route it to the floor drain and secure it with tubing straps.

Fix a clogged condensate drain

If water is puddling near the furnace with the A/C running, you have a clogged condensate drain tube. Condensation from air conditioning coils contains bacteria that can form slime and clog the condensate pan drain tube. You can prevent slime and eliminate drain tube clogs in two easy steps. First, remove the drain tube and fitting from your A/C condensate pan. Toss them. Next, buy a package of slime preventing tablets (one choice is AC-Safe Air Conditioner Pan Tablets). Follow the package dosing directions and insert the tablets right in the drain pan (Photo 1).

Next, buy a 3/4-in. MIPT barb fitting, a small coil of 3/4-in. I.D. vinyl tubing, and several tubing straps. Then install the larger tubing (Photo 2). The pan tabs will reduce slime formation, and the larger-diameter tubing will enable faster condensate flow. That usually eliminates clogging for good.

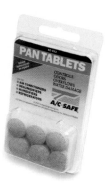

Replace baseboard heater covers

Got old, rusty "hydronic" (hot water heat) baseboards? You could replace them in their entirety, but that's expensive and time consuming. You could also sand and paint them, but that's a lot of work.

The easiest option is to replace just the front covers and end caps with aftermarket ones made of plastic or metal, which are available at home centers and online. Supplyhouse.com (formerly pexsupply.com) sells several styles of replacement covers, called "baseboarders." End caps are sold separately. The company's site has easy-to-follow installation videos.

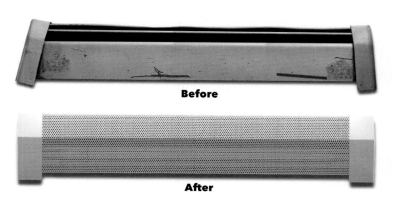

Before

After

Fight allergies with furnace filters

The claims made by furnace filter manufacturers are true: A high-efficiency filter can provide some relief from allergies. By trapping smaller airborne particles, these filters make the air in your home cleaner and less irritating to allergy sufferers. But before you install a high-efficiency filter, there are a few things worth knowing:

▶ High-efficiency means higher cost. If you're currently spending $20 per year on cheapie filters, prepare for sticker shock. You can easily spend $100 per year on high-efficiency filters.

▶ **What the numbers mean.** Furnace filters are labeled with a numerical efficiency rating. A higher number indicates higher "efficiency." That simply means the filter traps smaller particles. When it comes to furnace filters, "efficiency" does not mean energy savings.

▶ **The numbers are tricky.** MERV is the most common rating system. But some filters carry "MPR" or "FPR" ratings (see "How Furnace Filters Are Rated," below). A MERV 13 is roughly equivalent to an FPR 10 filter. Luckily, there are several charts online to help you convert the numbers. Just search for "MERV vs MPR vs FPR."

▶ **Higher isn't always better.** If no one in your home suffers from allergies, there's no reason to go higher than MERV 7. For allergies, MERV 11 is your best choice because higher-rated filters cost more but don't provide much extra relief.

▶ **Don't trust the life-span claims.** Filters carry claims like "lasts up to 90 days." But the life span of a filter depends on

how clean the air is in your home and how much your heating/cooling system runs. No manufacturer can possibly know that.

How furnace filters are rated

Many filter manufacturers follow the Minimum Efficiency Reporting Value (MERV) rating system established by the American Society of Heating, Refrigerating and Air-Conditioning Engineers (ASHRAE). The MERV number is an indication of the filter's effectiveness at trapping particles. A MERV 1 filter traps dust bunnies but allows most dust to pass right through, while a MERV 16 traps bacteria and particles as small as .30 to 1.0 micron and is used mostly in operating rooms. If you don't have allergies, a MERV 7 furnace filter will work just fine in your home. And if you do have family members with allergies, go up to a filter with a MERV 11 rating.

However, some filter manufacturers and retailers have developed proprietary rating systems like Microparticle Performance Rating (MPR) or Filter Performance Rating (FPR). Before you buy a filter based on an MPR or FPR rating, look for a MERV to FPR/MPR chart online or contact your furnace service company for a filter recommendation based on your particular furnace.

► **Filters are not enough.** Furnace filters help, but for allergy sufferers, reducing dust in your home is even more important. That mostly consists of frequent vacuuming with high-quality vacuums and filters and/or eliminating carpeting and rugs as much as possible. For tips on dust control, go to family-handyman.com and search for "allergies."

► **"Efficiency" can wreck your furnace.** High-efficiency filters have smaller pores, which can reduce airflow when new and even more as they clog. That can make the furnace overheat, causing it to shut down or burn out the expensive blower motor. The repair bills can easily run hundreds of dollars, not to mention the increased energy costs to run the stressed blower motor. (To protect your system, see below.)

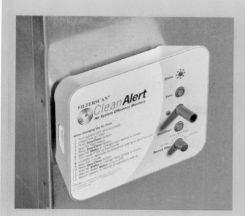

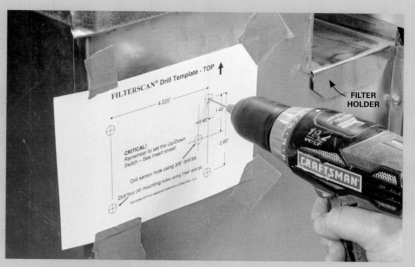

FILTER HOLDER

1 **DRILL MOUNTING HOLES**
Tape the template to the return air duct between the filter holder and the furnace. Stay at least 6 in. away from the filter holder. Then drill screw holes in the duct.

Prevent furnace damage with a filter monitor

A filter that's plugged with particles may not look dirty. And the manufacturers' life-span estimates are nearly worthless. So how can you tell when a filter is dirty enough to stress your heating/cooling system? You can't unless you install a filter monitor. They're available in two versions:

► Mechanical filter monitors are inexpensive and take about five minutes to install, even if you're a beginning DIYer. They're available online (search for "furnace filter monitor"). The downside is that it relies on your memory. If you forget to check it, you won't know when the filter is clogged.

► Electronic filter monitors let you know when the filter needs replacing. The unit shown (the FILTERSCAN WiFi), for example, connects to your home's Wi-Fi and sends an alert to your smartphone. Installation is as simple as driving a few screws. Just find a location on your return air duct and predrill holes (Photo 1). Then mount the unit (Photo 2) and follow the calibration and Wi-Fi setup instructions.

2 **MOUNT AND CALIBRATE THE MONITOR**
Screw the monitor to the duct and install the batteries. Turn off the furnace and press the calibrate button. Then install a new filter, turn on the furnace, raise the thermostat setting and wait until the blower kicks in. Press the calibrate button again. Then install the cover.

Replace a furnace humidifier

1 **DISCONNECT AND REMOVE THE OLD UNIT**
Remove the screws from the bottom of the old humidifier. Then unscrew the fasteners at the top. Tilt the top out and lift it off the duct or plenum.

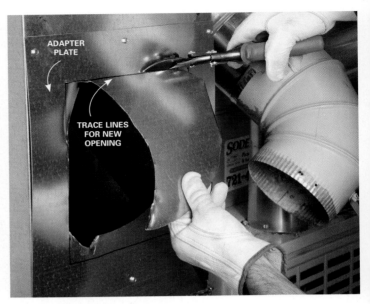

2 **CUT THE NEW OPENING**
Slice an opening into the new metal by hammering the narrow edge of a screwdriver into it. Then jam tin snips into the "slice" and cut out and along the edges of the trace. Leave the corners for last.

Furnace humidifiers are pretty simple gadgets. When they fail, the cause is usually a clogged or burned-out solenoid water valve or a bad drum motor. You can replace those parts yourself—if you can find them at an affordable price. The price of the parts for a humidifier that's 20 years old or older can be shocking. In that case, you may be better off replacing the entire unit with a newer and more efficient model. Many of the newer models come with a digital humidistat and automatic outdoor temperature compensation. The compensation feature automatically dials down humidifier output as outdoor temps drop. That reduces any condensation on your windows.

If you can operate tin snips and read a wiring diagram, you can do the entire job yourself in about two hours.

Turn off the power to the furnace and humidifier. Next, disconnect the round bypass duct (if equipped) coming into the old unit. Then turn off the water valve and disconnect the old water line. Disconnect the wiring to the solenoid valve and humidistat and remove the old humidifier (Photo 1).

Refer to the installation manual and compare the new opening size to the old opening. If the new humidifier requires a smaller opening (most do), you'll have to make an adapter plate. Cut a piece of sheet metal to completely cover the old opening. Attach it with No. 6 x 1/2-in. self-drilling sheet metal screws. Then trace the new opening onto the plate, making sure your lines are level. Cut the new opening (Photo 2). Use caution to avoid damaging the A/C coil. Hook the bottom edge of the new humidifier onto the opening and tilt the top toward the duct. Level the unit and

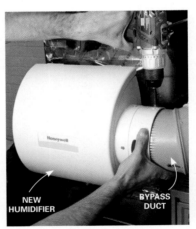

3 **INSTALL THE BYPASS**
Install the summer/winter damper (provided with the new unit) and insert the bypass duct. Secure it with sheet metal screws.

4 **INSTALL THE OUTDOOR SENSOR**
Connect the thermostat cable to the sensor. Then push the extra wire back into the hold and caulk the hole. Mount the sensor to your house.

secure with self-drilling sheet metal screws. Then attach the bypass duct (Photo 3).

Locate the new humidistat on the return air duct. Then run 18-2 thermostat cable to a shady non-south-facing side of the house for the outdoor temperature sensor. Mount the outdoor sensor (Photo 4).

Connect the water line to the solenoid valve and hook up the humidistat wiring. Turn the power back on and test the entire system.

Replace a noisy bath fan

If the bath fan in your home is more than 20 years old, chances are it's pretty loud. A loud fan may be good for masking bathroom noise, but the jet engine roar is downright annoying the rest of the time. Worse yet, your old bath fan may not be moving enough air to keep your bathroom free of mold and mildew.

Newer-style bath fans, on the other hand, are so quiet you can hardly hear them running, and they cost very little to operate. It's easier than you think to swap out that noisy, inefficient bath fan, especially if you choose one that's designed to be installed without ripping out the bathroom ceiling.

Of the many replacement models to choose from, we picked the NuTone No. RN110 Ultra Pro Series because the fan can be installed from inside the bathroom.

It's not the quietest model available, but at 0.6 sones (about 25 decibels), it's a huge improvement over the old 4-sone (about 60 decibels) fan we're replacing. If you can locate a joist, cut drywall and handle basic electrical work, you can do the whole job in about two hours and save about $200 on the installation. You'll need a stud finder, a drywall saw, a drill and screws, and aluminum duct tape.

Buy the right size for your bathroom

There's no such thing as a "one-size-fits-all" bath fan. For bathrooms up to 100 sq. ft., calculate the required cubic feet per minute (cfm) by multiplying the room's length x width x height. Multiply that result by .13 and round up to the nearest 10. Example: 10 ft. wide x 9 ft. long x 9 ft. high x .13 = 105. Round up to 110 and buy a 110-cfm bath fan. For bathrooms larger than 100 sq. ft., simply add up the cfm requirements for each of these plumbing fixtures: toilet, 50 cfm; shower, 50 cfm; bathtub, 50 cfm; jetted tub, 100 cfm.

Turn off the power before proceeding

You'll have to remove the power cable from the old unit and connect it to the new fan. This must be done with the power off. Don't rely on turning off the fan switch; flip the breaker as well. Then double-check that the power is off with a voltage sniffer. If you're not comfortable working with electricity, hire an electrician to remove and connect the wires.

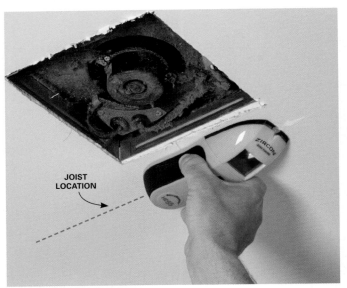

1 FIND THE JOISTS

Slide a stud finder along the ceiling until you find the joist nearest the old fan. Mark the location. Then find the joist on the opposite side of the fan.

JOIST LOCATION

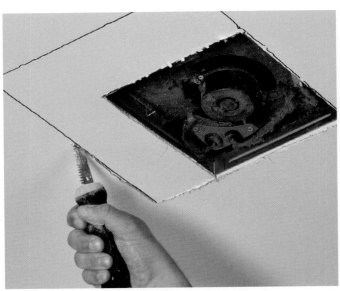

2 MARK AND CUT THE CEILING OPENING

Using the template provided, trace the new opening onto the ceiling. Then cut along the lines using a drywall saw. Cut shallower strokes around the flexible duct so you don't puncture it.

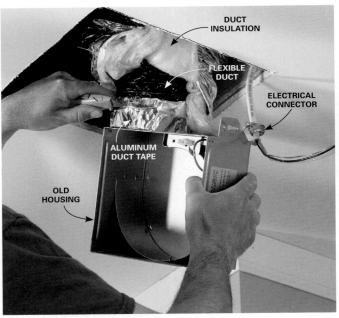

DUCT INSULATION

FLEXIBLE DUCT

ELECTRICAL CONNECTOR

ALUMINUM DUCT TAPE

OLD HOUSING

3 DISCONNECT AND REMOVE OLD PARTS

Unscrew the old fan housing from the joist. Then disconnect the electrical cable from the housing. Finally, slice through the duct sealing tape with a utility knife and disconnect the duct.

NEW BRACKET

4 MOUNT THE BRACKET

Slide the bracket through the opening and extend it so it contacts the joists on each side of the opening. Secure both sides to the joists with drywall screws.

You may have to go into your attic

The installation we show here is all done from inside a bath with a floor above it. However, if you're replacing a bath fan in a bathroom with an accessible attic above it, you have the option of doing some of the work from up there. Use your judgment. You may save some mess by going into the attic and moving the insulation aside before you remove the old fan. Then rearrange the insulation after the installation is done. Or, eliminate the second trip by making the electrical and vent connections at the same time.

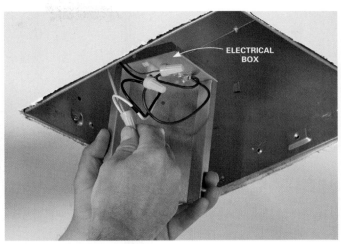

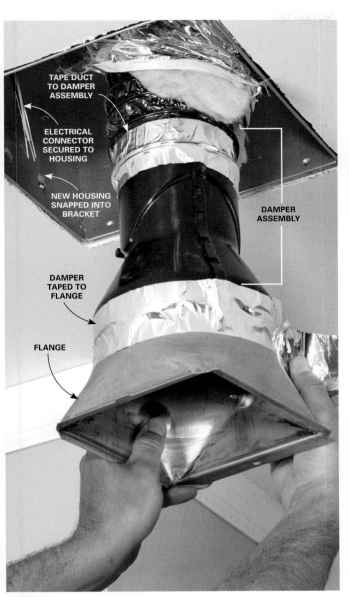

6 CONNECT THE WIRES
Secure the hot (black), neutral (white) and ground (green/bare copper) wires with wire nuts. Then slide the metal electrical box into place in the housing and attach it with the screw provided.

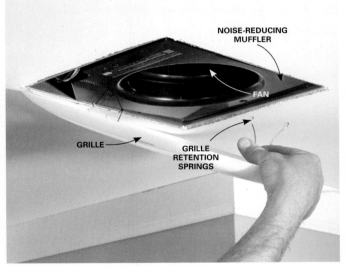

5 CONNECT THE DUCT
Pull the old duct through the housing and into the room. Then tape the duct to the damper assembly. Slide the damper onto the flange and secure with aluminum duct tape. Push the duct, damper and flange back into the ceiling and secure the flange to the housing using the screw provided.

7 INSTALL THE FAN AND GRILLE
Slide the fan assembly into the housing until it snaps in place. Secure with screws. Plug the electrical connector into the electrical box mounted earlier. Then screw in the noise-reducing muffler. Squeeze the grille springs and snap the grille into place.

Find the joists and duct and enlarge the opening

Most bath fans are mounted to a ceiling joist with the duct running parallel to the joist. Start by locating the direction of your ceiling joists (Photo 1). Then locate the damper (you may have to remove the fan motor and blade from the housing). That'll tell you where the duct lies in the ceiling. Mark the duct location. Then enlarge the opening (Photo 2).

Remove and replace the housing, duct and fan

With the opening now enlarged, you'll have room to disconnect the old duct, electrical cable and old housing (Photo 3). Install and secure the new mounting frame (Photo 4). Connect the electrical cable to the new housing and snap the housing into the frame so the duct opening is facing the existing duct. Then connect the duct, damper and flange using aluminum duct

tape (Photo 5). Finish the rough-in by connecting the power wires and ground to the electrical box provided (Photo 6).

Then simply slide the fan into the housing and add the muffler and grille (Photo 7). Turn on the power and test. Apply a bead of fire-resistant (intumescent) caulk around the fan housing and drywall to prevent moisture intrusion into the attic.

Chapter 4

DOOR & WINDOW Rx

Replacing window and door screen

It's easy to replace the screen fabric in an aluminum frame. What's hard is figuring out which diameter spline to buy and how tight the fabric should be stretched. No problem—here's how to conquer both of those issues.

Spline replacement

Let's start with spline basics. Don't reuse the old spline unless it's fairly new. It's probably dried and brittle, so install new spline when you install new fabric. New spline is more pliable and will slip into the channel easier and hold the fabric tighter. Besides, it's cheap.

There are nine different sizes of spline (yikes!), but most home centers only carry the four most common sizes. Forget about measuring the spline channel width. Just bring a small section of the old spline with you and visually match it to the new spline. If none of the options are dead-on, buy the two closest sizes. Then test-fit each one using a small patch of new screen. The spline should take just a bit of effort to snap into the frame. If you have to use a lot of muscle, the spline is too large.

Installing the screen

You may be tempted to buy aluminum fabric. Don't. It's harder to install and is overkill for residential applications. Instead, take your old screen fabric with you to find new screen that matches the color and mesh size. That way it'll match your other screens. Then buy a concave spline roller and a roll of screen fabric.

Cut the screen 1 in. larger than the opening. Then clip off a corner of the fabric and place it over a corner of the aluminum frame. Press the spline and fabric into the channel and continue rolling it into the long edge of the screen (Photo 1). Round the corner (don't cut the spline at the corners), and use the same technique along the second edge of the screen frame. Next, place a heavy object in the center of the screen fabric (Photo 2) and finish installing the screen. **Note:** Don't overstretch the screen trying to get it "banjo"-tight. That'll bend the frame. Finish the job by trimming off the excess screen (Photo 3).

CONCAVE ROLLER

1 Roll in the screen and spline. Align the screen squarely to the frame along the longest edge. Lay the spline directly over the channel ahead of the roller. Lightly stretch the screen away from the starting corner as you roll the spline into place.

2 Depress the center with a heavy object. Load a brick in the center of the screen to create the proper amount of slack. Then continue installing the fabric along the third and fourth sides of the screen frame. Remove the brick.

3 Cut off the excess screen. Use a brand-new utility blade and position the knife at a steep angle against the frame. Then trim off the excess screen.

Auto body fix for a dented steel door

Fill a dent or hole in a steel door the same way a body shop would fix your car. You can do this with the door in place, but it will be easier with the door lying flat on sawhorses. Remove an area of paint a couple of inches larger than the damaged spot (Photo 1). Sand away the paint with 60- or 80-grit paper, or do the job faster with a small wire wheel in a drill. Next, fill the wound with auto body filler (at hardware stores and home centers). To mix the filler, place a scoop of resin on a scrap of plywood or hardboard. Then add the hardener. Mix the two components thoroughly; unmixed resin won't harden and you'll be left with a sticky mess. A plastic putty knife makes a good mixing tool.

Apply the filler with a metal putty knife that's wider than the damaged spot (Photo 2). The filler will start to harden in just a couple of minutes, so you have to work fast. Fill the repair flush with the surrounding surface. Don't overfill it and don't try to smooth out imperfections after the filler begins to harden. Adding another coat of filler is easier than sanding off humps. When the filler has hardened completely (about 30 minutes), sand it smooth (Photo 3). After priming the repair, you could paint over the primer only. But the new paint won't perfectly match the older paint, so it's best to repaint the entire door.

Tip

If the damage is near the bottom of the door, you can skip the repair and cover it with a metal kick plate (available at home centers and hardware stores). Kick plates are about 8 in. wide and come in lengths to match standard doors.

1 Remove paint around the dent with a wire wheel. Roughen the bare metal with 60-grit sandpaper.

2 Mix auto body filler and fill the dent using a wide putty knife. Avoid leaving humps or ridges. If necessary, add more filler after the first layer hardens.

3 Sand the filler smooth with 100-grit paper. Use a sanding block to ensure a flat surface. Prime the repair and paint the entire door.

Adjust a dragging shower door

If the sliding doors on your shower or bathtub don't glide smoothly, you can repair them. A door that drags on the lower track will eventually do permanent damage to both the door and the track. A dragging roller at the top of the door will wear and require replacement.

First, make sure the rollers on both doors are riding on the tracks inside the upper rail. Sometimes, one roller falls out of the track and the bottom edge of the door skids along the lower rail. In that case, you only have to lift the door and guide the roller back onto the track.

If an off-track roller isn't the problem, you'll have to remove the doors to adjust and possibly replace the rollers. Many doors have a small plastic guide at the middle of the lower rail. To remove this type of guide, just remove a single screw. Others have a guide rail screwed to the door (Photo 1).

With the guide removed, lift the doors out of their tracks (Photo 2). Then make sure the rollers turn easily. If not, apply a little silicone spray lubricant. Some lubricants can harm plastic, so check the label. If the lubricant doesn't do the trick, replace the rollers. Most home centers and some hardware stores carry replacements. Take an old roller with you to find a match. In many cases, you can use a replacement that's slightly larger or smaller than the original. But be sure the original and replacement edges match—either rounded or flat (see photos, left). If you can't find rollers locally, search "shower door parts" online to find a supplier.

Screw the new rollers into place and rehang the doors. You'll probably have to remove doors once or twice to adjust the rollers for smooth operation (Photo 3).

1 Unscrew the guide at the lower edge of the sliding door. Protect the shower or tub from scratches with a drop cloth.

GUIDE RAIL

2 Lift the door out of its track inside the upper rail. Tilt each door in or out to remove it. Wipe both tracks clean.

UPPER RAIL

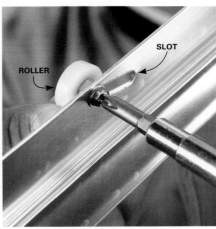

ROLLER
SLOT

3 Raise or lower each door by repositioning the roller in its slanted slot. Loosen the screw to move the roller.

ROUND EDGE
FLAT EDGE

Three garage door fixes

1. Replace rotting trim

Wood garage doorjambs and trim often rot near the bottom or get crunched by bumpers.

A good, long-lasting solution is to replace the wood jamb, brick mold trim and doorstop with paintable solid vinyl pieces that won't crack or decay. Available at home centers and lumberyards, the cost of solid vinyl is comparable to clear wood. The vinyl can be cut, nailed and painted just like wood. It's available in white, but you can order brown, bronze and tan. Fill nail holes with white caulk or exterior wood filler, then, if desired, prime and paint with acrylic latex. Use a light paint color over white vinyl to keep it from overheating.

Remove the old jamb and trim (Photo 1), then nail the vinyl jamb to the frame, beginning with the top piece (Photo 2). Fasten every 12 to 16 in. with 8d galvanized nails or stainless steel trim screws. Precut the miters on the top piece of brick mold trim and nail it to the framing every 12 in. with 10d galvanized casing nails. Use 6d casing nails for the stop molding, nailing it at the premarked points on the trim.

If the temperature is below 40 degrees F during installation, predrill nail holes and leave a 1/8-in. gap at the ends of the jamb for expansion.

Glue the brick mold corners with PVC cement (Photo 3), then nail them into place after the glue sets. To avoid breaking the joint, wait at least an hour for the glue to fully cure before nailing within a foot of the corner. Splice long runs with glued butt joints.

The edge of the vinyl stop molding should be 2-1/2 in. back from the garage door so the rubber seal fits loosely against the door (Photo 4).

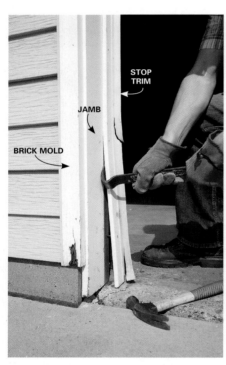

STOP TRIM

JAMB

BRICK MOLD

1 Cut through any caulk lines with a utility knife, then pry off the old garage doorstop, brick mold and jamb.

8D GALVANIZED CASING NAIL

HELPER CLAMP

2 Use a clamp to hold up one end of the top jamb, then nail the jamb to the framing with 8d galvanized casing nails.

3 Spread PVC cement on both sides of the mitered corners, then hold them together until they bond.

4 Mark the width of the trim piece at several points on the jamb, then nail. Trim the overlapping rubber seal at the corners.

2. Clean up rusty door track

Garage door tracks often rest directly on damp concrete floors, where they eventually rust. However, there's no reason they can't be slightly above the floor and stay dry: The garage rafters carry the weight of the track and the angle brackets hold the track in place.

Clean up the tracks and prevent rusting by simply cutting off the bottom 1/2 in. First make sure all the angle bracket bolts are tight, then cut the track bottoms off (Photo 1). Use a rag dipped in mineral spirits to remove any lubricant on the first 6 in. of track, then scrape and brush off as much rust as you can. Finally, paint the bottom with a metal spray paint that's formulated to bond to rusted areas (Photo 2). Rust-Oleum Rust Reformer is one choice.

1 Mark the bottom of the track, then cut the metal with a reciprocating saw or hacksaw.

2 Clean the bottom of the track with mineral spirits, wire-brush the rust, and then paint the area.

3. Install new weather seal

If the weather seal attached to the bottom of your steel garage door is torn or completely flattened, it's time to replace it with a new piece. Home centers sell two types: a nail-on style for wood doors and a slide-in "bulb" type for steel doors.

Lift the door just enough that the garage door track doesn't get in the way of the weather seal, then slide out the old rubber bulb (Photo 1). You may need to pry the track ends open with a flat screwdriver if they've been crimped. If it's especially stubborn, cut it and remove it in pieces.

Clean the door bottom (Photo 2), then cut the new rubber seal to length with a razor knife. Thread the T-shaped edges into the weather seal track, then slide the seal across the door. Be patient—it takes a lot of pushing and pulling even with a helper.

1 Lift the garage door to about 6 ft. high and pull the old weather seal out through the gap behind the door track.

WEATHER SEAL TRACK

2 Scrape dirt and corrosion out of the weather seal track with a screwdriver and a stiff brush.

DISH SOAP HERE

3 Lubricate the rubber with a few drops of dish soap, then push and pull the new weather seal into the track.

Great goofs

A close call

In the double garage of our first home, we had a one-piece swing-up garage door, also known as a "kick-out" garage door. The door pivots up instead of rolling on tracks. I decided to replace the springs one day, and I opened the door and propped it with a 2x4 to secure it while I did the job. The old springs were stretched out and not too hard to remove. I soon discovered that I couldn't stretch the new springs enough with the door in the open position, so I reached for the 2x4 to let the door down.

Yiiiiiikes! The door was so heavy that it came down with a crash and sent me sliding on my keister halfway across the garage floor. Fortunately, I only had some bruises on my backside and scraped elbows. When my wits came back, I realized how lucky I was not to be in the back of an ambulance. I now leave garage door spring replacement to the pros!

—John Gray

Repair a cranky window

When a casement (crank-out) window is hard to open or close, people blame the operator (crank mechanism). It may have gone bad, but an operator usually doesn't fail on its own. Operator gears strip out when you crank too hard while trying to open or close a binding or stuck sash. If you just replace the operator without fixing the root cause of the binding, you'll be replacing it again—and soon.

We'll show you how to get to the bottom of most casement window problems and explain how to fix each one. The parts are fairly inexpensive, but, as with many other home repair projects, you'll spend more time searching for the right parts than you will on making the repairs.

First, the usual suspects

A sash can sag and bind in the frame from worn, dirty or corroded hinges; loose or stripped screws; or settling. Loose or stripped screws are the easiest to fix, and they're usually the most common cause of binding, so start there. If you have interior hinges (hinges located in the head and sill area and covered by the sash), open the sash all the way to expose screws. Tighten each one. If the screw holes are stripped, you'll have to remove the sash first to fix them (Photo 1). Next, remove the hinge, enlarge the holes and refill them with toothpicks and epoxy filler (Photo 2). Then reinstall the hinge screws and sash and see if that solves the problem.

Next, check the condition of the hinges. It's much easier to spot wear if the hinge is clean and lubricated. So clean away dirt

1 **REMOVE THE SASH**
Disconnect the operator arm and hinge arm locks from the sash while holding the window firmly. Then slide plastic hinge sleds toward the release area and lift the sash out of the frame. Tilt the sash sideways and bring it into the room.

and grease buildup with household cleaner and then lubricate the hinges (Photo 3). Open and close the window and examine the hinge pivots (top and bottom) as they move. If you see "slop," replace the hinge. Exterior mounted hinges (common on windows from the '50s) are especially prone to corrosion and binding since they're constantly exposed to the elements. You can try lubricating them, but if the binding recurs, you'll have to replace them (see "Find Parts for Old Windows," below). Remove the old screws (Photo 4). Then, following the hinge profile, slice through the old paint with a utility knife. Pry off the old hinge and install the new one.

If the hinges are in good shape, or you've replaced them and the sash still binds, the window frame has probably settled and is out of square. Resquaring the window frame is a big job. But you can try to fix the problem by relocating the hinges. To learn how to move a hinge, go to familyhandyman.com and search for "repair old windows."

Finish by checking the operator

Now that the sash is opening and closing smoothly, turn your attention to the condition of the operator. First remove the sill operator cover trim (Photo 5). Then loosen the crank handle setscrew and remove the handle and operator cover. Reinstall the crank handle and rotate it while checking the condition of the gears. Look for gray dust or rough, chipped or missing teeth. Those are all signs the operator needs to be replaced. However, if the operator looks clean and moves smoothly, just tighten the screws, apply a dab of lithium grease to the gears, and reassemble all the trim. Now your window should be in tip-top shape.

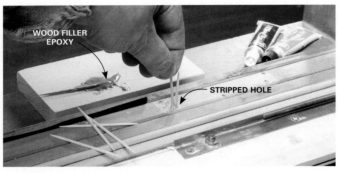

2 **FILL THE STRIPPED HOLES**
Mix a small batch of two-part epoxy wood filler and use a toothpick to spread it inside the enlarged hole. Then dip each of the toothpicks into the filler and jam them into the hole. Slice off the extended portions with a utility knife once the filler sets.

3 **LUBRICATE THE HINGES**
Saturate each hinge with silicone or dry Teflon spray lube. Wipe up the excess. Then work in the lube by opening and closing the window several times.

5 **REMOVE THE OPERATOR TRIM**
Slide a flat bar under the sill operator trim piece and gently pry it up slightly on one end. Then move the flat bar to the opposite side and pry that up. Next, remove the operator screws and the operator.

Find parts for old windows

You won't find these 1950s-era hinges (or other window parts) at many hardware stores, but they're available online. The new parts may not be an exact match for your old hardware, but they'll do the job and put your window back in the swing of things. Just measure the old parts, shoot digital photos of the top and bottom pieces (they may be different) and email the info to an online window parts seller (blainewindow.com is one very reputable source).

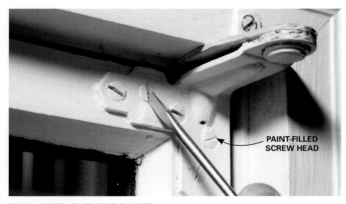

4 **CHIP OUT THE PAINT**
Tilt a flat-blade screwdriver at a 45-degree angle and hammer it along the slotted head to chip out the paint. Then slice through any remaining paint with a utility knife.

Stop patio door drafts

Patio door weather-strip seals slowly degrade and wear, letting in small drafts that are barely noticeable. If you spent the winter kicking up the thermostat (or grabbing a blanket) just to be comfortable near the door, you've already wasted enough money on heat to buy several sets of weather-strip seals. If you open your patio door frequently or the door is exposed to sunlight, it pays to replace the weather stripping every 10 years.

We bought all the seals for this early '90s Marvin sliding patio door for less than $100 including shipping. Replacing the seals is a one-person job, but enlist a friend to help lift the heavy door in and out of the track. You just need a screwdriver, a hammer, hooks and picks, and a putty knife. The entire job takes just a few hours. Here's the process.

Find the make and model

Some patio door manufacturers engrave their logo on the door pull lock hardware, but others hide the branding and model information. If you can't find a manufacturer logo or model label, look along the door edges or jamb for a gold sticker from the American Architectural Manufacturers Association (AAMA). If you find the label, shoot a digital photo and go to aamanet.org and click on "Product Directory" to decipher the codes and get the brand and model information.

If you can't locate the label, copy the numbers on the metal strip between the panes of glass. Then go to igcc.org to decipher the codes. If neither approach works, or the manufacturer no longer sells replacement weather-strip seals, you'll have to use off-the-shelf weather stripping and come up with a custom fix (see "If You Can't Find Factory Parts," at right).

Next, measure the stationary and movable sections. Take a digital photo of the entire door, track and jamb. Then contact the manufacturer's customer service/parts department to order replacement parts.

Remove the door

Most sliding patio doors tilt into the room from the top and then lift off the bottom track. The door is usually held in place with a removable header strip, which has to come off first. Brace the door or have a helper hold the door upright while you

If you can't find factory parts

If you can't locate manufacturer weather-strip seals in stores, try these sources:

- ▶ amweatherguard.com
- ▶ biltbestwindowparts.com
- ▶ strybuc.com
- ▶ swisco.com

If you've checked all online sources and still can't find an exact match, you'll have to improvise with off-the-shelf materials. V-seal can be used in place of factory jamb, header and track leaf seals. Just fold along the score line to form a "V." Remove the backing and stick it in place. Place EPDM foam rubber on the jamb and adjust the latch to accommodate the thickness. Use entry door seal strips to replace factory pile strips in mating areas.

1 UNSCREW AND REMOVE THE HEADER
Open the patio door so the sliding door is in front of the stationary section. Start removing the header screws from that end. As you reach the open part of the door, have a friend brace the movable door so it doesn't tip out. Then remove the entire header strip. (If the door trim overlaps the header strip, you'll have to remove it.)

2 TILT AND LIFT
Tilt the top of the sliding door out far enough to clear the frame. Then lift the door up and off the bottom track (get help—it's heavy). Set the door on a drop cloth and lean the door against a wall.

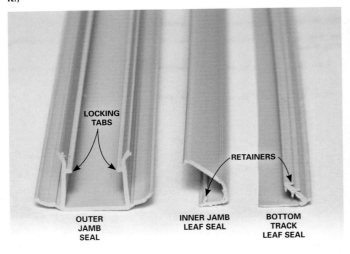

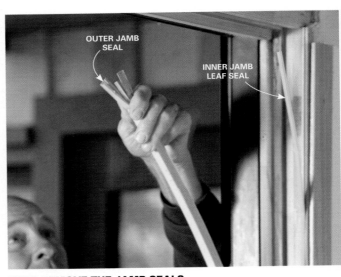

3 IDENTIFY AND LOCATE THE SEALS
The outer jamb seal is hard plastic with locking tabs and rubber sealing wings. The inner and track seals are made from a softer flexible material and are held in place with retainers.

4 REMOVE THE JAMB SEALS
Grab the outer jamb seal at the top and pull it off. Then pull the leaf seal out of the inner part of the jamb.

remove the header retaining screws (Photo 1). Lean the door against a wall in a safe place after you lift it out of the track (Photo 2). The bottom rollers are usually dirty and the door latch can be greasy, so spread a drop cloth over the floor to prevent stains.

Remove and replace the jamb, header, track and pile seals

Although weather-strip styles vary among manufacturers, this Marvin patio door is pretty common. The jamb has two seals: a hard plastic outer seal with locking tabs that snap into grooves on the jamb and a flexible "leaf" seal that's wedged into a groove on the inside part of the jamb (Photo 3).

Remove both jamb seals (Photo 4). Then remove the header seal (Photo 5). Next, cut the new seals to length and install them (Photos 6 and 7). Then replace the pile seal on the stationary and sliding doors (Photo 8).

Clean and lubricate the bottom rollers using an all-purpose oil (Photo 9) and thoroughly clean the plastic or metal track that the rollers ride on. Then reinstall the sliding door and retaining header piece.

5 **REMOVE THE HEADER SEAL**
Starting at one side, slide a hook or pick behind the header seal and pry it away from the wood. Then slide the pick along the header as you pull off the entire header seal.

6 **CUT THE NEW SEALS**
Using the old seals as templates, mark and cut the new seals to the proper length. Cut with scissors, a utility knife or hacksaw.

7 **INSTALL THE NEW SEALS**
Spread the locking tabs and snap the outer and header jamb seals into place. Push the inner leaf seal into the groove. Then slide the bottom seal into the track.

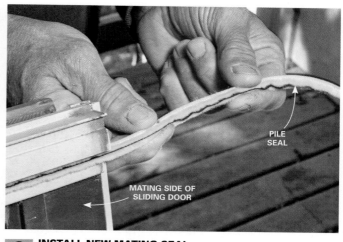

8 **INSTALL NEW MATING SEAL**
Slide the new pile seal into the groove on the mating side of the sliding door. Then attach new self-adhesive pile strips at the top and bottom of the stationary door.

9 **LUBRICATE THE ROLLERS**
Clean the bottom rollers with a grease-cutting household cleaner. Then apply a few drops of oil to the roller axles. Wipe off the excess before installing the door.

Great goofs

A bit too close

Our new patio door looked great, but I wanted to add some security hardware. Easy enough, except that I drilled my first hole too close to the glass. When the drill bit hit the glass, the entire pane shattered into thousands of pieces. All I could do was to watch in horror as the fragments fell like rain. I thought I would have to replace the entire door assembly. Fortunately, the store where I bought the doors just happened to have a set of doors with no frame. The manager gave me a deal. I also purchased a different security lock!

—Lloyd Lehn, Ph.D.

Fix a rattling door

If your interior doors are out of adjustment, they'll rattle every time a breeze kicks up. The problem is always caused by a gap between the door stop and the door. Here are three simple fixes.

The simplest fix of the three is to bend the little tang on the strike plate toward the door (photo, bottom left). When the door latches, it pushes the door toward the stop just a bit and holds the latch a little tighter, sometimes enough to silence the door. It doesn't always work, but it's worth a shot. A pair of pliers always hacks up the finish on the plate, so use two adjustable wrenches instead.

The next easiest fix is to shim any gaps with self-adhesive "dots" (bottom right), which are usually used to soften cabinet door and drawer closes. You'll find them near the cabinet hardware at a hardware store. The least obvious are the clear dots that blend in with the door finish.

The harder, but more elegant fix is to actually shift the door stop so it's tight against the door (top photo). If there's paint and/or caulk, score it first with a utility knife. Then use a block and smack the stop tight against the door. The existing nails will shift quite a bit but may hold the stop away from the jamb when they bend. If that happens, use the block again to smack the stop flat to the jamb to flatten the nails. Check the door operation to make sure it doesn't drag on the stop before you renail it. Here's the downside: With painted or stained trim, there may be a bit of retouching to do.

THE MOST ELEGANT FIX: SHIFT THE DOOR STOP
Close the door and hold a block of wood against the door stop. Smack the wood until the door stop moves enough to touch the door. Then secure the door stop with 1-1/4-in. finish nails.

OR, BEND THE TANG GENTLY
Tighten one adjustable wrench onto the curved "latch" side of the plate to hold it while you bend the tang. Then tighten the second wrench on the tang. Bend it toward the door and reinstall the strike to test the fit. Make several small bends rather than "overshooting" and having to bend it back and forth.

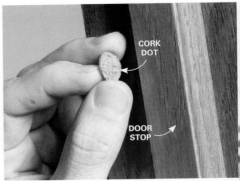

CORK DOT

DOOR STOP

OR, FILL THE GAP WITH A "DOT"
Close the door and look for the largest gap between the door and the door stop. Fill the gap with a dot that matches the size of the gap. Just press the dot onto the door stop and cut off any overlap with a utility knife.

CHAIN TENSION ADJUSTING ROD AND NUT

Rebuild your garage door opener

If you press the garage door opener button and hear either a humming or a grinding sound, but the door won't open, you may think you need a new opener. And you might. But before you give up on the old unit, pop off the cover and check for stripped gears. That's a common problem and one that you can fix yourself for less than about $25.

You'll have to get a replacement gear kit (two new gears, grease and washers), which may take some running around. But once you have the kit in hand, you can do the repair in about two hours. You'll need a 2x4, a small drift punch, a standard 1/4-in. drive socket set, hex wrenches, a circular saw, a drill and a hammer. We'll show you how to remove and replace the gears without damaging the shafts.

Start by unplugging the opener. Then remove the retaining screws for the metal cover and put it aside. Shine a flashlight directly at the gear set. If you see chewed-up teeth, you've nailed the problem. If the gears are in good shape, you've got a more serious problem and your best bet may be to just replace the entire unit. To find a replacement gear kit, write down or snap a photo of the make, model and serial number of your opener (you'll find it on a label on the back of the opener). Then call a garage door opener repair company. They'll probably charge a bit more than an online source, but you'll have the parts right away and be up and running the same day.

1 REMOVE THE CHAIN

Unscrew the outer nut on the chain tensioning rod. If necessary, use pliers to prevent the chain from turning. Then slip on a pair of gloves and remove the greasy chain from the sprocket at the top of the opener.

RETAINING SCREWS

SHREDDED HELICAL GEAR

2 REMOVE THE HELICAL GEAR ASSEMBLY

Unscrew the hex-head screws that hold the helical gear assembly in place. Save the screws for reassembly. Then lift the entire assembly (sprocket, plate, shaft and helical gear) up and out of the top of the unit.

3 **REMOVE THE HELICAL GEAR FROM THE SHAFT**
Support both ends of the helical gear assembly with the two jigs. Hold a small drift punch over the roll pin and tap the pin out of the shaft with a small hammer.

ROLL PIN

GROOVE IN
2x4 BLOCK

HOLE IN
2x4 BLOCK

Getting out the gear shafts

Use a combination wrench to loosen and remove the chain (Photo 1). Next, use a 1/4-in. drive socket, extension and ratchet to remove the helical gear assembly retaining screws (Photo 2). Snap a photo of the wiring connections from the motor or label them with masking tape. Disconnect the motor wires and remove the entire motor assembly. Move the helical gear assembly and the motor assembly to your workbench.

Remove the helical and worm gears Cut a shallow groove into a 2x4 with a circular saw. Then slice off about a 3-in. section to make a jig to hold the helical gear assembly circular plate (Photo 3). Place the plate in the groove, hold the gear assembly level and mark the end of the shaft on another 2x4. Drill a hole in the wood and insert the end of the shaft. Then remove the roll pin (Photo 3). Slide the old gear off the shaft and replace it with the new gear. Reinstall the roll pin using the same jigs.

Next, remove the retaining collar and thrust washers on the end of the motor shaft (Photo 4). Pull the motor out of the chassis and slide the worm gear off the shaft (the roll pin stays in place on this shaft). Slide on the new worm gear with the notched end facing the roll pin.

Reassemble the motor assembly and place it back in the opener. Then install the helical gear assembly. Coat the gear teeth with new grease. Reattach the chain and tighten it to the proper tension (see your owner's manual). Test your repair with the garage door disconnected from the opener trolley.

MOTOR
RETAINING
SCREWS

WORM GEAR

4 **REMOVE THE WORM GEAR**
Loosen the collar setscrews with a hex wrench and slide the worm gear off the shaft. Then remove the motor retaining screws.

Four fixes for a noisy garage door

When a garage door makes noise, it's usually just screaming for a bit of TLC. We'll show you some fixes to quiet down any garage door. And, if you have a tuck-under or attached garage, we'll show you how to reduce the vibrations and noise that transfer to the living space.

Test the noise level by opening the door after each fix and quit when things are quiet enough for you.

Before you get started, pick up a Prime Flo garage door lubrication kit for $7. You'll get all the lubricants you need for this job. Also pick up rollers if you need them for Fix #4.

1. Isolate the opener

If you have an attached or tuck-under garage and your opener seems loud inside the house, try this step.

Mechanically isolate the opener from the garage rafters/trusses with rubber pads. Cut rubber pads out of an old tire, or buy specially made rubber/cork anti-vibration pads. (Four 5-1/2- x 5-1/2- x 3/8-in. pads are $16 at amazon. com. Just search for "anti vibration pads.") You'll be adding about an inch in thickness, so you'll need four longer lag screws and four fender washers.

ADD ANTI-VIBRATION PADS
Slide one anti-vibration pad between the mounting bracket and the ceiling and the second pad under the bracket. Then slip a fender washer onto the new lag screw and drive it into the rafter with a socket wrench or impact driver. Repeat on all four corners of the opener bracket.

OPENER BRACKET

ANTI-VIBRATION PAD

FENDER WASHER

2. Tighten the chain and lube the opener

A loose garage door opener chain makes loud slapping sounds and causes jerky door movements that smack the rollers against the track. So start by tightening the chain (find the procedure in your owner's manual).

If you have a track drive opener, the next step is to lubricate the opener track with grease. If you have a screw drive opener, grease the threads.

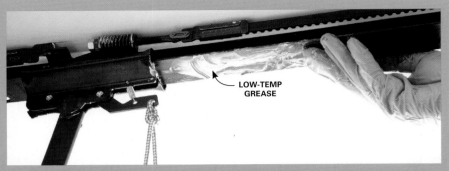

GREASE THE TRACK
Squeeze a large dollop of grease onto your gloved hand and wipe it onto the track. Operate the opener several times to spread the grease along the track and into the trolley.

3. Lube the hardware

Next, quiet all the garage door's moving parts with garage door lube spray. It works much better than spray-on oils because it stays in place and dries to a greaselike consistency. The grease also does a better job of quieting moving parts. Repeat this step every six months.

LUBE EVERYTHING THAT MOVES
Spray the roller shafts and hinges first. Wipe off the drippy excess. Then slip a piece of cardboard behind the torsion springs and soak them, too.

4. Install quieter rollers

If your garage door has steel track rollers, they're part of your noise problem. Buy eight "quiet" nylon rollers. They're equipped with bearings and cost a few bucks more than nylon "bearingless" rollers or nylon rollers without end caps, but they're quieter, roll smoother and last longer. You can find them at home centers and online at garage-doors-and-parts.com.

Swap out the steel rollers for the new nylon ones (one at a time). If your door uses torsion springs mounted on the header above the door, do NOT attempt to replace the rollers in the two bottom brackets. Those brackets are under constant spring tension and can cause serious injury if you unbolt them. That's a job for a pro.

INSTALL NEW ROLLERS
Remove the hinge retaining nuts and tilt the hinge/bracket toward you. Swap out the rollers and reverse the procedure to reinstall. Then reinstall the nuts and snug them up with a wrench (but don't overtighten).

Reinforce a door

Burglars don't usually pick locks. That takes too long. Instead, they kick or pry the door open. The dead bolt usually survives that brute force, but the door or strike plate gives way. Here's how to beef up those weak spots:

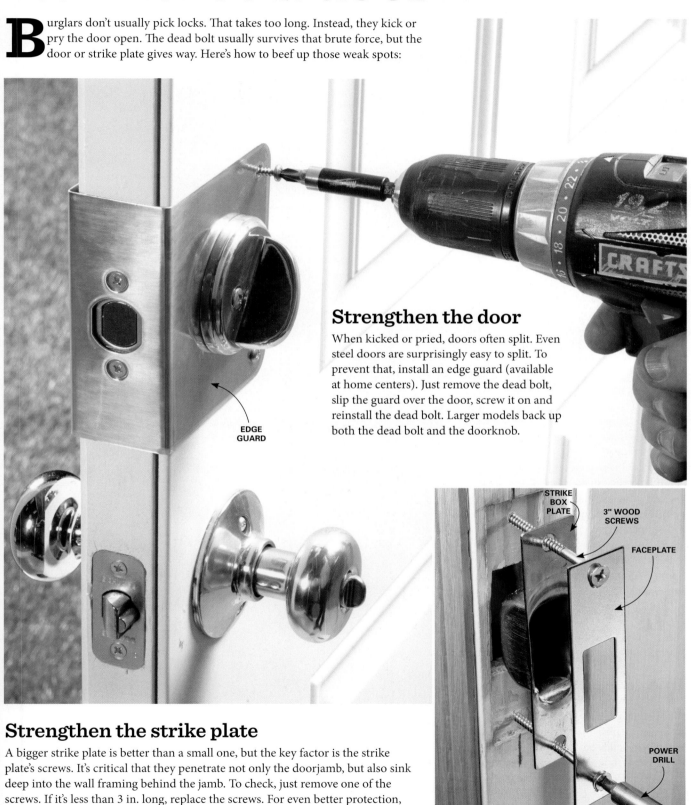

Strengthen the door

When kicked or pried, doors often split. Even steel doors are surprisingly easy to split. To prevent that, install an edge guard (available at home centers). Just remove the dead bolt, slip the guard over the door, screw it on and reinstall the dead bolt. Larger models back up both the dead bolt and the doorknob.

EDGE GUARD

STRIKE BOX PLATE

3" WOOD SCREWS

FACEPLATE

POWER DRILL

Strengthen the strike plate

A bigger strike plate is better than a small one, but the key factor is the strike plate's screws. It's critical that they penetrate not only the doorjamb, but also sink deep into the wall framing behind the jamb. To check, just remove one of the screws. If it's less than 3 in. long, replace the screws. For even better protection, install a larger strike plate that allows for more than two screws.

Fix a broken window jamb liner

Modern double-hung windows (the upper and lower window sashes slide up and down past each other) don't use pulleys and sash weights to support the sash (the moving part of the window). Instead they have liners on each side that contain a spring assembly. If your sash won't stay in the raised position, chances are that some part of the jamb liner hardware is broken. You might be able to spot a broken cord or other sign of problem by looking closely as you open and close the window. If you determine that the jamb liner mechanism is broken, you can fix it by replacing both jamb liners.

The first step is to find a source for the new jamb liners. The original manufacturer is the best source of replacement parts. If you don't know what brand your window is and can't find a label, search online for a window repair parts specialist that can help you. Companies like Blaine Window Hardware at blainewindow.com can identify the jamb liner and send you new ones. But you may have to remove the jamb liner first and send in a sliver of it. Another option is to scan or photocopy the end profile of the jamb liner and e-mail the image to the parts supplier. Temporarily reinstall the old jamb liner and sash to secure the house while you're waiting for the new parts to arrive.

The photos show how to remove a common type of jamb liner on a Marvin window. Photo 3 shows where to find the information you'll need to order a new Marvin jamb liner. Start by tilting out the sash (Photo 1). Then remove the jamb liner (Photo 2). If you're handy and want to save money, you can repair the jamb liner instead of replacing it. To see how, go to familyhandyman.com and search for "window repair."

JAMB LINER

SASH

1 **REMOVE THE SASH**
Push in on the jamb liner while you pull out on the top corner of the sash. Release the opposite side using the same technique. Then pivot the sash downward and tilt it sideways to remove it.

WINDOW STOP

JAMB LINER

BROKEN
CORD

2 **PRY OUT THE JAMB LINER**
Starting at the bottom, wedge a stiff putty knife into the crack between the jamb liner and the window stop. Pry the jamb liner flange out from under the stop. Then slide the putty knife upward to release the jamb liner.

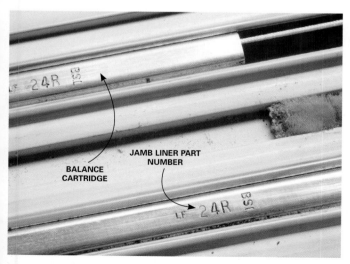

BALANCE
CARTRIDGE

JAMB LINER PART
NUMBER

3 Find the information you'll need to order new jamb liners stamped on the metal balance cartridges.

Living in a goldfish bowl

While painting our house, I removed the aluminum storm windows to get at the main window and frame. My goof came in reinstalling the storms. I caulked completely around the storm windows, including the little drain slots at the bottom. The first time it rained, water was blown in through an opening near the top of the storm windows—and the space between the main window and the storm window filled with water. Glug, glug.

—Al Diemer

Replace door-bottom weather strip

O lder wood doors usually rely on a non-adjustable threshold to keep the weather out. If your old door doesn't seal tight against the threshold, you're wasting energy. You could screw a surface-applied weather strip to the face of the door, but a door-bottom weather strip is a less obtrusive way to create a good seal.

The door bottom we're using is available at most home centers and hardware stores. If you can't find a door bottom that's smooth on one side, you can slice off the barbed flanges from bottoms designed for steel or fiberglass doors.

Cut the bottom of the door to allow enough (but not too much) clearance to install the new door bottom. The goal is to create an even 3/8-in. space between the top of the existing threshold and the bottom of the door. Close the door and measure the largest gap between the door and the threshold. If the gap is less than 3/8 in., calculate how much you'll have to cut off the bottom to equal 3/8 in. Mark this distance on the door at the point you measured. Then use a scribing tool to extend a mark across the bottom of the door (Photo 1).

Remove the hinge pins and move the door to a set of sawhorses. Mount a sharp blade in your circular saw and cut along the line. Protect the surface of the door with masking tape. If you have a veneered door, score along the line with a sharp utility knife before sawing it to avoid chipping the veneer.

Cut the door-bottom weather strip about 1/8 in. shorter than the width of the door and tack it to the bottom of the door with a staple gun. Rehang the door to test the fit. If it's too snug, remove the weather strip and trim a bit more from the door. When the fit is perfect, remove the staples and mount the weather strip (Photo 2).

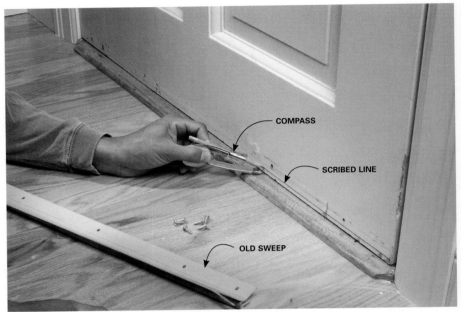

1 Scribe a line on the door 3/8 in. above the top of the threshold. Remove the door and carefully cut along the line with a circular saw.

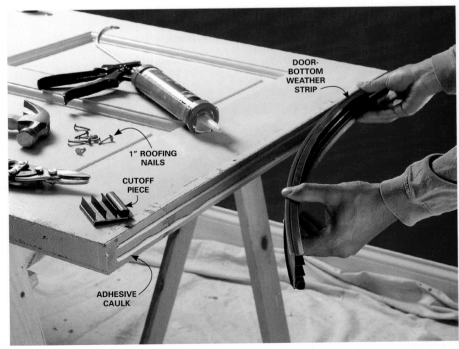

2 Cut the door bottom to length with tin snips or a utility knife. Apply two parallel beads of adhesive caulk the length of the door and nail the door bottom to the door.

Remove a heavy door

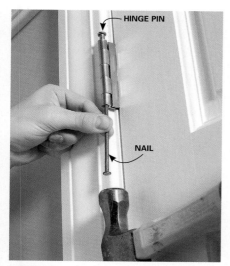

1 Close the door and tap the hinge pins loose with a hammer and nail.

HINGE PIN

NAIL

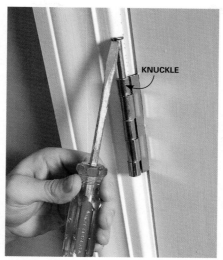

2 Tap the pin up until it's loose enough to pull out.

KNUCKLE

3 Open the door partway and pull it to the side so it drops off the hinges.

Laying new carpet, stripping or painting a door, sanding down a rubbing edge—there are any number of reasons to take a door off its hinges. And although it looks simple enough, it can turn into a finger-pinching hassle, especially when you're dealing with a heavy, solid-wood door.

To make this job go smoothly, first close and latch the door. Then remove the hinge pins by tapping on the bottom of the hinge pin with a nail (Photo 1). Don't try to drive the pins all the way out with the nail—you might damage the trim with the hammer. After they pop up an inch or so, try pulling them free with your fingers. If they're stubborn, just drive up on the underside of the knuckle with a flat-blade screwdriver (Photo 2).

Slide a piece of cardboard under the door to protect the floor, then ease the door off the hinges by lifting slightly at the knob with one hand and under one of the hinges with the other hand (Photo 3). If the weight of the door makes it difficult to separate the hinges, wedge a pry bar under the door to take the weight off the hinges.

To put the door back on the hinges, grab the door at the center and tip it slightly toward the top, engaging the knuckles of the top hinge. With the weight of the door hanging on the top hinge, work the other hinges together. Push a hinge pin into whichever hinge lines up first, then tap in the remaining pins. If one of the hinges seems slightly low and the other hinges won't fit together, place a pry bar under the center of the door and—with the lowest set of hinge leaves engaged—lever the door up until the other hinge leaves fit together (Photo 4). Close the door most of the way and hold it firmly for this step—the pry bar may try to push the door in or out as well as up.

4 Replace the door on the hinges, using a pry bar if necessary to get the hinge leaves to fit together.

WOOD FULCRUM

PRY BAR

Fix a sticking sliding door

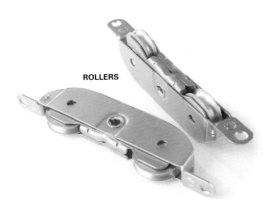

ROLLERS

Years of dirt, exposure to the elements and hard use can turn sliding doors into sticking doors, but the problem is usually easy to fix.

Start with a good cleaning. Scrub caked dirt and grime out of the track with a stiff brush and soapy water. If the door still doesn't slide smoothly, the rollers under the door either need adjusting or are shot.

Locate the two adjusting screws at the bottom of the door (on the face or edge of the door) and pry off the trim caps that cover the screws. If one side looks lower, raise it until the door looks even on the track (Photo 1). If the door still sticks, turn both screws a quarter turn to raise the whole door. Then slide the door just short of the jamb and be sure the gap is even.

If the door still doesn't glide smoothly, you'll have to remove the door and examine the rollers. Get help for this—the door is heavy! Unscrew the stop

1 Lift or lower the door on the track with a screwdriver or Allen wrench. Raise it just enough to clear the track and roll smoothly.

HIDDEN ADJUSTING SCREW

TRIM CAP

STOP MOLDING

2 Remove the screws that hold the stop molding. Cut the paint or varnish line on the room side of the stop molding so the molding will pull off cleanly.

3 Grip the door by the edges and tip it about a foot into the room. Lift it up and out of the track one edge at a time.

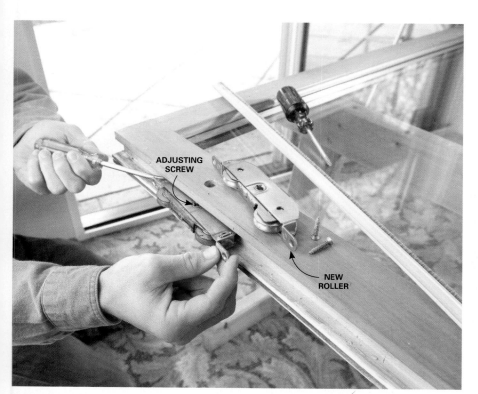

ADJUSTING SCREW

NEW ROLLER

4 Unscrew and pry out the screws that hold the roller in, then carefully lever it out with a screwdriver. Clean or replace the rollers.

molding on the inside of the jamb (Photo 2). Be sure to hold the door in place once the stop is removed—if you forget and walk away for a moment, the door will fall in, requiring a much bigger repair! Tilt the door back (Photo 3) and set it on sawhorses. Inspect the rollers for problems. If they're full of dirt and debris, give them a good cleaning and a few drops of lubricant and see if they spin freely. However, if the rollers are worn, cracked or bent, remove them (Photo 4) and replace them with a new pair.

You can order rollers and other door parts through lumberyards and home centers or online (alcosupply.com or blainewindow.com). Look for the door manufacturer's name on the edge of the door or the hardware manufacturer's name on the roller.

Fix a door latch that won't catch

When a door latch won't catch, it's because the latch doesn't align with the hole in the strike plate. Sometimes you can clearly see the misalignment. If not, do the "lipstick test" (Photo 1).

Tighten the hinges first. If you find that the latch contacts the strike plate too high or too low, make sure all the door's hinge screws are tight. If that doesn't solve the problem, try this trick: Remove one of the screws on the jamb side of the hinge and drive in a 3-in. screw. The long screw will grab the wall framing and draw in the whole doorjamb slightly. To raise the latch, do this at the top hinge. To lower the latch, do it at the bottom hinge.

Enlarge the strike plate hole. If long screws don't solve the too-high or too-low problem, measure the misalignment of the lipstick marks on the strike plate. If the latch misses the strike plate hole by 1/8 in. or less, remove the strike plate and enlarge its hole with a file (Photo 2). A half-round file matches the curve of the latch hole.

Move the strike plate. If the latch contacts the strike plate at the correct level but doesn't go in far enough, or if the latch strikes more than 1/8 in. too high or too low, you'll have to reposition the strike plate. You can move it up or down and in or out. Use a sharp chisel to enlarge the strike plate mortise (Photo 3). Then hold the strike plate in place and drill new 1/16-in. holes for the screws. Install the strike plate and fill the gap in the mortise with wood filler. Remove the strike plate to paint or finish the patch.

STRIKE PLATE

LATCH

1 Smear lipstick on the latch and stick masking tape to the strike plate. Close the door to determine where the latch contacts the plate.

2 Remove the strike plate, place it in a vise and enlarge the hole with a file. You may also have to enlarge the hole in the jamb.

LATCH HOLE

MORTISE

3 Mark the new position of the strike plate and enlarge the mortise with a chisel. You may also have to enlarge the latch hole in the jamb.

Kid-proof storm door closer

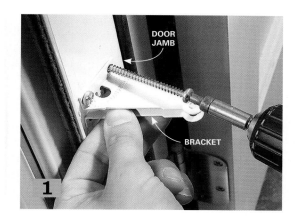

A gust of wind (or a high-velocity kid on his way outside) can swing a storm door open so hard that it tears the closer's bracket out of the jamb. If the closer is unharmed, you can refasten it. If the closer has a bent arm or other damage, take it to a home center or hardware store and find a similar replacement. Either way, toss aside the short bracket screws provided by the manufacturer and buy No. 10 x 3-in. pan head screws. Long screws pass through the doorjamb and bite into the 2x4 framing inside the wall, so they won't pull out as easily. Drill pilot holes as deep as you can with a 3/16-in. bit and drive in the screws (Photo 1). Don't drive the screws too tight; they can pull the doorjamb toward the framing and alter the fit of your entry door. While you're at it, make sure the screws that fasten the door bracket are tight. If they're stripped, drive in larger-diameter screws of the same length (Photo 2).

Renew single-pane windows

On older single-pane windows, the glass is usually surrounded by putty called "glazing compound," which holds the glass in place and seals out the weather. This putty often lasts decades, but over the years it becomes rock-hard, cracks and even falls off the window. Loose or missing compound lets wind and rain leak in around the glass.

Replacing the putty around one pane of glass will take 15 minutes to an hour, depending on the size of the pane and the stubbornness of the old putty. Replace broken glass while you're at it. This adds only a few minutes and a few dollars to the job.

It's possible to replace glass and putty with the window in place, but you'll save time and get better results if you can remove the window and clamp it down on a flat surface. If you have broken glass, get it out of the way before you remove the old putty. Put on heavy gloves and eye protection, place a cloth over the broken pane and tap it with a hammer. With the glass thoroughly broken up, pull the shards out of the frame by hand. Pull out the old glazing points with pliers. If the old glass is in good shape, leave it in place.

The next step is to get rid of the old putty. If the putty is badly cracked, you can pry away large chunks quickly (Photo 1). Putty in good condition takes longer to remove. With a heat gun in one hand and a stiff putty knife in the other, heat the putty to soften it and gouge it out. Wear leather gloves to protect your hands from burns. Keep the heat gun moving to avoid concentrating heat in one spot. Otherwise the heat will crack the glass. If your heat gun doesn't have a heat shield attachment, protect the glass with a scrap of sheet metal. When the putty is removed, prime any bare wood inside the window frame. A shellac-based primer such as BIN is a good choice because it dries in minutes.

If you need new glass, measure the opening, subtract 1/8 in. from your measurements and have the new glass cut to size at a full-service hardware store. Take a shard of the old glass with you to match the thickness. Also buy a package of glazing points to hold the glass in place while the new compound hardens. Glazing compound is available in oil-based and latex/acrylic versions. The latex products, which usually come in a tube, have a

GLAZING POINT

CAULK

NEW GLASS

LOOSE PUTTY

HEAT GUN

HEAT SHIELD

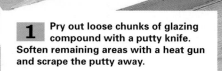

1 Pry out loose chunks of glazing compound with a putty knife. Soften remaining areas with a heat gun and scrape the putty away.

2 Set new glass onto a bead of latex caulk. Press glazing points into the wood every 8 in. Let the excess caulk that oozes out under the glass harden and slice it off with a utility knife later.

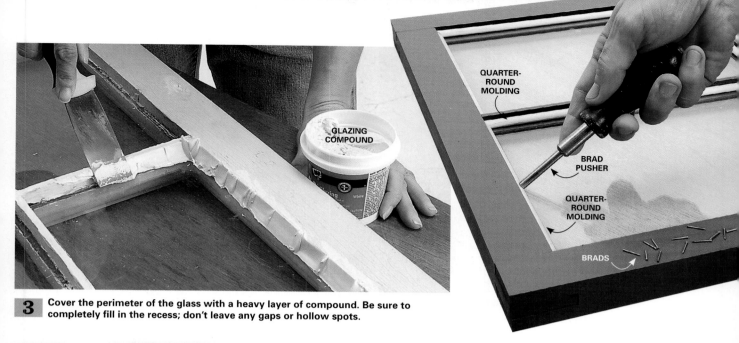

QUARTER-ROUND MOLDING

BRAD PUSHER

QUARTER-ROUND MOLDING

BRADS

GLAZING COMPOUND

3 Cover the perimeter of the glass with a heavy layer of compound. Be sure to completely fill in the recess; don't leave any gaps or hollow spots.

4 Dip a putty knife in mineral spirits to lubricate it and smooth out the compound. Wet the knife again and run over the compound as many times as it takes to create a smooth surface.

5 Drag the ridge of excess compound away from the finished joint and scrape it up. Be careful not to touch the smoothed surface.

An alternative to putty: mitered moldings

Applying a smooth, perfect bead of glazing compound is fussy, time-consuming work. So when good looks matter, consider wood moldings rather than putty to hold glass in place (1/4-in. quarter-round works for most windows). Set the glass in place over a light bead of latex caulk (see Photo 2). There's no need for glazing points. To nail the moldings in place, you can carefully drive in tiny brads with a hammer or carefully shoot in brads with a pneumatic brad nailer. But the safest method is to use a brad pusher. A brad pusher is simply a metal tube with a sliding piston inside. Drop a brad in the tube, push hard on the handle, and the piston pushes the brad neatly into wood—with little danger of breaking the glass. Most hardware stores and home centers don't carry brad pushers, but you can order one online.

longer life expectancy and you don't have to wait days before painting them as you do with oil-based putty. But they often begin to dry before you can tool them smooth. If neat, smooth results are important, choose an oil-based putty (such as DAP 33).

For installation of new glass, the directions on glazing compound may tell you to lay a light bead of compound inside the frame and then set the glass over it. That works well with soft latex compound. But if you're using stiffer oil-based compound, lay in a light bead of acrylic latex caulk instead. Set the glass onto the caulk, then wiggle and press down to firmly embed the glass. Then apply new putty as shown in Photo 3.

To complete the job, smooth out the new glazing compound (Photos 4 and 5). Oil-based putty is easier to work with when it's warm. To heat it, set the can in a bowl of hot water for a few minutes. Remember that oil-based putty remains soft for days, so be careful not to touch it after smoothing. You'll have to wait several days before you can prime and paint oil-based putty; check the label.

Free a sticking storm door

If your storm door won't close without a firm tug—or it won't close at all—it's probably rubbing against the frame, wearing off the paint and grating on your nerves. Most storm doors are mounted on a metal frame that's screwed to wood molding surrounding the door. When the metal frame on the hinge side of the door comes loose, or the molding itself loosens, the door sags and scrapes against the other side of the frame, usually near the top.

Before you grab your tools, partly open the door from the outside and push the door up and down. Watch the hinge side of the door frame. If the molding moves, secure it with extra nails (Photo 1). Start by adding a couple of nails near the top of the wood trim. Then add nails farther down if necessary. Sink the nailheads slightly with a nail set, cover the heads with acrylic caulk and touch up the molding with paint.

More often than not, it's the metal frame that comes loose, not the wood trim. To fix the metal frame, buy a few No. 8 x 1-in. pan head screws. Stainless steel screws are best. Stick a shim between the door and the frame (as in Photo 1), tighten the existing screws and drill new screw holes through the frame. Press lightly as you drill the metal; you don't want to drill into the wood molding with the 3/16-in. bit. Then drill a 3/32-in. pilot hole into the wood and add screws (Photo 2). In most cases, two or three screws added near the top of the frame will do the job.

1 Position the door by wedging a shim between the door and the frame. Predrill and drive 10d galvanized finish nails to firmly fasten the molding.

SHIM KNOB SIDE

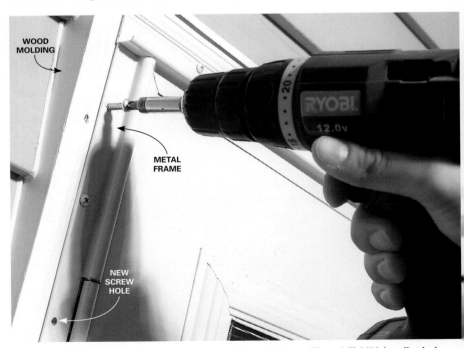

WOOD MOLDING

METAL FRAME

NEW SCREW HOLE

2 Drill new 3/16-in. screw holes through the metal frame. Then drill 3/32-in. pilot holes into the wood and drive in No. 8 x 1-in. screws. For a neater look, spray-paint the screw heads first.

Fix a sagging self-closing door

We get a lot of questions about how to fix a door that closes by itself. We'll show you a couple of fixes that carpenters have been using for years that just might do the trick. These tips work only if a door slowly "creeps" closed. If it swings freely, the door or wall is out of plumb and will require trickier fixes, which we won't cover here.

Check the gap at the top of the door. If it's wider at the doorknob side, remove the center screw at the top hinge and replace it with a 3-in. screw (Photo 1). The screw will pull the jamb and door tighter to the framing and hopefully fix the problem.

If the door still creeps closed (but less so), go to the thin cardboard shimming technique (Photo 2). Put one shim behind the middle hinge and two shims behind the bottom hinge.

1 DRAW IN THE TOP HINGE
Draw the doorjamb toward the framing with a 3-in. screw. An impact driver works best, but if you don't have one, predrill first with a 1/8-in. drill bit.

2 SHIM THE HINGES
Slip one shim behind the center hinge and replace the screws. Then place two shims behind the bottom hinge.

Adjust a storm door for a perfect close

If your storm door slams shut or won't close hard enough to latch, try a few simple adjustments to make it close just right.

First, change the mounting position of the closer's connecting pin (Photo 1). To remove the pin, you have to first lock the door open with the hold-open washer to release the tension on the pin. But there's a good chance that your hold-open washer won't work. In that case, open the door and snap locking pliers (such as Vise-Grip pliers) onto the closer shaft to hold the door open. To repair the washer, slip it off the shaft, put it in a vise and make a sharper bend in it using a hammer. Or you can take the entire closer to a home center or hardware store and find a similar replacement. Some closers mount a little differently from the one we show. For example, you may find that the door bracket, rather than the closer, has two pinholes.

If moving the pin makes matters worse, return it to its original position and try the adjustment screw (Photo 2). Turn it clockwise for a softer close, counterclockwise for harder. If your door has two closers, treat them exactly alike. Adjust both screws equally and make sure their pins are in the same position.

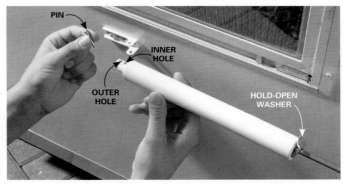

1 Lock the door open and remove the pin. Connect the closer at the inner hole to make the door close harder. For a softer close, use the outer hole.

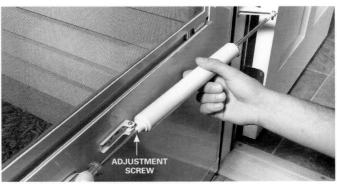

2 Turn the adjustment screw to make the door close harder or softer. Make a quarter turn, test the door and continue making quarter turns until the door closes just right.

Bifold door fix

Slam a bifold door too many times and you can split the wood where the top and bottom anchor and pivot pins sit. Then the door either sags or falls out of the track. You can try gluing and clamping the wood, but the wood can split again in a different spot. Or you can fix the problem permanently by installing corner braces. Buy a corner brace kit at a home center. Take the old anchor/pivot pins to the store to match up to new ones.

Start by marking the anchor pin hole location on the new brace (Photo 1). Then finish the corner brace installation (Photo 2) and install the door.

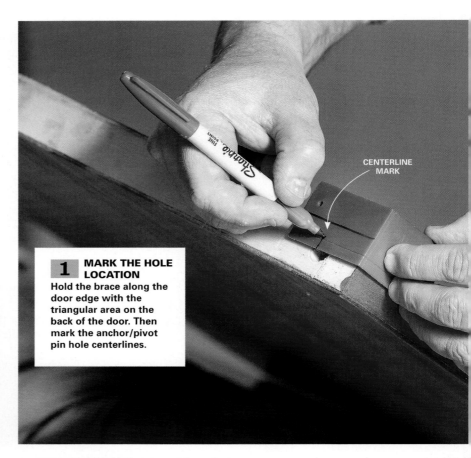

1 MARK THE HOLE LOCATION
Hold the brace along the door edge with the triangular area on the back of the door. Then mark the anchor/pivot pin hole centerlines.

CENTERLINE MARK

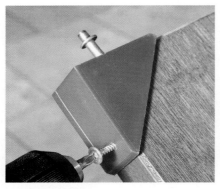

2 SECURE THE BRACE
Slide the brace onto the corner and secure it at the top with one screw. Drill a hole for the anchor/pivot pin. Tap in the new anchor/pivot pin and secure the jamb side of the brace with one additional screw.

BIFOLD DOOR REBUILDING KIT
A kit like includes everything you need to fix the hanging hardware for a closet door that has blown-out corners. Since the brackets are on the back side, they're barely noticeable.

Bifold doorknob fix

You're supposed to mount hollow-core bifold doorknobs along the edge closest to the hinge because that area is reinforced with solid wood. But that's also a "pinch zone," so many people mount the knobs in the middle of the hollow section. Eventually the screw head pulls through the thin veneer and the knob dangles out the front side. The fix is easy. Just buy a 3/16-in. x 1-in. fender washer (15¢) at any hardware store. Remove the screw. Slide the washer down to the screw head and reinstall.

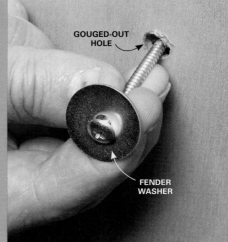

GOUGED-OUT HOLE

FENDER WASHER

One common problem with bifold doors is the hardware—it wears out. This is simple and inexpensive to fix. You can buy new pivots and rollers, and installing the new hardware is straightforward enough. Sometimes the particleboard that the hardware fits into gets stripped out from years of use. If this is the case, simply fill the hole with a quick-set, two-part epoxy before installing the new hardware. Let the epoxy set up for a minute or two. If you try to apply it when it's too runny, the epoxy will run right down through the hole or make a big mess on the floor.

Here's one important caveat: When you push the new hardware into the hole, the epoxy may gum up the works, preventing the new roller or pivot from compressing, which is necessary to reinstall the door. Wrap the bottom side of the new hardware with masking tape to prevent this.

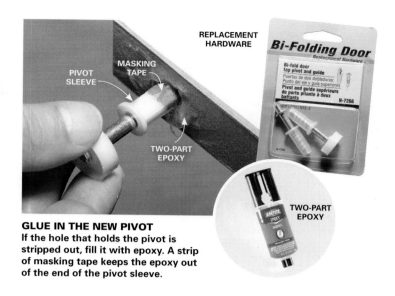

GLUE IN THE NEW PIVOT
If the hole that holds the pivot is stripped out, fill it with epoxy. A strip of masking tape keeps the epoxy out of the end of the pivot sleeve.

Turn four screws to seal a drafty door

ADJUSTABLE THRESHOLD

Those big screwheads in the threshold of a newer entry door aren't just decorative; they raise or lower a narrow strip set in the threshold. So if you've noticed a draft under the door, try this: On a sunny day, turn off the lights and close nearby curtains. Lie down and look for daylight under the door. A sliver of light sneaking in at both corners of the door is normal. But if you see light between the threshold and the door, grab your screwdriver. Raise the threshold where light enters by turning the nearest screws counterclockwise. Set a straightedge (such as a framing square) on the threshold and adjust the other screws to make sure the adjustable strip is straight. Close the door and check for light. Readjust the threshold until you've eliminated the light. But don't raise the threshold so high that it presses too hard against the weatherstripping on the door. A too-tight fit will wear out the weatherstripping quickly.

Chapter 5

EXTERIOR MAINTENANCE & REPAIR

How to seal a driveway

An asphalt driveway can last almost 30 years. But you can't achieve that long life span unless the driveway was installed properly and you perform regular maintenance, like filling cracks annually and applying sealer when needed. Here, we'll show you how to clean and prepare the driveway so you get the longest life and best protection from driveway sealer.

Preparation can take a full day (including drying time), and it's tedious. The application phase is much faster, taking only a few hours per coat for a typical driveway. Most sealer manufacturers recommend two coats with a minimum drying time of eight hours between coats, so this project will fill an entire weekend.

The materials cost about $100, but you'll save a few hundred bucks in labor over a professional job. A power washer speeds the cleaning process, but you can do the job without it. In addition to a squeegee or application brush, you'll need a broom, drill, mixing paddle, duct tape, dashing brush and poly sheeting to protect painted surfaces.

Buying the right materials

Driveway sealer is available in various grades and price ranges, from as little as $15 per 5-gallon pail to about $35 per pail for a premium product. Some bargain products contain almost 50 percent water and have lower coverage rates and a correspondingly shorter guarantee, so they're not the most cost-effective solution over the long term. Use one of them if you're trying to spiff up the driveway before selling your home. Premium products, on the other hand, are made with higher-quality resins and UV stabilizers and contain filler and elastomeric material, so they last longer and carry a longer guarantee.

Avoid these common driveway-sealing mistakes

▶ **Depending on the sealer to fill cracks.** It won't. Fill them properly before applying sealer.

▶ **Failure to clean and prep the driveway before applying the sealer.** If you don't want to spend time cleaning the driveway, you may as well skip the sealer too, because it won't stick to a dirty driveway.

▶ **Failure to stir properly.** Don't depend on a stir stick. It simply won't blend the water and solids enough to get a consistent mixture.

▶ **Use of the wrong applicator.** Using a brush when the manufacturer specifies a squeegee (or vice versa) will cause premature sealer failure.

▶ **Applying sealer too often.** Too much sealer will flake off. Wait until you begin to see asphalt aggregate before you apply a new coat of sealer.

Manufacturers also make different formulas for different driveway conditions: one formula for newer driveways in good condition and another formula for older driveways that haven't been well maintained. The two formulas also vary in their coverage, so read the labels carefully and choose the correct sealer and quantity for your particular driveway. Follow the manufacturer's directions for the type of applicator to use (brush or squeegee). Using the wrong one can cause premature failure.

You'll also need liquid driveway cleaner/degreaser to remove oil and tree sap. If your driveway has visible oil stains, pick up a bottle of oil spot primer.

Check the weather before you start

You'll need at least two days of dry weather to seal your driveway. Temperatures must be above 50 degrees F during application and throughout the night. And, it's best to avoid scorching-hot sunny days (the sealer may dry too fast). If you ignore the weather forecast, you may see $100 worth of sealer wash away in a heavy rain.

Start with cleaning and priming

Even if you think your driveway is clean, trust us, it isn't. Exhaust gas contains combustion byproducts that deposit a light, sometimes oily film on your driveway. That film, along with dirt and tree sap, must come off if you want the sealer to stick. So clean the driveway first (Photo 1).

Next, rinse the driveway with clear water (Photo 2). Let the driveway dry completely. Then perform a final sweep with a push broom. Treat any oil stains with an oil spot primer (Photo 3).

Mask, stir, and trim

Driveway sealer will splash onto your garage door and sidewalks as you pour it. And it'll get all over your shoes and clothes. It's very difficult (often impossible) to remove later,

1 **SOAP AND SCRUB**
Use the soap nozzle on your power washer or a garden hose applicator to apply the driveway cleaner. Then scrub the entire driveway with a stiff-bristle push broom.

40-DEGREE NOZZLE SETTING

2 **RINSE WITH A STRONG STREAM**
Flush the soap and dirt residue with a 40-degree power washer nozzle or a strong stream of water from your garden hose.

3 **PRETREAT THE OIL STAINS**
Pour the oil spot primer on the damaged areas and brush it into the pores with a disposable chip brush. Apply a second coat to heavier stains. Let the primer dry fully before applying the driveway sealer.

4 **MIX THE SEALER**
Start the mixing paddle near the top of the pail and slowly lower it into the contents settled at the bottom. Cycle the mixing paddle up and down while it spins to combine the water and solids into a smooth consistency.

5 **CUT IN THE EDGES**
Dip the dashing brush into the sealer and apply a liberal coating to all four edges of the driveway. Don't spread it too thin; you want it to fill in all the pores.

Driveway sealers: Real protection or just black paint?

Some asphalt driveway companies tell their customers that driveway sealer is a waste of money, that it's cosmetic and doesn't do anything to extend the life of the asphalt.

It's true that driveway sealer can't replace the liquid asphalt (oil/tar) that oxidizes and bakes out of the mixture from heat and sun exposure. But a high-quality sealer can dramatically reduce future heat and UV damage. Plus, it seals the pores to prevent aggregate breakup damage caused by water penetration, freeze/thaw cycles and chemicals. So it really does extend the life of your driveway.

POLY SHEETING TO MASK DOOR

STAGED PAILS

6 **STAGE THE PAILS**
Guesstimate the coverage of each pail and stage each additional pail along the driveway. That saves time and reduces the need to walk through wet sealer to get the next pail.

7 **POUR ONTO THE DRIVEWAY**
Start at the top left or right edge of the driveway and pour the sealer in an upside-down U-shape pattern.

8 **SPREAD THE SEALER**
Start at one leg of the upside-down "U" and apply even pressure to spread the puddle across the driveway and down along the opposite leg. Then pick up the excess sealer on the down leg and start the next row.

so wear old work clothes and shoes. Mask the garage door with poly sheeting and apply strips of duct tape to concrete walks where it butts up to the asphalt.

Choose an area on the driveway for mixing and cover it with poly sheeting to protect against spills (dried spills will show through the sealer). Remove the pail lids and cut a small hole in the center of one lid. Use that lid to prevent splashing during mixing. Stir until the mixture is smooth (Photo 4).

Next, cut in all four edges of the driveway with a large dashing brush (Photo 5). Clean the brush with soap and water as soon as you're done cutting in the edges—you'll need it again the following day. Then stage the pails, equally-spaced, down the driveway (Photo 6).

Pour and spread

Pour the sealer onto the driveway (Photo 7). Then spread the puddle with a squeegee or broom, depending on the manufacturer's directions (Photo 8). Pour enough sealer to maintain a puddle in front of the applicator tool.

When you reach the bottom of the driveway, cap the remaining pails and clean the squeegee or brush. Set the empty pails along the curb to prevent cars from ruining the job. Then let the sealer dry overnight.

Repeat the sealer application the next day. Let the sealer dry for 48 hours before driving on it (better safe than sorry). Don't ask how we learned that lesson.

Fix driveway cracks

Buy the supplies and tools

We used melt-in 1/2-in.-diameter Latex-ite Pli-Stix Crack and Joint Filler and Latex-ite Trowel Patch for this project. Our driveway had several 25-ft.-long cracks. So we bought four 30-ft. packages of the crack filler and four 2-gallon pails of the trowel patch. We already had a propane torch. But we bought an extension hose to eliminate the flame-outs that occur when you tip a propane cylinder upside down.

Check the weather and prep the cracks

Choose a sunny day with no rain in the forecast for at least 24 hours. Start by rolling the crack filler rope onto a sunny section of the driveway so it warms and softens. While it's warming, remove all the dirt, weeds and old crack filler from the cracks. Scrape out the old material with a flat-blade screwdriver or 5-in-1 paint tool. It's a painstaking process, but it's critical to getting a successful repair. So don't skip it or take shortcuts. Cleaning and filling hairline cracks are more time consuming, and the fix won't last. unless you widen them with an angle grinder and diamond wheel (Photo 1, p. 216).

Once you finish digging out all the cracks, blow the dust and debris out of the cracks and off the driveway using a leaf blower or compressed air gun.

Add the filler and melt it

Push the melt-in filler deep into the cracks (Photo 2). If any filler bulges above the surface of the driveway, cut off the excess with a knife or compress it so it sits below the surface (Photo 3).

Then screw the extension hose onto your propane tank and mount the torch to the other end and fire it up. The melt-in

O ver time, every asphalt driveway develops cracks. They're more than just an eyesore; they actually speed up the demise of your driveway if you ignore them. And in cold climates, water seeps in and destroys the asphalt when it expands during freezing. If you plan to topcoat your driveway you'll need to fix the cracks first.

You can buy squeeze bottle and caulk tube–style crack filler products from any home center. They're quick and easy to apply, but they shrink and crack and don't last very long. However, there's another way to fill asphalt cracks: with melt-in filler

that doesn't shrink—the same type used by highway crews. The melt-in material and trowelable cover mix cost about $100 for a typical driveway.

It'll take almost a full day to repair several cracks if they're 20 ft. long or so, but the repairs will last much longer than other quick fixes. In addition to the melt-in and trowel mix products, you'll need a propane torch with an extension hose, and a leaf blower or compressed air gun. Use an angle grinder fitted with a diamond wheel to widen hairline cracks and to quickly remove previously applied crack fillers.

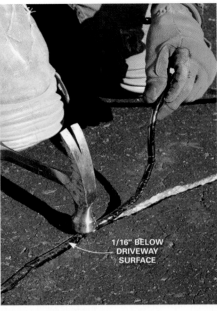

1 WIDEN HAIRLINE CRACKS
Plunge the diamond wheel into one end of the crack and drag backward to dig out any old filler and widen the crack.

2 STUFF THE CRACK WITH FILLER
Jam the filler deep into the crack using a flat-blade screwdriver. Add a second layer to fill deeper or wider cracks.

3 COMPRESS THE FILLER
Hammer the filler so it sits at least 1/16 in. below the surface of the driveway. Don't overfill.

4 MELT THE FILLER
Sweep the torch flame side to side slowly over a 12-in. section until the filler begins to melt. Then move on to the next section. Return to the previous section and heat again until the filler levels out and seeps into the crack.

5 ADD TROWEL MIX AND THEN SMOOTH IT
After the filler has cooled, scoop up the trowel patch and tap it onto the crack filler to create a small mound. Smooth it with a trowel and let dry overnight. If a depression remains the next day, apply a second coat.

filler burns easily, so don't try to melt it in one fell swoop. Using just the tip of the flame, slowly melt the filler (Photo 4). If the filler starts to burn, blow out the flames and use a faster sweeping motion or move the flame farther from the crack.

Allow the filler to cool to the touch (at least 20 minutes) before covering it with the trowel patch material. Then lay down a bead of trowel patch and smooth it (Photo 5). Let the trowel patch dry overnight. Apply a second coat if you see a depression where the crack was filled.

Patch pitted asphalt

Asphalt driveways can develop pitted areas from motor oil and coolant contamination and repeated freeze/thaw cycles. If the pits are 1/2 in. or less, you can fill them with a spreadable filler product. (Latex-ite Trowel Patch is one choice available at home centers.)

Clean oil stains and prime with oil stain primer. Then coat the entire pitted area with patch material and let dry overnight (Photo 1). Apply a second coat to top off any partially filled pits (Photo 2) and smooth the surface. Let dry.

1 FILL THE PITS
Force the filler material into the cracks and pits with a trowel. Then smooth the streaks with an old broom.

2 ENLARGE THE AREA AND SMOOTH
Pour more filler material onto the pitted area and spread it with a floor squeegee to smooth the surface.

Great goofs

Screwing up in the driveway

I decided the driveway was a perfect spot to lay out the pieces for the simple collapsible miter saw table I was building. This was such an easy project...my 10-year-old could have done it! All I needed was 2x4s, hinges and two different lengths of screws—1-in. screws to attach the hinges to the single 2x4 and 2-1/2-in. screws to attach two 2x4s. The assembly zipped right along, and after finishing the main section of the table, I stood back to admire my work. It looked perfect. But when I bent down to lift it off the driveway, it wouldn't budge. No matter how hard I pulled, it was stuck fast! Turns out I'd used the longer screws for the hinges, and they had bored straight down through the 2x4 and into the asphalt. I guess I should have let my 10-year-old build the rack after all.

—Gary Leger

Fix a driveway apron

I t's normal for asphalt driveways to sink a bit over time. But when your driveway has sunk to the point where it's 4 or 5 in. lower than your garage floor, it's time to fix it. If you don't, water will pool in the depression, seep into the soil below, and eventually destroy the driveway.

Having it done professionally can easily cost $1,000 or more to dig out the old portion and install a new apron. Concrete contractors charge even more. But you can rebuild your asphalt driveway apron yourself. The entire job takes a full day and it's not much fun. But the materials and tools only cost about $250, so the savings is worth it.

You'll need a diamond blade for your circular saw, a tamper, a pry bar and a short square-blade shovel. Plus, you'll need enough cold patch material to fill in the trench you make (one choice is Quikrete Asphalt Cold Patch). To figure out how many bags you'll need, refer to the depth and width tables on the bag. Finally, you'll need mineral spirits and rags for cleanup. Here's how to make the repair.

First check the weather

Cold patch cures by solvent evaporation, and it takes about 30 days to reach a full cure. So the best time to do the project is during an extended warm, dry spell. You can do it in spring or fall, but cold weather and rain will greatly extend the cure time.

Wear old clothes and protect your floors

This is a messy job, and no matter how careful you are, you're going to get tar on your clothes and shoes. You can't wash off the tar with soap and water. So wear old clothes and shoes that you can toss into the trash when you're done. If you have to go into the house during the project, leave your shoes outside so you don't track tar into the house.

Cut out the sunken area

Cold patch works only when it's compacted and "keyed" into at least two vertical surfaces. So don't think you can build up the driveway height by pouring cold patch on top of the old sunken asphalt—the patching material will just break off in chunks. Instead, you'll have to cut out the sunken asphalt (Photo 1). After it's cut, lay a block of wood on the soil at

1 CUT OUT THE SUNKEN ASPHALT
Slap a diamond blade into your circular saw and set it to its maximum cutting depth. Then snap a chalk line out from the garage floor to a maximum distance of 24 in. Wear an N95 respirator and safety glasses and cut out the old asphalt.

SUNKEN PORTION

DIAMOND BLADE

CHALK LINE

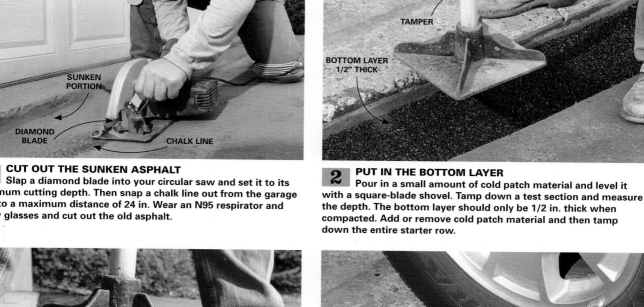

2 PUT IN THE BOTTOM LAYER
Pour in a small amount of cold patch material and level it with a square-blade shovel. Tamp down a test section and measure the depth. The bottom layer should only be 1/2 in. thick when compacted. Add or remove cold patch material and then tamp down the entire starter row.

TAMPER

BOTTOM LAYER 1/2" THICK

1/2" OVERFILL

3 BUILD ADDITIONAL LAYERS
Add and compact the cold patch in 1-in. layers until you reach the garage floor. Then overfill with an additional 1/2 in. of material and tamp to get a smooth surface.

4 DRIVE OVER IT TO COMPACT
Cut a piece of plywood slightly wider than the trench. Lay it over the patch material and cover it with 2x4s. Then drive over it several times with your vehicle until the patch is level with the garage floor.

the edge of the driveway, shove a pry bar under the old asphalt, and pry against the wood block. The old asphalt will lift up and break off in sections.

Remove all the cut asphalt and scrape off any caulking material sticking to the edge of the garage floor.

Next, build a starter row of patch material (Photo 2). Once the starter row is in place and tamped, apply additional patch material in 1-in. layers (Photo 3). Resist the temptation to completely fill the area and compact it in one fell swoop. You simply can't exert enough compaction force with a tamper to properly key it into the vertical surfaces—the patch material will just creep out the sides when you drive on it.

Once your tamped layers are level with the garage floor, add a final topping layer. Then lay down wood scraps and use your vehicle to do a final compaction (Photo 4). Clean all your tools with mineral spirits and dispose of the rags properly to prevent spontaneous combustion.

The instructions say you can drive over the patch immediately. But tires may still make slight depressions in the asphalt until it's fully cured, which takes 30 days. So leave the plywood in place for a few weeks at least.

Make your garage floor last

Sealing your concrete garage floor is the best way to prevent damage from road salt and freezing temperatures. With so many concrete sealing/ waterproofing products on the market, choosing the right product can be confusing.

To get the scoop on choosing the right sealer, we contacted Dave Barnes, president of Saver Systems Inc., a manufacturer of concrete sealing/waterproofing products. Here's what we learned about the pros and cons of each concrete sealing technology.

Four types of sealers

Film-forming acrylic, epoxy and polyurethane products seal the concrete pores and impart a sheen or "wet-look" gloss to the entire garage floor for a really sharp look. These coatings are easy to clean, but they require more rigorous surface preparation. They're also slippery, especially when wet.

Silane/siloxane formulas penetrate the concrete and react with minerals to form a "hydrophobic" surface that repels water, road salt and other deicing chemicals. The product won't darken the concrete or look shiny, so your garage floor will still look like dull concrete.

We chose silane/siloxane

This garage is in Minnesota, so preventing damage from freezing water and road salt was critical. We didn't care about gloss, but we wanted to avoid two steps that are required for many film-forming sealers: acid etching and roughening the surface. We chose MasonrySaver All-Purpose Heavy Duty Water Repellent, a water-based silane/siloxane. It took 5 gallons to seal the floor of this three-car garage.

It's all about surface prep

Always start by cleaning the floor with a concrete cleaner and power washer (Photo 1). If you have oil stains, treat them before you power wash (search "oil stain removal" at familyhandyman.com). Then apply the sealer with a paint pad to get an even application and avoid puddles (Photo 2). After it dries, fill floor cracks with a polyurethane crack filler (Photo 3).

Caution

To avoid electrical shock or carbon monoxide poisoning, always locate your power washer in an open area outside the garage.

POWER WASHER

1 APPLY CLEANER, SCRUB AND POWER WASH
Mask the walls with poly. Then use the power washer to apply concrete cleaner. Scrub with a push broom. Then rinse with high pressure and a 40-degree nozzle. Squeegee and let dry.

PAINT PAD

2 APPLY AND SPREAD
Dip the paint pad into the sealer and spread it evenly across the floor to avoid puddling. Let the product soak in and dry.

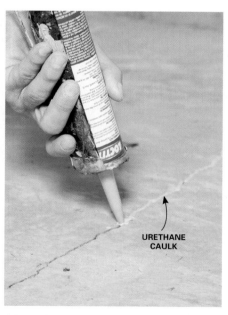

URETHANE CAULK

3 FORCE FILLER INTO THE CRACKS
Cut a small opening in the tube tip. Then hold the caulk gun perpendicular to the floor, pressing the tip into the crack. Squeeze the trigger and force the crack filler deep into the crack.

Resurface a pitted garage floor

A spalled (pitted) garage floor looks horrible. And patches will just pop out eventually. But you can resurface the concrete yourself, usually in less than a day, and for less than $300. You'll need a pressure washer, concrete cleaner (such as Quikrete Concrete & Stucco Wash), a push broom and a floor squeegee. Buy enough concrete resurfacer material (such as Quikrete Concrete Resurfacer) to coat the entire floor. Refer to the coverage specs on the bag to determine how many bags you need.

The resurfacing material won't bond to loose concrete, paint, grease, algae or mildew. So pressure-wash the entire floor with concrete cleaner and a clean-water rinse. Next, prefill any cracks and pits that are more than 1/4 in. deep (Photos 1 and 2).

Saturate the concrete with water and then use a broom to push out any puddles from the pitted areas or low spots. Follow the mixing directions on the resurfacer bag. Then pour out a puddle and spread it (Photo 3). If the pits still show, let the material set up and apply a second coat later in the day. But you can stop with one coat if it provides good coverage. To apply a nonslip texture, lightly drag a clean push broom in one direction across the still-wet material (allow no more than five minutes of setting time before applying the broom finish).

Let the new floor dry for at least 24 hours before you drive on it. Follow the manufacturer's directions for additional hot-weather misting procedures or extra drying time for cool weather.

1 **FIND THE DEEPEST PITS**
Make a mark 1/4 in. from the tip of a pencil. Use it as a depth gauge to locate pits that need filling.

—TAPE

2 **FILL CRACKS AND JOINTS**
Apply tape to each side of the crack or joint and fill with crack sealer. Then level the sealer with a trowel and remove the tape.

POWER MIXER

3 **APPLY RESURFACER**
Spread from the middle of the puddle and apply moderate squeegee pressure to force the resurfacer into the pores and pits. Then drag the squeegee backward to eliminate the edge ridges. Continue spreading until you get even coverage.

Tips for maintaining your chimney

Most homeowners never think about masonry chimney maintenance beyond the occasional flue cleaning (which we'll show you how to do in an upcoming issue). But ignoring your chimney can cost you big-time. A cracked chimney crown or spalling bricks can easily cost $1,000 to repair. And, if left untreated, the damage can accelerate quickly, and cost you upward of $3,000.

It doesn't have to be that way. By simply sealing the bricks and the crown and adding a chimney cap, you'll greatly extend your chimney's life. The materials cost less than $300, and you can complete all three procedures in just a few hours. You'd pay a pro about $1,000 to do all three, so the savings is huge.

You'll have to climb up on your roof twice (once to measure the flue liner to order the correct chimney cap and once to perform the procedures). And, you must be able to safely reach the chimney crown from your roof. If you can't reach the chimney crown, have a very steep roof pitch or aren't comfortable working on your roof, call a pro. If you decide you can handle the heights, make sure you wear a safety harness.

Start at the chimney crown

Masonry chimneys are capped with a mortar "crown" to prevent water from getting behind the bricks and alongside the flue, and into the house. Over time, normal expansion and contraction cycles can cause cracks to form, as shown at left. Sealing the chimney crown with crown sealer, a flexible elastomeric coating, is the best way to stop existing cracks from spreading and prevent new ones.

Choose a clear or overcast day for the project (no rain in the forecast for at least four hours). Prepare the crown by cleaning it with a stiff poly or nylon brush. Fill any

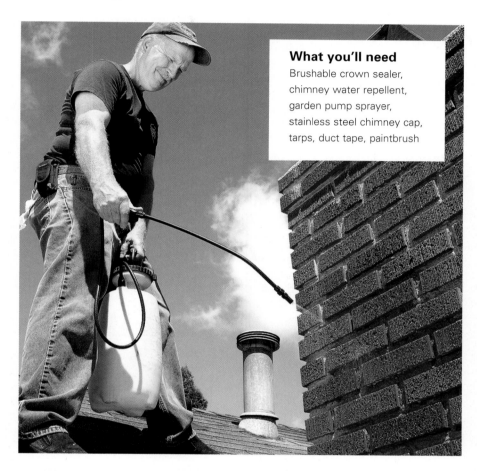

What you'll need

Brushable crown sealer, chimney water repellent, garden pump sprayer, stainless steel chimney cap, tarps, duct tape, paintbrush

SPIDER CRACKS

MISSING CHUNKS

The cracks in this chimney crown have reached a critical point. If not sealed soon, they'll destroy the crown and eventually the chimney.

large cracks with patching cement or 100 percent silicone caulk (they'll cure even after you apply the crown sealer).

Next, wrap duct tape all around the crown about 1/4 in. below the edge of the crown-to-brick seam. Press the tape into the vertical brick joints. Then tape around each flue liner 1 in. above the crown. Lay canvas (not plastic) tarps around the base of the chimney to protect the shingles from crown sealer drips.

Our chimney repair expert applies crown sealer by hand so he can force it into cracks and get the first coat done faster. If you choose that method, just slip on a disposable glove and apply the sealer (Photo 1). (One brand is Chimney RX Brushable Crown Repair.) Cover the entire crown and then smooth it with a paintbrush (Photo 2). Wait until the sealer dries tacky to the touch, then apply a second coat with a brush. Clean up with water.

Seal the bricks

Once the crown sealer feels dry to the touch (30 to 60 minutes), remove the duct tape but leave the roof tarps in place. Then mask off any painted chimney flashings before applying the water repellent. Spray on the repellent (one brand is Chimney RX Masonry Chimney Water Repellent) with a low-pressure, garden pump sprayer (Photo 3).

Finish it off with a chimney cap

A chimney cap keeps water and critters out of your flue and extends flue life. Many codes require a mesh cap, so check before buying. Chimney expert Jim Smart recommends spending extra to get a stainless steel cap because it will last much longer than the galvanized type. One source for stainless steel caps is efireplacestore.com.

You'll need the outside dimensions of the flue liner to get the right size cap for your chimney. Then install it on the flue liner (Photo 4).

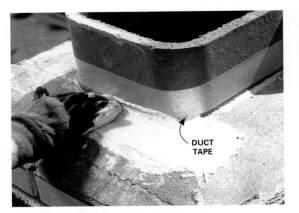

1 APPLY THE FIRST COAT BY HAND
Scoop up a handful of the sealer and wipe it onto the crown. Force the sealant into the cracks and into the crown-to-brick seam.

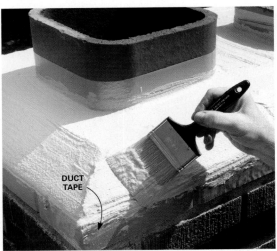

2 EVEN OUT THE FIRST COAT
Stroke the wet sealant with a brush to level the high and low spots and create a smooth surface.

3 SPRAY THE BRICK WITH WATER REPELLENT
Start at the bottom of the chimney and spray the brick until the excess repellent runs down about 8 in. below the spray line. Work your way up to the top. Apply a second coat within five minutes using the same technique.

4 INSTALL THE CAP
Set the cap over the flue liner and secure it with screws. Tighten until snug, but no more. Excessive pressure can crack the clay liner.

Restore a wood deck

If your deck is still solid, give worn deck boards a new life!

Keeping a wood deck in good shape takes a lot of work. Even if you stain or seal it, the boards can still crack and splinter, making the deck look old and worn. Switching over to composite decking is one option, though the cost may be prohibitive. But there's another, far more affordable solution. You can save your existing deck by applying a deck restoration product.

Deck restoration coatings are thick enough to fill all cracks, knotholes and splinters, and they provide a completely new textured surface that can last as long as 13 years without additional applications. You can do the prep work in one day, then apply the product over a two-day period the following weekend. You'll need a power washer (rent it if you don't own one), a jug of deck cleaner, a special roller, masking materials and a roller extension. Here's how to buy the product, prepare the surface and apply it.

1 PROTECT THE HOUSE AND RAILS

To avoid splattering the post rails, wrap them with masking tape and apply poly sheeting to the rails and siding. Spread poly sheeting under the deck to catch the product that oozes between the board gaps.

MASK UP 4'

TAPE POSTS

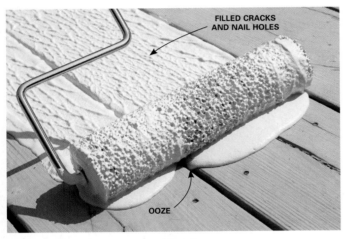

FILLED CRACKS AND NAIL HOLES

OOZE

2 ROLL ON THE DECK COATING

Dunk the entire roller in the pail, place it on the deck boards and press down to form a puddle. Then roll the puddle forward to force the product into the cracks. Then lift, reload and do the next section. Don't back-roll.

3 COAT THE ENTIRE LENGTH OF THE BOARDS

Start at one end of a few boards and apply the entire length of the boards, to maintain a uniform texture. Clean the gaps as you go with a stir stick or a 5-in-1 style paint tool.

What is a deck restoration coating?

Deck restoration coatings are made from a long-lasting tintable acrylic base material with UV inhibitors and added solids (aluminum oxide or sand). The solids provide texture and hold the product together (like aggregate in concrete). Some brands allow the wood to breathe yet repel water, while others form an impermeable barrier. The coverage ranges from 20 sq. ft. to as much as 75 sq. ft. per gallon. All brands require rigorous surface preparation. The procedures vary by manufacturer; read the product label. Apply two coats for the best performance.

Pick the brand and get it tinted

Shop for deck restoration products at home centers and paint stores. Some retail brands are Restore 10X and 4X by Rust-Oleum, Deckover by Behr, Rescue IT! by Olympic, and RockSolid Deck Restoration by Rust-Oleum. Discuss the surface preparation requirements for each brand with the sales associate—each brand is different.

Rust-Oleum's Restore 10X, the type we used, is 10 times the thickness of paint. Restore 4X, as well as the other products, are about four times the thickness of paint. The extra thickness of 10X makes it more durable and better at covering cracks, knots and surface flaws. However, that thickness also means less coverage per gallon. If your deck is in decent shape and you'd like to save money, choose a thinner-viscosity product.

Next, choose the color carefully because deck coatings absorb a lot of heat and retain it longer than plain wood. If you pick a dark color and your deck gets direct sunlight, it may be too hot to walk on with bare feet.

Some deck restoration products (such as Restore 10X) can be used only on horizontal surfaces, so you'll need a matching or complementary product designed for the deck's vertical surfaces. And, if you're buying 4 or more gallons, buy it in pails instead of individual gallons. You won't have to refill your roller tray constantly (the product goes fast!). Before you leave the store, buy the manufacturer's recommended deck wash to ensure compatibility with the deck coating. And buy enough application

4 FILL IN MISSED SPOTS

Dunk a brush into the pail and dribble it into missed spots or depressions to build them up.

TEXTURED

4" BRUSH

SMOOTH

5 **SMOOTH WITH A BRUSH**
Start at one end of the board and walk the brush down the entire length in one continuous motion. If you lift the brush, you'll leave marks.

rollers (one roller for every 4 gallons of material). Ask for extra stir sticks—you'll need them to clean the product from the gaps between boards.

Prepare the surface

Start by breaking off any large splinters. Then reset any protruding nail heads or remove them and secure the boards with deck screws instead. If you've applied a solid stain or clear sealer and then covered areas of the deck with planters or furniture, those

sun-shielded areas must be sanded. Use 80-grit sandpaper to remove the gloss and rough up the surface in those areas.

Next, dilute the deck cleaning product, apply it, and let it soak in for the recommended time. Then scrub the entire deck using a stiff scrub brush and extension handle. Pay extra attention to any greasy areas; get all the grease off. Then power wash the entire deck to remove ground-in dirt and loose stain. Aim the nozzle into the board gaps to clean them out too.

Before applying the restoration product, let the wood dry for a week and mask off all vertical surfaces (Photo 1).

Apply the first coat

Start by filling knotholes, splinters and cracks with latex caulk or the restoration product. Let it set until it's stiff. Then apply the deck coating with the special roller (Photo 2). You'll have to reload the roller every few feet to get the proper coating thickness. Don't try to make the product go further by working it back and forth—that'll thin it and load it with air bubbles. Coat several boards at a time (Photo 3). Some product will fill the gaps and some will fall through and be wasted (get over it; it's part of the cost of the job). Refill holes along the way (Photo 4). If you prefer a smooth finish, level the coating right away with a brush (Photo 5).

Clean up with soap and water and let the first coat dry for three to six hours (or until dry to the touch). You probably won't like the look of the first coat. Don't worry; it's just the primer coat. The second coat is the "magic coat" that fills in all the gaps and provides the smooth texture you saw at the store. Apply the second coat using the same method. Then let the deck dry for two full days before walking on it.

For the longest-lasting results, clean the coating in the spring and fall using the manufacturer's cleaner.

Stiffen wobbly deck railings

Deck posts and railings screwed to a single rim joist feel wobbly because the rim joist flexes whenever you lean against the railing. Adding blocking will stiffen the rim joist and make the railing feel much more solid.

First, tighten any loose bolts and screws. If the post doesn't have bolts, add them—carriage bolts work best.

Cut pressure-treated 2-by blocking (the same width as the floor joists) to fit tightly between the rim joist and the next joist. Place the blocking directly behind the post and toe-screw it into both the rim joist and the neighboring joist. Fasten additional blocking every 4 ft. along the rim joist.

WOBBLY POST

RIM JOIST

JOIST

CARRIAGE BOLT

2x BLOCKING

Toe-screw blocking to the rim of the deck with three 3-in. deck screws at both ends.

Stiffen a bouncy deck

A deck that bounces when you walk across it won't feel strong and solid, even if it meets structural requirements. The cause is usually long joist spans between beams or between a beam and the house.

To stiffen a deck, you have to be able to get to the framing underneath. You can add another beam, along with posts, to support the joists. However, this is a big job. We recommend that you first add rows of solid blocking every 3 to 4 ft. along the span (Photo 1). Run the first row down the middle of the span, check the deck for bounce, then add rows to further reduce it.

Use treated lumber blocking that's the same size as the joists (usually 2x8 or 2x10). Install the blocking in rows along a chalk line snapped at a right angle to the joists. You'll have to measure and cut each block separately to get a snug fit, since the joists are never exactly the same distance apart. Staggering the blocking in a step pattern (Photo 2) allows you to easily drive nails from both sides, rather than having to toenail.

1 Snap lines for blocks every 3 to 4 ft. along the joist span. Measure and cut the blocks to fit tightly. Tap them into place in a staggered pattern.

2 Square each block to the joist and drive three 16d galvanized box nails through the joists into each end of the block. Repeat for each row.

7 fixes for a safer deck

A well-built deck will last for decades. But a deck that's rotting or missing fasteners, or that moves when you walk on it, may be dangerous. Decks built by inexperienced do-it-yourselfers, not inspected when they were built, or more than 20 years old (building codes may have been different) are susceptible to serious problems. Every year, people are severely injured, even killed, when decks like these fall down. This has usually happened during parties when the deck was filled with guests. Now for the good news. Most of the fixes are quick, inexpensive and easy. Home centers and lumberyards carry the tools and materials you'll need.

We'll show you the warning signs of a dangerous deck—and how to fix the problems. If you're still not sure whether your deck is safe, have it inspected by your local building inspector.

NEW LAG SCREWS
(WITH WASHER)

LEDGER

EXISTING LAG SCREW
(WITHOUT WASHER)

Fasten the ledger to the house with lag screws. Drive them fast with a corded drill and socket. Every lag screw must have a washer.

1. No lags in the ledger

SOCKET

The ledger board holds up the end of the deck that's against the house. If the ledger isn't well fastened, the deck can simply fall off the house. A building inspector we talked with said the most common problem with DIY decks is ledger boards not properly fastened to the house. For a strong connection, a ledger needs 1/2-in. x 3-in. lag screws (or lag bolts if you have access from the inside to fasten the washers and nuts) driven every 16 in. This ledger board was fastened mostly with nails instead of lag screws (and no washers).

Starting at one end of the ledger board, drill two 1/4-in. pilot holes. Offset the holes so the top isn't aligned with the bottom hole. Then drive the lag screws (with washers) using a drill and an impact socket (you'll need a socket adapter that fits in your drill). Don't countersink the screws—that only weakens the ledger board.

2. Missing nails in joist hangers

Granted, there are a lot of nail holes in a joist hanger—but they all need to be filled. Otherwise, the hangers can pull loose from the ledger board or rim joist. Deck builders sometimes drive a couple of nails into the hangers to hold them in place, then forget to add the rest later. This deck had only a single nail in some joist hangers. In other areas, it had the wrong nails. Joist hanger nails are the only nails acceptable. These short, fat, galvanized nails are specially designed to hold the hangers in place under heavy loads and resist corrosion from treated lumber.

INSTANT FIX
Fill every nail hole in joist hangers, using joist hanger nails only. If you find other types of nails, replace them with joist hanger nails.

JOIST HANGER NAILS

CORRODED NAIL

MISSING NAILS

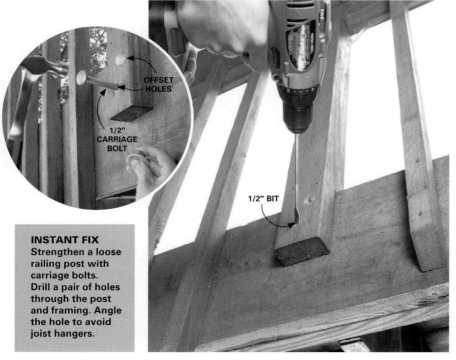

OFFSET HOLES

1/2" CARRIAGE BOLT

1/2" BIT

INSTANT FIX
Strengthen a loose railing post with carriage bolts. Drill a pair of holes through the post and framing. Angle the hole to avoid joist hangers.

3. Rickety railing posts

Loose railings won't lead to your deck falling down, but you could tumble off your deck. Railing posts attached only with nails are bound to come loose, and no matter how many new nails you drive into them, you won't solve the problem. Instead, add carriage bolts.

Measure the thickness of the post and rim joist, then buy 1/2-in.-diameter galvanized carriage bolts that length plus 1 in. Also get a nut and washer for each. Drill two 1/2-in. holes through the post and rim joist. Offset the holes, keeping one about 1-1/2 in. from the top of the joist and the other the same distance from the bottom (make sure to avoid drilling where a joist abuts the rim joist). Tap the carriage bolts through the holes, then tighten the nuts until the bolt heads are set flush with the post.

4. Rotted posts

Deck posts that rest directly on footings soak up water and then they rot, especially posts that aren't pressure treated (like this one, which is cedar). As the post rots, it loses its strength and can't support the deck's weight. Newer decks keep the concrete footings a few inches above ground and use a special base bracket to keep the posts dry. Replacing a rotted post is the best solution. Before removing the post, be sure you have everything you need for the replacement, including a wedge anchor.

Clear grass or stone away from the bottom of the deck post. Prod along the bottom of the post with a screwdriver or an awl. If the wood is spongy or pieces easily peel away, you'll need to replace the post. Start by nailing 2x4s or 2x6s together to use as temporary braces. Place scrap wood on the ground for a pad within 3 ft. of the post being replaced, then set a hydraulic jack over it. Cut the brace to size, set one end on the jack and place the other end under the rim joist. Slowly jack up the brace until it's wedged tight. Be careful not to overdo it. You're just bracing the deck, not raising it. If you hear the joist boards creak, then stop. Then place a second brace on the other side of the post (Photo 1). (If you don't have jacks, you can rent them. Or you can set your temporary braces directly on the pads and drive shims between the posts and the rim joist.

Mark the post location on the footing, then remove the post by cutting through the fasteners that tie it to the rim joist. Use a metal blade in a reciprocating saw (or knock out the post with a hammer). If there's already a bolt sticking out of the footing, use it to install a new post base. If not, you'll need to add a 3/8- by 4-in. wedge anchor. Do this by placing the post base at the marks where the old post sat, and then mark the center. Remove the post base and drill the center mark with a 3/8-in. masonry bit. Drill down 3 in., then blow the dust out of the hole. Tap the anchor into the hole with a hammer (Photo 2). Install the post base over the anchor. As you tighten the nut on the anchor, the clip expands and wedges tight against the hole walls to hold itself in place.

1 Prop up the deck with temporary braces so you can remove the rotted post. Stop jacking when you hear the deck begin to creak.

2 Tap a wedge anchor into a predrilled hole in the footing, then tighten the post base over it.

3 Set the new post into place and nail it to the base. Then plumb the post and fasten it to the rim joist or beam.

Cut a treated post to fit between the post base and the top of the rim joist. Set the post into place and tack it to the post base with 8d or 10d galvanized nails (Photo 3). Place a level alongside the post. When it's plumb (straight), tack it in place to the rim joist. Then install a connector and drive carriage bolts through the rim joist (see the next repair).

5. Wimpy post connections

Ideally, posts should sit directly under the beam or rim joist to support the deck. If the posts are fastened to the side of the beam or rim joist, like the one shown here, the weight is put on the fasteners that connect the post to the deck. This deck had only three nails in the post—a recipe for collapse. Nails alone aren't strong enough for this job, no matter how many you use. For a strong connection, you need 1/2-in.-diameter galvanized carriage bolts.

Add two of these bolts by drilling 1/2-in. holes through the rim joist and post. Use an 8-in.-long 1/2-in. drill bit. The length of the bolts depends on the size of your post and the thickness of the rim joist (add them and buy bolts at least 1 in. longer than your measurement). We used 8-in. bolts, which went through two 1-1/2-in. rim joists and a 3-1/2-in. post. Tap the bolts through with a hammer, then add a washer and nut on the other side.

INSTANT FIX
Strengthen post connections with carriage bolts. Drill holes, knock the bolts through, then tighten a washer and nut on the other side.

INSTANT FIX
Stiffen a wobbly deck with a diagonal brace run from corner to corner. Drive two nails per joist.

6. Wobbly deck syndrome

If your deck gets a case of the shakes when you walk across it, there's probably no reason for concern. Still, in some cases, the deck movement puts extra stress on the fasteners and connectors. Over time, the joists can pull away from the rim joist or ledger board and twist out of their vertical position, which weakens them. Fastening angle bracing under the deck will stiffen it and take out the sway. The braces are mostly hidden from view and let you walk on your deck without feeling like it's going to fall down at any moment.

Run a treated 2x4 diagonally from corner to corner, under the deck. Drive two 16d galvanized nails through the brace into each joist. If a single board won't span the distance, use two, overlapping the braces by at least two joists. Cut the bracing flush with the outside edge of the deck.

7. Missing ledger flashing

The area around the ledger board should be watertight. Even small leaks can lead to mold inside the walls of the house and, even worse, the house rim joist (which supports the ledger) will rot and the ledger will fall off. Stand or crawl under the deck and look at the ledger board. If you don't see a metal or plastic lip over the top of the ledger board, add the flashing. Flashing was completely missing from this deck.

To add flashing, first remove the deck board that runs alongside the house. If the boards run diagonally, snap a chalk line 5-1/2 in. from the house, then set the blade in a circular saw to the depth of the decking boards and cut off the board ends. (Replace the cutouts at the end of the job with a 5-1/2-in.-wide board installed parallel to the house.)

For vinyl, wood or other lap siding, work a flat bar under the siding and gently pull out the nails (Photo 1). Insert the flashing behind the siding (Photo 2). If you have a brick or stucco house, you probably won't see any flashing because the ledgers are often installed directly over brick or stucco.

We used vinyl flashing, but you can also use galvanized metal or aluminum flashing. At each joist location, make a small cut in the flashing lip with a utility knife so it'll lie flat over the joists. The rest of the lip should fit over the top edge of the ledger board.

You should have flashing under the bottom edge of the ledger too. But since there's no way to add it without removing the ledger board, run a bead of acrylic caulk along the bottom of the ledger board to seal out water (Photo 3).

1 Pry the siding away from the house and remove the deck board that's over the ledger to clear the way for new flashing.

2 Slide the flashing behind the siding so the lip covers the top of the ledger. Reattach the siding.

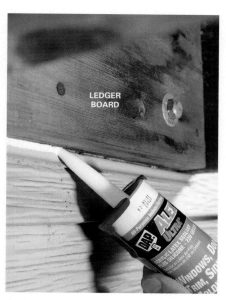

3 Seal out water along the bottom edge of the ledger, if the bottom flashing is missing, by running a bead of caulk.

Replace popped deck nails

1 Grab slightly protruding nails directly under the head with a diagonal cutter. Roll the cutter back onto thin blocking to pry the nail up slightly.

Decking swells and shrinks as it goes through repeated cycles of wet and dry seasons. This frequently causes nails to loosen and pop up above the deck boards. You can drive them down again, but chances are that's only a short-term solution. They'll probably pop up again after a few years. The long-term solution is to remove the popped nails and replace them with deck screws.

The trick is to pull the old nails without marring the decking. Always use a block or shim under your prying tool (Photos 1 and 2). And work on tough-to-get-out nails using several steps. A diagonal cutter works well for nails that only protrude slightly (Photo 1). The slim jaws can slip under the head. You'll only raise the nail a slight amount, so you may have to repeat this process two or three times. Once the nailhead is high enough, you can grip it with a cat's paw or hammer claw without marring the deck board (Photo 2). Be sure to use thin wood blocks to protect the decking. Minor dents will disappear when the wood swells after the next rain.

There's no need to drill a pilot hole if you send the screw down the old nail hole. However, one drawback of screws is that their heads are larger than nailheads and can be unsightly. We recommend that you buy deck screws in a color that most closely matches the aged decking.

2 Tap the claw of a cat's paw under the nailhead and lever the nail up. Finish pulling with a hammer or pry bar. Protect the deck board with a shim or thin block.

3 Stand on the deck board to hold it down. Then drive a 2-1/2 in. deck screw down into the old nail hole. Set the screwhead flush to the surface.

Solutions for stubborn nails

If the head breaks off a stubborn nail and you can't get it with a pry bar, try pulling it with locking pliers. Grip the nail tip and roll the pliers over to get it going (photo at left). If the nail shank breaks off, don't worry. Just drill a pilot hole beside the nail and drive in a screw. The screwhead will cover the nail (photo at right).

Great goofs

Decorator flooring

My husband and I put a smooth, flawless coat of epoxy on our garage floor. Then we lowered the overhead door, leaving it high enough that it wouldn't touch the wet floor but low enough that the cat couldn't squeeze in under it.

The next morning I peeked into the garage and my eyes grew to the size of silver dollars! We didn't keep the cat out of the garage; we kept her in—all night! (She must have been hiding on top of the rafters.)

It's a goof we're unlikely to forget; hundreds of little paw prints across the floor's mirror finish remind us every day.

—Lisa Marie Raby

Stained pride

We finished building our new deck in the late fall, but because the weather was too cold for staining, we decided to wait until spring. Under the deck was a perfect spot to store my canoe and keep it safe and snow free all winter long. That spring I was eager to stain the deck. I went to the home center, got the stain and roller, and got right at it. I let the stain cure for a couple of days, just to be sure. When I went to the back yard to get the deck furniture out of the shed, I saw my yellow canoe nestled beneath the deck—nicely camouflaged with brown stripes all over it!

—Clayton Hoelschen

Wash off ugly roof stains

1 SOAK THE SHINGLES
Saturate a large area of shingles with the cleaner. Start at the bottom row and work up to the peak. Spray until you see runoff. Respray any areas that dry out.

Choose the right chemicals

If you search online, you'll see hundreds of posts on roof-cleaning methods. In less than 10 minutes, you'll sign off convinced that all you need is a few gallons of household bleach and a power washer set at its lowest setting.

We don't recommend that approach. Even at low pressure, a power washer can seriously damage shingles. Plus, chlorine bleach is a corrosive agent that can damage metal roof flashings, gutters and downspouts. It can lighten the color of your roof and "bleach" anything the overspray contacts. And the runoff harms plants. But here's the kicker. Bleach may kill the top layer of algae and lighten the stains, but it doesn't kill the underlying algae. So the algae colony gets right back to work.

Sodium hydroxide (lye) products, on the other hand, work better than bleach and are less harmful to vegetation. But they're also corrosive, and using them requires you to don full protective gear.

So look for a roof-cleaning product that's noncorrosive and safe for the environment. We chose Defy roof cleaner, but there are other brands.

Choose the right day and prepare the area

Check the weather forecast and choose a cool or overcast day with little to no wind so the spray hits your shingles, not the neighbors'. Those conditions allow the cleaning solution to soak deep into the algae colonies without evaporating too quickly.

Next, repair any loose shingles or flashings, and clean the gutters and downspouts so they can drain freely.

Then prepare the area by moving lawn furniture and covering vegetation, because you're going to have overspray. Even though the product we chose isn't toxic, the runoff can be pretty ugly. So a little prep work will save you cleanup time later.

The cleaning process

Mix the product with water for a 1:7 dilution ratio (a gallon covers about 700 to 900 sq. ft). Pour it into a pump sprayer,

HARNESS

TIE-DOWN

SPECIALIZED RINSING TOOL

2 BLAST OFF THE CRUD
Drag the rinsing tool in a forward-and-back motion as if you're vacuuming. That places the three water jets at the correct angle to blast off the dead algae colonies.

Black streaks on the north- and west-facing and shaded areas of your asphalt-shingled roof can really wreck the appearance of your home. The streaks look like mold, but they're actually algae colonies that form in your shingles and feed on moisture and the limestone filler agents in the shingles.

Using shingles that have been treated with algicide keeps the growth at bay for about 10 years (thus the 10-year algae warranty). But once the algicide wears off, your roof hosts an all-you-can-eat buffet for the neighborhood algae spores. As the algae eat away at the limestone, they dig into the asphalt and dislodge the light-reflecting granules. That's the

beginning of the end of your roof. So it pays to clean your shingles as soon as you spot algae growth.

Professional roof cleaners charge $300 to $500, depending on the size of the roof. And they have to repeat the cleaning every few years. If your roof slope isn't too steep and you're comfortable working on it, you can clean it yourself and save money.

You'll need a full-body harness, a garden sprayer, a garden hose and a nontoxic, noncorrosive roof-cleaning chemical. Some manufacturers sell a special tool applicator and rinsing tool. But if the staining isn't severe, you may not need them (see "Tools That Make the Job Easier", p. 238). Here's how to do it.

strap yourself into a full-body harness, tie it down and climb to the roof.

Before applying the cleaner, spray the roof with water to cool it down. That'll prevent the cleaner from drying out too quickly. Then spray the cleaner onto the shingles (Photo 1, p. 236). Wait about 20 minutes, then rinse.

If the staining is fairly light, you can rinse off the cleaning solution with just a garden hose sprayer. But go slowly and use even strokes. If you don't, you'll wind up with clean patches that were rinsed properly alongside dirty patches that you skipped over too quickly. For severely stained roofs, a garden nozzle won't exert enough pressure to dislodge the stains. In that case, you'll want to invest in a specialized rinsing tool (Photo 2, p. 237; also see "Tools That Make the Job Easier").

Prevent regrowth

Depending on weather conditions, you can expect algae regrowth in as little as one year. There are two ways to slow the regrowth process. One is to install zinc or copper strips along the entire ridge. Theoretically, rainwater picks up algae-killing ions and spreads them over the roof. In reality, the protection falls short because algae can still feed off humidity when it's not raining. But you don't have a lot to lose by trying it.

The second method is to spray on a coating of stain-blocking solution (Defy

PRESSURE-BOOSTING PUMP

CLEANER APPLICATOR

Tools that make the job easier

One manufacturer (Saver Systems) has taken roof cleaning to a new level and developed a special rinsing tool to dislodge dug-in algae colonies. Their Roof Rinsing Tool is far more effective than an ordinary garden spray nozzle. If your household water pressure isn't enough to generate the proper nozzle pressure at the jets, the manufacturer recommends boosting it with a supplemental 1/2-hp pump. (One choice is the Wayne PC4 transfer pump shown above.

If you really want to speed up the cleaning process and are willing to spend more, buy the Defy Roof Cleaner Applicator. Pour in the concentrated cleaner, and the special sprayer dilutes the cleaner as you spray, eliminating the need to continually pump and refill a traditional garden sprayer.

Stain Blocker for Roofs is one product, but there are other brands as well.) A stain-blocking product can buy you up to three years of protection from algae. If you decide to try it, apply it shortly after you've cleaned the roof.

Whether you install the metallic strips or apply the stain-blocking solutions, you're still going to experience algae regrowth sometime down the road. Get back up on your roof and clean it early, so the stains don't set in permanently.

Great goofs

Going down?

While reroofing my house, I decided to add a rooftop turbine for extra ventilation. After stripping the shingles, I cut the big round hole for the turbine and then started rolling out sections of tarpaper. When I got near the top, I walked over to start the next run of tarpaper. Within four steps, my foot zeroed in on the section I'd just laid over the hole. Yikes! One foot went through the covered hole and I fell backward. My leg hooked in the hole, fortunately stopping my downhill plummet. My nail pouches emptied themselves all over the roof, adding to the commotion. I finally managed to right myself and discovered I'd escaped serious injury. I relaid the strip of tarpaper and this time cut out the hole as I rolled over it and even circled it with a red grease pencil. Once is enough!

—Wes Gilbreath

Replace a shingle

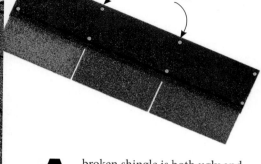

TYPICAL NAIL LOCATIONS

1 Gently tap a flat bar under the shingles to break the seal-down strips free. Don't force it—shingles rip easily.

NAIL REMOVAL ZONE

NAIL

2 Wedge the notch of the pry bar under the shingle at the nail head, then pry up both shingle and nail.

EDGE OF NEW SHINGLE

3 Nail down the new shingle, propping the tabs above as you nail to avoid breaking them.

A broken shingle is both ugly and a leak waiting to happen. But as long as you can find matching shingles (and you're not afraid of heights), the repair is straightforward.

Pick a day when the weather is moderate to do the repair—too cold and the shingles can crack; too warm and the shingle sealants are tough to break.

Loosen the tabs under the broken shingle and the next two courses above it (Photo 1). Shingles are fastened with eight nails each—four at the center just above the tab slots and four through the shingle above it—and you have to lift up all the shingles that cover those nails to remove them.

After all the tabs are loose, push the flat bar up under the damaged shingle to each nail, centering the nail in the flat bar notch (Photo 2). To avoid ripping shingles, gently work the pry bar under both tabs as you push it up.

Pop out the nails by prying underneath the shingle instead of trying to dig the nail head out from the top of the shingle; that will wreck the shingle. Then push the shingle down from the nail head and pull out the nail. After removing the center row of nails on the damaged shingle, lift the undamaged shingles above it and remove the next row of nails. Then pull out the damaged shingle.

Slide the new shingle up into place. Nail the center row first, then the center row of the course above it, nailing 1/2 in. over from the old holes (Photo 3). Nail at the top of the slots between the tabs, just above the sealant strip.

Replace vent flashing

All-metal plumbing vents present two opportunities for leaks—first, where the flashing meets the roof, and second, where the vent pipe meets the flashing. When the latter situation occurs, caulking and similar fixes will prove to be only temporary cures. You'll have to replace the flashing, either with a rubber-sleeve version or the telescoping two-piece type shown below.

1 Carefully remove any shingles that lap over the top half of the flashing base. Pull the nails that secure the old flashing and remove it.

LEAD CAULKING RING

ADJUSTABLE SLEEVE

BASE FLASHING

2 Fit the new base flashing over the pipe and nail along the edges. Slide the adjustable sleeve over the base flashing and vent pipe.

PLIABLE RING

3 Notch and reinstall shingles to cover upper portion of base flashing. Apply roofing cement to overlapping tabs and exposed nail heads. Fold pliable ring over top of vent pipe.

Seal a valley joint

Occasionally, a flashing that's still intact can allow water passage; this is especially true for valley flashing that doesn't have a raised fin or ridge in the center to help prevent fast-moving water from sloshing. If the roofer didn't cement the joint—and many don't—the shingles can curl up at the edge and eventually create a gap that water can easily penetrate.

1 Starting at the bottom edge, lift the shingle and apply a heavy, consistent bead of roofing cement along the flashing.

2 Drop and embed the first shingle into the cement. Lift the next shingle and lay another long bead of cement on the flashing and the top edge of the previous shingle.

3 Continue applying cement to both the flashing and the shingles as you work your way up. Press the shingles down to seat them.

Great goofs

The tar 'pits'

Last winter, my roof developed some leaks. As soon as the snow melted, I went up to pinpoint the problem. The section of roof in question had damaged roll roofing, so I decided to get a bucket of roofing tar and fix it. The cool, 50-degree day was great for working but the tar seemed a bit too stiff to spread thinly. I worked the tar in along the edge of the roof over the leak. All was fine until we got our first day of 80-degree heat. My dog came into the house with tar all over his feet. I went out to investigate and saw melted tar dripping all over the siding and windows.

—William Fronckiewicz

Mother knows best

I needed help installing a metal roof on my high, steep roof, and my stepson begged to help. He needed the money and wanted the experience. His mother, the worrywart, agreed only after he promised to wear a safety harness. Since no one else was wearing one, I disagreed, thinking it was unnecessary. But she held firm, so I went ahead and bought one for him.

All was going well for a few days until I happened to walk around the corner of the house and saw him dangling off the edge of the roof. When he saw me, he screamed, "Don't tell Mom!" After a touch-and-go rescue, we finally could laugh about the ordeal. But we didn't tell his mother about it until after we finished the roof....

—Charles Oakes

Hookin' ladder

About three or four times a year, my wife and I climb up on the roof of our house to blow off the leaves and pine needles that have accumulated, and as long as we're up there, clean our skylights. I usually place the ladder and go up first, blowing off debris while she rakes and cleans below. Then she joins me with a garden hose and cleaning supplies for the skylights and we work as a team.

The last time we were up there, the hose tangled with the ladder and sent it to the ground. The skylights were sealed, we had no cell phone and there were no neighbors within earshot. I had an idea: Lasso the ladder with the hose and pull it up! After several unsuccessful attempts, I hooked one of the ladder rungs with the handle of the hose sprayer and was able to gently pull the ladder back safely. We still work as a team, but from now on, it's one up and one down!

—Dan Brown & Kellie Hogan

Touch up a vinyl-clad fence

Vinyl-clad chain-link fence keeps its appearance for a long time. But the vinyl can get scuffed and worn where the gate latch locks onto the post. The repair is a little tricky because you're trying to paint over vinyl and metal. If you use a spray paint formulated for metal, it won't bond well to the vinyl. Instead, coat the damaged area with spray paint specifically designed for plastic (Krylon Fusion is one brand).

Start by cleaning the damaged area and beyond with a household spray cleaner. Then rough up the surface (Photo 1). Finish the repair with special paint for vinyl (Photo 2). Let the repair dry at least 24 hours before operating the gate latch mechanism.

1 **SAND THE AREA**
Lightly scuff the vinyl and metal with 120-grit sandpaper. Then wipe with a tack cloth.

2 **COAT WITH PAINT**
Apply a first coat of vinyl/plastic paint and allow it to set up the recommended time shown on the label. Then apply a finish coat.

Great goofs

Shrinking green lumber

When we built our deck, we took great pains to make sure we had only a 3/8-in. space between the boards. We wanted gaps narrow enough to keep things from falling through, yet wide enough for drainage. Several months later, the gaps were almost an inch wide! When we got tired of crawling under the deck to retrieve things, we bit the bullet and reinstalled the boards. We learned the hard way that green-treated lumber is often wet, and it shrinks as it dries. We should have placed the boards right next to each other when we first installed them.

— **David Myers**

Repair a bent fence rail

When a tree limb falls on your property, you can bet it's going to damage something. And if that something happens to be a chain link fence, consider yourself lucky, because fixing a chain link fence is an easy DIY repair. You could hire a pro or fix it yourself for less than $100.

We asked our friends at Premier Fence in St. Paul, MN, to evaluate the damage on this fence and walk us through the repair. Here's how to proceed.

CRIMPED END

CUTTING LINE

MARK A CUTTING LINE
Slide the new rail down so the crimped end is located over a straight section of the damaged rail. Then mark the cutting line.

Get a new section of top rail and some wire ties from a home center or fence supplier. The top rail should have one open end and one crimped end. Grab a hacksaw, file and pliers—and a helper.

Start by removing the wire ties that hold the fence fabric to the top rail. Then rest the new rail on top of the damaged rail and have your helper hold it in place while you mark a cutting line on the old rail as shown in the photo on p. 243. Then mark a cut on the opposite end of the new rail where it meets a joint.

Cut the damaged rail at the cutting line (Figure A), slide it off the joint and toss it. Then cut the excess off the top rail to mate with the existing joint. Create some maneuvering room by unbolting the top rail from the corner post and sliding it away from the damaged area. Install the larger end of the new rail onto the crimped end of the old rail. Then make the final connection. Reconnect the rail end cap to the corner post.

Figure A
Cutting guide

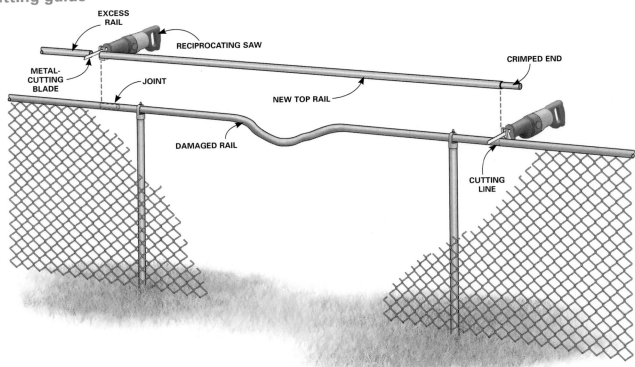

EXCESS RAIL

RECIPROCATING SAW

METAL-CUTTING BLADE

JOINT

NEW TOP RAIL

CRIMPED END

DAMAGED RAIL

CUTTING LINE

Great goofs

Lattice lesson

After finishing my porch deck, I decided it needed a skirt to hide the ugly footings. After cutting a couple of 4 x 8-ft. lattice sheets to size, I crawled underneath the deck to nail them up. Relieved that the job was nearly done, I started to wiggle out through the last open portion—only to realize it was too small. I had jailed myself in!

Fortunately I was able to pull free a good-size section and make my hasty escape before the neighbors could catch the show.

—Randall Deane

Special delivery

I was helping a friend build a three-rail fence around his horse pasture. Since the local home improvement store was only about a mile from his house, we decided there was no need to rent a flatbed truck or have the wood delivered. It would only take a few trips.

On the first trip, we loaded about thirty 16-ft. 2x6s into the back of his pickup. We anchored the ends of the boards under his toolbox and let the boards rest on his closed tailgate. We got about a block from his house when we hit a pothole, the boards bounced, and BAM! The tailgate broke, the toolbox catapulted into the air and crashed back down into the truck bed, and wood spilled all over the road. Needless to say, the other drivers were not very pleased, and we ended up having to go and rent that flatbed truck after all.

—Jessica Johnson

Don't fence me in

When my sister and brother-in-law recently bought a new house, the only thing missing was a backyard fence for the dogs. The first weekend we put in all the fence posts. The following weekend, we hired a guy with a pickup to help us haul all the preassembled panels from the home center to the backyard and assemble the panels. He pulled the truck into the center of the yard to save on carrying materials. Finally, after a long day turned to evening, we were admiring the finished job. Then we suddenly looked at each other and immediately realized our mistake. We'd fenced in the truck!

—Ralph Tremato

Straighten sagging gutters

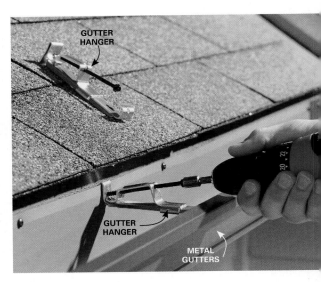

If your metal gutters have developed a middle-age sag, it's time for a little tummy tuck! Find some version of a gutter support bracket that'll work on your gutters to lift the low spots. It'll help drain water better and help keep debris from accumulating. The style shown is very easy to install. Another style of gutter hanger slides under the shingles and is nailed to the roof under the shingles. But test-bend your shingles first. Older shingles can be brittle and could break off when you lift them for the installation.

Hook the gutter hanger under the front edge of the gutter and over the back edge. Then drive the hex head screw through the wood trim behind the gutter. The hangers will be stronger if you screw them into a rafter. Look for nailheads, which indicate rafter locations. Add new gutter hangers about every 3 ft. along the entire length of the gutters if the old ones have let go.

Stop overflowing gutters

If rainwater cascading down your roof valley causes a waterfall that washes out the petunias every time it storms, install a splash guard. It takes about 20 minutes to complete. You can find these precut splash guards in both brown and white aluminum at a home center, but you could easily make your own out of aluminum or sheet metal and spray-paint them to match your gutters. If you don't own a Pop riveter, attach the guards with 1/2-in. sheet metal screws instead.

1 Drill 1/8-in. holes through both the splash guard and the gutter to accommodate the Pop rivets used in the next step. Self-tapping 1/2-in. sheet metal screws will also work.

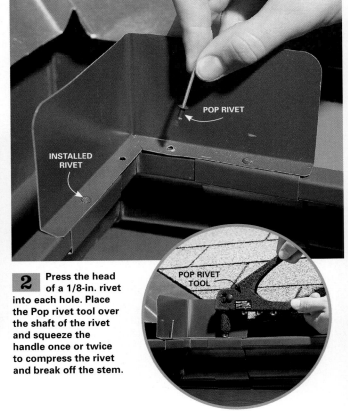

2 Press the head of a 1/8-in. rivet into each hole. Place the Pop rivet tool over the shaft of the rivet and squeeze the handle once or twice to compress the rivet and break off the stem.

Patch leaky gutters

Gutter leaks usually start at rusty spots or seams that have opened up because of expansion and contraction. If your gutter is still basically sound, the easiest way to stop the leak is by covering the damaged area with roof and gutter repair tape.

Prepare the gutter by scraping out as much old tar or caulk as possible. Wire-brush the metal thoroughly to get rid of rust and to give the tape a clean surface for bonding (Photo 1). If the gutter is badly rusted or has been heavily coated with tar that you can't scrape out, spray on a special adhesive primer before applying the tape.

Cut the tape with scissors or a razor knife (Photo 2). Tear the paper backing off the tape and lightly adhere one edge of the tape to the top of the gutter. Roll the tape down the wall of the gutter, pushing it firmly into curves and corners (Photo 3). Work wrinkles and bubbles flat. Overlap long seams by at least 1 in. and end seams by 4 in.

OLD TAR

LEAKY SEAM

1 Clean the area around the leak with a stiff scraper and a wire brush, then rinse off all dust and wipe completely dry.

1" MINIMUM OVERLAP

3 Starting at the center, press tape firmly into place. Follow the contours of the gutter and smooth out all wrinkles.

GUTTER TAPE

2 Cut the gutter repair tape long enough to overlap the leaky area by at least 6 in. in each direction.

Reattach a rain gutter end cap

For a long-lasting repair of those annoying gutter leaks, turn to silicone sealants. Silicone will act as an adhesive to keep the end cap securely in place, as well as a sealant to stop leaks and drips. Attach the end caps using the caulking and riveting techniques shown in Photos 1 – 3. Well-stocked home centers and hardware stores will have everything you need.

Easier gutter cleaning

An old plastic spatula makes a great tool for cleaning debris from gutters! It doesn't scratch up the gutter, and you can cut it to fit gutter contours with snips. Grime wipes right off the spatula too, making cleanup a breeze.

1 Pry off the end cap and chisel off all old gutter sealant from both the end cap and the lip of the gutter. Use a straight-slot screwdriver that's narrow enough to work down into the cap's groove. Wipe them clean. Restore any bent adjoining metal edges with a screwdriver and pliers. Dry-fit the parts to make sure they will join properly.

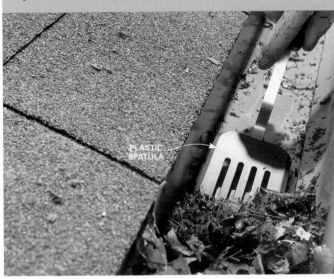

2 Fill the groove in the end cap with clear silicone caulk. Attach the end cap to the gutter by pressing the cap solidly against the lip, making sure the two are firmly seated together.

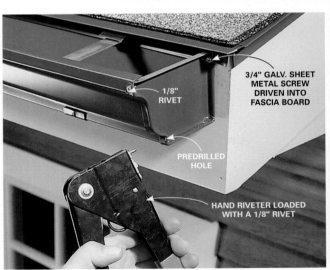

3 Maintain steady pressure on the end cap and drill three 1/8-in. holes as shown through the cap's flange. Then install the screw and two 1/8-in.-dia. rivets. Wipe away excess silicone on the outside before it dries.

Making paint last

Pressure washers clean deep and fast

1 Pressure washing removes loose paint and built-up grime and improves paint adhesion. Use the high pressure carefully, especially around windows. High-pressure water can break the glass. Avoid directing water up under the laps, and keep the nozzle at least 16 in. away from the wood.

Paint just won't stick to dirty or dusty surfaces. You'll need to clean it even if there's very little scraping to do, and the fastest way is with a pressure washer. You can rent a pressure washer (Photo 1) from a rental store for about $60 a day and get a lot of loose paint and grime off your old painted surfaces fast.

These washers kick out a hard stream of water, so try it out on an inconspicuous spot on the house to get the hang of handling the wand. Be careful not to hit windows (they can break), and don't work the spray upward under the laps of siding. Remember, this is for cleaning, not blasting all the old paint off. Of course, some of the old loose paint will fall off, but too much pressure will gouge the wood.

Don't try to pressure-wash while standing on a ladder. The recoil can knock you off balance. And finally, keep in mind that you won't be able to do any scraping and sanding for a couple of days until the surface dries thoroughly.

If the prospect of using a pressure washer is just too intimidating, you can get a stiff brush on a pole and a bucket with mild detergent and scrub the surfaces. Follow the scrub immediately with a rinse from your garden hose.

> **CAUTION**
>
> Houses built before 1978 may contain lead paint. Before disturbing any surface, get a lab analysis of paint chips from it. Contact your local public health department for information on how to collect samples and where to send them.

2 Some loose paint will flake off while you wash the surface. But don't try to strip the paint—you'll gouge the wood.

Patch rotted wood

Do you have rotted wood? It's usually better to simply tear out the old board or molding and replace it than to repair it. But for window-sills and door jambs that are hard to remove and molding that would be tough to duplicate, patching with wood filler makes sense.

Fillers for repair of rotted wood generally fall into three categories. For small holes and cracks, there are fillers like DAP Latex Wood Filler or MH Ready Patch that harden as the water or solvent evaporates. Other fillers, such as Durham's Rock Hard Water Putty, harden by a chemical reaction when water is mixed in. Finally, two-part fillers like Minwax High Performance Wood Filler (polyester) and Abatron's WoodEpox (epoxy) harden after you mix the two parts.

Two-part fillers are the most durable, and the best choice for long-lasting repairs. Although polyester and epoxy are both two-part fillers, they have unique character-istics that make them quite different to work with. We'll show you the differences and give you some tips for working with these two excellent wood repair fillers.

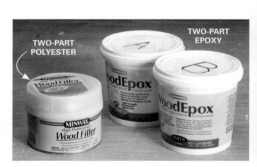

Epoxy and polyester fillers are two-part formulas that harden after you mix the parts. They're both excellent fillers, though with slightly different characteristics.

1 Gouge out rotted wood with a chisel, screwdriver or other pointy tool.

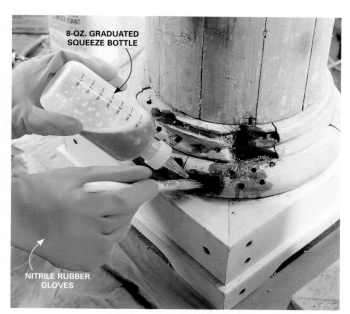

8-OZ. GRADUATED SQUEEZE BOTTLE

NITRILE RUBBER GLOVES

2 Mix two-part epoxy consolidant in a squeeze bottle. Squirt it into the holes and repair area. Use a disposable brush to spread the consolidant and work it into the wood fibers.

Use epoxy for a premium repair

One common brand of epoxy wood filler is Abatron WoodEpox (abatron.com). Unlike polyester filler, epoxy wood filler has a dough-like consistency, so it will stay put even on vertical repairs.

Prepare for an epoxy repair by removing as much rotted wood as possible. Use an old screwdriver, chisel or 5-in-1 painter's tool to gouge out the damaged wood (Photo 1). If the wood is wet, cover it loosely with a poly tent and let it dry completely before starting the repair. Drill a series of 1/4-in. holes around the rotted area if you suspect rotted wood below the surface, but don't drill all the way through. You'll fill these with consolidant to solidify the wood around the repair.

Start the repair by soaking the damaged area with epoxy consolidant (Photo 2). Mix the consolidant according to the directions. Wear rubber gloves and safety glasses when you're working with epoxy. You can mix the consolidant in a squirt bottle or a small plastic container. Use a disposable brush to work the epoxy consolidant into the wood fibers. Epoxy is difficult to remove after it hardens, so clean up drips and runs right away with paper towels. You don't have to wait for the consolidant to harden before applying the epoxy filler.

Next, mix the two-part epoxy filler on a mixing board (Photo 3). Then apply it with a putty knife or simply press it into place

Tips for working with epoxy

▶ Label the caps "A" and "B" and don't mix them up.
▶ Start with a clean container or mixing board each time you mix a new batch.
▶ Save epoxy by filling most of the cavity with a scrap of wood. Glue it in with epoxy filler.
▶ Carve the epoxy before it becomes rock hard.

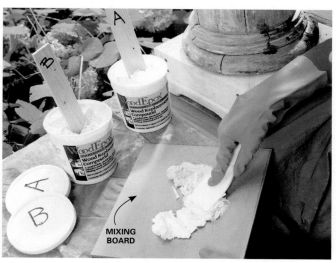

MIXING BOARD

3 Mix the two-part epoxy wood filler on a smooth board according to the manufacturer's directions.

SOFT EPOXY WOOD FILLER

4 Press the epoxy filler into the repair. Leave enough protruding so you can shape the repair after it starts to harden.

HARDENED EPOXY WOOD FILLER

5 Rough out the shape with a rasp. Mix another batch of epoxy filler and add another layer if necessary. Fine-tune the repair with sandpaper, then prime and paint.

with your fingers (Photo 4). Roughly shape the epoxy, making sure it protrudes beyond the final profile. When the temperature is 70 degrees F, you'll have about 30 minutes before the epoxy starts to harden. Increase the working time by spreading the epoxy in a thin layer on your mixing board and keeping it cool. On a warm day, the epoxy will harden enough in three or four hours to start shaping it with a Surform plane, rasp and sandpaper (Photo 5). After rough-shaping with a plane or rasp, sand the filler with 80-grit and then 120-grit sandpaper. If you sand off too much (or didn't add enough epoxy to begin with), dust off the repair and add another layer. You can make a more spreadable filler by mixing a small batch of consolidant and a small batch of filler and then adding some of the consolidant to the filler to reach the desired consistency.

Polyester is readily available and less expensive

If you've done any auto body repair, you've probably worked with two-part polyester filler. Minwax High Performance Wood Filler is one brand formulated for wood repair, but a gallon container of Bondo or some other brand of two-part auto body polyester will also work and may be less expensive for larger fixes.

The process for repairing wood is much the same whether you're using polyester filler or epoxy. Instead of epoxy consolidant, you'll use High Performance Wood Hardener to solidify and strengthen the wood fibers (Photo 1). Polyester begins hardening faster than Abatron WoodEpox. Depending on the temperature, you'll have about 10 to 15 minutes to work before the filler starts to harden.

Also, unlike WoodEpox, polyester tends to sag when you're doing vertical repairs. One trick is to build a form and line it with plastic sheeting. Press the form against the filler and attach it with screws. Then pull it off after the filler hardens. Or you can wait until the sagging filler reaches the hardness of soap and carve it off with a putty knife or chisel or shape it with a Surform plane or rasp (Photo 2). Most medium to large repairs will require at least two layers of filler. Complete the repair by sanding and priming the filled area and then painting.

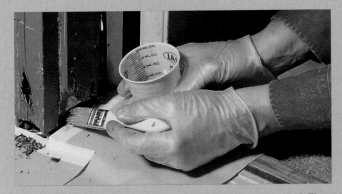

1 Remove rotted wood with a 5-in-1 or other sharp tool. Then coat the area with wood hardener as shown. Mix polyester wood filler and press it into the recess with a putty knife.

2 Carve the partially hardened sagging wood filler with a putty knife or chisel. Add another layer of filler if necessary.

Stop rot with kick-out flashing

The solution to rotting sidewalls is a small piece of bent metal called a kick-out flashing, which simply directs all that water away from the wall. It installs just like standard step flashing, except that half of it hangs over the edge of the roof.

Inspect the sidewall around and underneath the fascia and inside the house for signs of moisture damage, and repair any rotted areas. Add felt, if needed, before nailing the new wood on, and prime the new wood on all four sides before installing it.

Install the kick-out flashing underneath the first shingle (Photo 1). If the shingle already has flashing on it, the kick-out flashing has to slip beneath it, and you'll have to loosen or remove siding to do this. If the sidewall is stucco or solid wood like ours and you can't open it to get flashing behind it, continue the step flashing to the peak of the roof, then cover the step flashing with cap flashing (Photo 2).

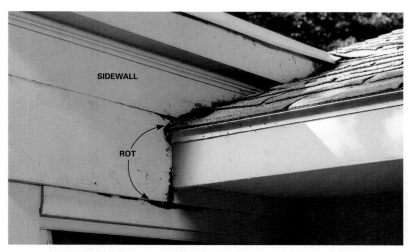

The intersection between a roof and a sidewall can be a rot problem waiting to happen. Even if the roof has been properly flashed against the sidewall (this one hasn't), water can still run down the side of the house and behind the siding, causing rot.

1 Lift the bottom shingle and slip in the kick-out flashing. Nail it to the sidewall (or glue it if nailing isn't possible).

2 If the kick-out and step flashing can't tuck behind the siding, screw on cap flashing to cover it, then caulk along the top.

How to repair mortar joints

Crumbling masonry joints start out ugly, and then things get uglier fast—bricks come loose, water seeps behind the wall and bees make their homes in the mortar holes. Let it go and the problem won't go away. In fact, the deterioration will accelerate and you'll have a much bigger fix on your hands. But you can mend the joints yourself with a process called tuckpointing.

Tuckpointing isn't difficult or expensive—the only real investment is your time. But you can pick away at it in your free time, area by area.

The steps we show here will work on any brick walls, chimneys and retaining walls. Tuckpointing won't fix cracking or crumbling bricks, or cracks in walls caused by a shifting foundation. Those problems call for more drastic fixes that we won't cover here.

Pick up tools and materials

First and foremost, you'll need an angle grinder with a 4- or 4-1/4-in. diamond blade. Don't bother renting one unless you only have several feet of bad joints. An inexpensive one will do the trick, so you might as well buy one.

You'll also need a few simple, inexpensive specialty tools that are available at masonry suppliers and some home centers. You'll need a brick trowel and a tuck pointer. If you have concave mortar joints, you'll need a masonry jointer that's the width of your joints. For flat joints, you'll need a joint raker. If you have just a few areas that need work, use a hammer and cold chisel to knock out the old mortar, but for more extensive work, plan on getting a rotary hammer drill fitted with a flat chisel to make the job go a heck of a lot quicker. You can rent one for a day. If you have multiple days' worth of work, rental costs can break the bank. In that case, it makes more sense to buy one.

You'll also need a 60-lb. bag of mortar mix. If you need colored mortar, take a small piece of the old mortar to a masonry supplier and ask for help finding a mortar dye to match. But be aware of this—fresh tuckpointing always stands out against older mortar. However, it will eventually weather to match.

Start small

If you only have a few joints to tuckpoint, dive right in. But if you have a large wall to tackle, start in a small area to get a feel for the operation before you start hogging out entire walls. You'll hone your skills and get a good idea of how much you can tuckpoint at one time. You'll have 30 to 60 minutes of working time once you mix the mortar.

Get ready for the dust

Tuckpointing is a dirty business. Grinding the joints creates a dust storm, with chunks of mortar covering the ground. Spread a drop cloth on the ground to catch the mortar so cleanup will take minutes instead of hours.

Close your house windows to keep out the dust, and tell your neighbors who might be affected to do the same.

Grind out the joints

Before you can put new mortar in the joints, you have to cut out the damaged material. Start by grinding the top and bottom of the horizontal (bed) joints with an angle grinder (Photo 1). Hold the grinder with both hands to keep it steady and avoid grinding into the bricks. You only need to grind 3/4 in. into the mortar.

Start at outside corners and work inward. That keeps you from putting extra pressure on the corner bricks, which could knock them out of the wall. After you've finished the horizontal joints, do the vertical (head) joints (Photo 2).

Knock out the mortar

Use the rotary hammer drill to pound the mortar out of the joints. Set the drill on the rotating mode (it puts less pressure on the bricks). Again, work from the outside corners inward (Photo 3). Keep the chisel point in the mortar joint and keep moving the hammer. The drill makes quick work of removing mortar, but be careful. The powerful tool can also knock out bricks. If that happens, take them all the way out, chisel off all the mortar, then reset them when you fill the joints.

1 **GRIND THE HORIZONTAL JOINTS FIRST**
Grind along the top and bottom of the horizontal joints. Get as close to the bricks as you can. If you accidentally grind against the bricks, the dust will turn the color of the brick.

2 **PLUNGE-CUT THE VERTICAL JOINTS**
Grind both sides of the vertical joints. Plunge the grinder into the joint and work it up and down to make the cuts. But be careful not to grind the bricks above and below the joints.

3 **HAMMER OUT THE MORTAR**
Keep moving the rotary hammer drill along the joints as you chisel out the mortar. Be sure to keep the chisel off the bricks so you don't knock them out of place.

There's really no secret to knocking out the mortar. Just hold the drill at about a 45-degree angle to the wall, squeeze the trigger and watch the mortar fall out. **Caution:** Wear eye protection—mortar pieces can go flying!

Clean out the joints

Once you've chipped out the damaged mortar, use a hand broom to sweep the joints. Sweep away mortar clumps and the dust (Photo 4). Use the rotary hammer drill to bust out stubborn chunks.

Then wash out the joints with water. But don't hose down the wall or you'll soak everything, including the ground where you'll be standing or kneeling. Instead, fill a bucket with water and brush the water into the joints (Photo 5). Don't worry about slopping water onto the bricks—you want them damp before you fill the joints anyway.

Mix the new mortar

If you're tinting the mortar, stir the dye and the mortar mix in a bucket before adding the water. Dye is typically sold in 1-1/2-lb. bags. Mix one-quarter of the dye with one-quarter of a 60-lb. bag of mortar mix. Stir in water until the mix is the consistency of peanut butter (Photo 6).

The mortar will last 30 to 60 minutes, but you may need to add water to keep it workable. After one hour, throw out what's left and mix a new batch.

Work the mortar into the joints

Use a brick trowel and a tuck pointer to pack the mortar into the joints. Most pros prefer this method to using a grout/ mortar bag. Mortar that is hand packed is more durable.

Scoop mortar onto the trowel. Hold the trowel next to the joint, then press the mortar into the joint with the tuck pointer (Photo 7). Pack the joint until it's flush with the front of the bricks.

4 SWEEP OUT THE JOINTS
Use a small broom to sweep debris and dust out of the joints. Inspect the joints for any remaining stubborn mortar and knock it out with the drill.

5 GIVE THE JOINTS A BATH
Stick a brush into a bucket of water and rinse out the joints. Your goal here isn't to make surfaces pristine, just to get rid of chunks and dust.

6 WHIP UP THE MORTAR BATCH
Mix the mortar to the consistency of peanut butter with no dry spots or clumps. You'll know the mix is right when it sticks to your trowel when you hold it at a 45-degree angle. Let the mortar sit for 10 minutes before using it.

TUCK POINTER

BRICK TROWEL

7 **FILL THE JOINTS**
Load your brick trowel and hold it next to the joint. Work the mortar into the joint with your tuck pointer. Pack the joint full before moving on to the next one.

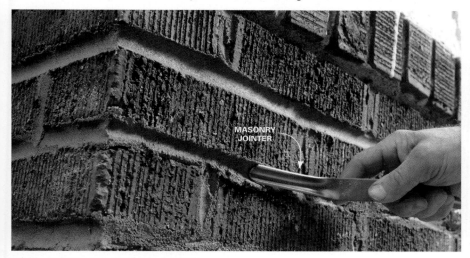

MASONRY JOINTER

8 **STRIKE THE MORTAR JOINTS**
Drag the jointer along the vertical joints and the horizontal joints. Apply gentle pressure to tool out the ridges where the joints intersect. Finish one joint before moving on to the next.

NEW MORTAR

9 **WIPE DOWN THE BRICKS**
Scrub the mortar off the bricks with a stiff brush. This also knocks down and smooths out any high spots along the joint edges.

Tool the joints

Let the mortar in the filled joints set for about 30 minutes. If you're tuckpointing a large area, continually check the first joints you filled to see if they're ready to tool (finish). Check by pressing the filled joint with your thumb. If your thumb leaves only a slight impression, it's ready to tool. If it goes in deeper, wait five minutes and try again. But don't let the mortar get too stiff—it can start to harden after just 30 minutes, making it difficult to tool the joints.

If you want rounded joints, press a masonry jointer into the top of vertical joints and pull the tool downward. The jointer will push out some of the mortar and leave a concave shape. For horizontal joints, start at a corner (Photo 8). Run the tool about halfway across the joint, then stop and finish tooling from the other side.

For flat joints, place a joint raker over an old joint to set the depth. Then run the raker along the new joints to make them flat.

Clean the bricks

Once the joints have set up (about 30 minutes after tooling), use a stiff-bristle brush to clean dried mortar off the bricks (Photo 9).

If the mortar refuses to come off, wait three days, then use muriatic acid. Use 10 parts water to 1 part acid (add the acid to the water, not the other way around). **Caution:** Be sure to wear eye protection and rubber gloves when working with acid. Brush the acid onto the bricks with a stiff-bristle brush, scrub the bricks and let the acid fizz. Then rinse the acid off with water. If there's still a little mortar residue left, treat it again.

The acid can slightly alter the bricks' appearance, so test it on a small area first. If it does alter the appearance, increase the ratio of water to acid.

Patch stucco

Stucco is a composite of portland cement, sand, lime and water. It has its origins in hand-troweled adobe plaster and other traditional low-tech masonry finishes, but now it's often applied professionally with specialized materials, tools and skills. But patching and repairing smaller areas can easily be managed by a competent do-it-yourselfer. The trick is building it up in layers.

You can buy premixed dry stucco in bags, just like concrete or mortar, and add water until the mix is stiff but pliable. Wait for a dry, mild day so excess heat doesn't shorten the mix's working time. Break or chisel away the damaged area of old stucco and cut away the old metal lath underneath. Remove any loose debris and use a mist sprayer to keep the working area from drying out.

1 Cut new metal lath for the repair, sizing it to overlap the old lath by 2 in. Fasten with roofing nails.

2 Trowel the first "scratch" coat on in layers that total 3/8 in. thick, working it vigorously into the metal lath.

3 While it's wet but starting to set, comb the scratch coat with a lath remnant to provide tooth for the next coat.

4 Trowel on the second "brown" coat until it's flush with the surrounding stucco. Use a straightedge to check its flatness.

5 Use a wet sponge float to feather the brown coat so it blends in with the edges of the surrounding area.

6 Knock down the bumps to create a matching texture, after using a dash brush to flick bits of stucco onto the surface.

Reattach loose vinyl siding

Hook the siding tool behind the locking face of the loose panel and pull down. Push the panel onto the locking face of the lower course to reattach it. If it doesn't reattach easily, check the nailing technique on the lower course. If the nails were driven too tight, the nailing flange may be dimpled. Its locking face won't be in a straight-line position to easily receive the next panel. Take a pry bar and carefully work it behind the nailhead. Back the nail out until the dimple is taken out of the nailing flange. The siding removal tool (shown) is a must for both removing siding panels and reconnecting them. When you're removing a locked panel, you'll have to wiggle the siding tool as you push it up to successfully grab the locking face's edge.

Vinyl siding is installed by interlocking the top and bottom edges of the panels. Properly installed, the panels should stay permanently locked together. If you have panels that have separated from poor installation, impact damage or severe weather, first check for clues that the siding was improperly installed. The installer may have tried to straighten unlevel courses by pulling the panels up taut, or pressing them down, then nailing them. Or perhaps the nails weren't driven straight and level, resulting in panels that later buckled.

Vinyl siding panels may come undone because these problems—or repeated temperature changes—allow the panels to expand, contract and loosen.

Buy a siding removal tool at a home center or a siding retailer. This tool (above) can be used for vinyl, aluminum or steel siding. As shown, the hook on the tool grabs the locking face under the bottom edge of each panel.

To reattach a panel, first use the siding tool to grab the panel's locking edge, then pull down. At the same time, use the heel of your hand to push the panel edge to catch the locking face on the lower siding course. Work the siding tool and heel of your hand along the edge of the loosened panel in this manner until the two courses of vinyl have snapped back together.

Turn down the heat

After trimming an overgrown tree in my yard, I piled the limbs into the back yard about 20 ft. from my garage. On a calm day a couple of weeks later, I decided to burn the pile. To be safe, I had the garden hose ready. The fire started just fine but soon it was so hot that I had to step back a bit. This hot fire didn't last long and when it was nearly out, I turned around toward the garage. Yikes! The vinyl siding on the whole side near the fire was curled and melted from the heat. I'm now doing a project that wasn't on my list.

—George DeLozier

Repair holes in aluminum and vinyl siding

All houses gradually accumulate holes in their siding from fasteners and cables. The only way to repair these holes perfectly in vinyl or aluminum is to replace the entire piece—a repair that ranges from challenging in vinyl to almost impossible in old aluminum.

For an easier, nearly-as-good fix that keeps water out and is almost invisible from several feet away, fill the hole with a color-matched caulk. Home centers don't usually stock it, but siding wholesalers that sell to contractors carry caulks specifically blended for dozens of different shades of siding. If you know the manufacturer and color name of your siding, you can get

the exact blend developed for that shade. Otherwise, bring a sample piece or take a photo and ask a salesperson to help you match it.

Before filling the hole, wipe the siding clean. Squirt enough caulk into the hole to fill the area behind the hole. Avoid smearing excess caulk all over the surrounding siding—the less you get on the siding, the less obvious the repair will be. Once the caulk is fully cured (which could be several days, depending on the type), trim it even with the siding with a razor blade.

To avoid making holes in the future, use vinyl siding clips instead of fasteners to hang decorations.

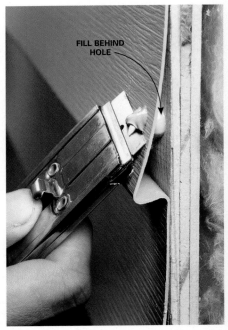

FILL BEHIND HOLE

Trim the hardened caulk flush with the siding using a straightedge razor blade.

COLOR-MATCHED CAULK

Replace damaged vinyl siding

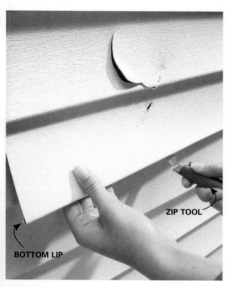

1 Slide the zip tool along the bottom edge to release the vinyl siding from the piece below it.

BOTTOM LIP
ZIP TOOL

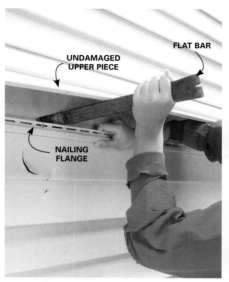

2 Slip a flat bar behind the vinyl siding and lever out the nails.

FLAT BAR
UNDAMAGED UPPER PIECE
NAILING FLANGE

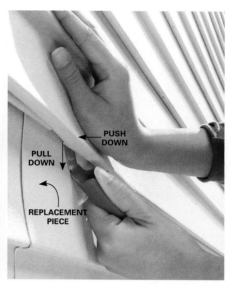

3 Install the replacement piece and hook the lip of the upper siding piece into the slot to lock it into place.

PUSH DOWN
PULL DOWN
REPLACEMENT PIECE

V inyl siding is tough, but not indestructible. If a falling branch or a well-hit baseball has cracked a piece of your siding, you can make it as good as new in about 15 minutes with a zip tool (available at any home center) and a replacement piece. It's as simple as unzipping the damaged piece and snapping in a new one.

Starting at one end of the damaged piece, push the end of the zip tool up under the siding until you feel it hook the bottom lip (Photo 1). Pull the zip tool downward and out to unhook the bottom lip, then slide it along the edge, pulling the siding out as you go. Then unzip any pieces above the damaged piece. Hold them out of the way with your elbow while you pry out the nails that hold the damaged piece in place (Photo 2).

Slide the replacement piece up into place, pushing up until the lower lip locks into the piece below it. Drive 1-1/4-in. roofing nails through the nailing flange. Space them about every 16 in. (near the old nail holes). Nail in the center of the nailing slot and leave about 1/32 in. of space between the nail head and the siding so the vinyl can move freely. Don't nail the heads tightly or the siding will buckle when it warms up.

With the new piece nailed, use the zip tool to lock the upper piece down over it. Start at one end and pull the lip down, twisting the tool slightly to force the leading edge down (Photo

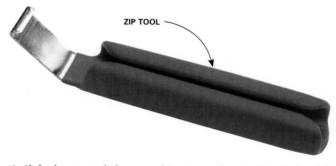

ZIP TOOL

3). Slide the zip tool along, pushing in on the vinyl just behind the tool with your other hand so it snaps into place.

It's best to repair vinyl in warm weather. In temperatures below freezing it becomes less flexible and may crack.

The downside of replacing older vinyl siding is that it can be hard to match the style and color, and siding rarely has any identifying marks. The best way to get a replacement piece is to take the broken piece to vinyl siding distributors in your area and find the closest match. If the old vinyl has faded or you can't find the right color, take the broken piece to a paint store and have the color matched. Paint the replacement piece with one coat of top-quality acrylic primer followed by acrylic house paint—acrylic paint will flex with the movement of the vinyl.

Special Section

TOOLS & EQUIPMENT

Rebuild a framing nailer

1 WORK FROM THE TOP DOWN
Remove the four hex screws and then the cap. Then remove the entire cylinder and driver assembly.

BAD TOP SEAL

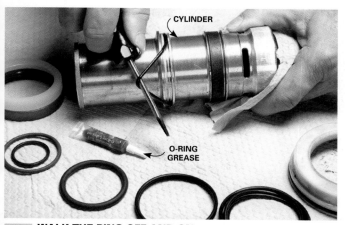

CYLINDER

O-RING GREASE

2 WALK THE RING OFF AND ON
Pry up the old O-ring. Then slide the round portion of the screwdriver under it. Circle the screwdriver around the O-ring to "walk" it off. Reverse the procedure to install the new, freshly greased ring.

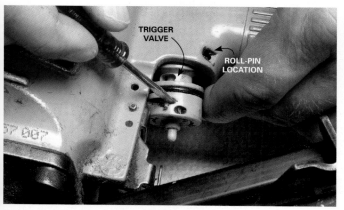

TRIGGER VALVE

ROLL-PIN LOCATION

3 SWAP OUT THE TRIGGER VALVE
Locate the roll-pin driver tool and tap it out with a small hammer. Then pull out the valve and install the freshly greased replacement.

Nothing beats a top-quality nailer for cutting hours out of a framing project. But all that heavy-duty nailing depends on a handful of rubber O-rings. When they fail, your project grinds to a halt. You don't have to wait a week for the shop to rebuild it. You can do the entire job yourself in about two hours with an o-ring rebuild kit. Here, we'll show you how to rebuild a Bostitch framing nailer with a master O-ring kit and a trigger valve assembly. If you have a different brand, don't worry. The rebuild is similar for others.

Framing nailers usually fail in one of these ways: deteriorated O-rings that cause air leaks, a trigger valve that won't fire, or a leaking cylinder seal or a worn driver bumper, which prevents the gun from making a complete stroke. A complete rebuild fixes all those problems. Buy the rebuild kit at a local service center or online. It'll come with all the O-rings and seals. If you've put a lot of nails through your gun, buy new bumpers and a trigger valve at the same time. Then download the gun schematic from the manufacturer (bostitch.com, senco.com or, for Duo-Fast and Paslode brands, itwserviceparts.com).

Start the disassembly at the cylinder cap (Photo 1). Lay out the pieces on a spotlessly clean workbench in the order you removed them. Then remove the old O-rings using a blunt, straight-blade screwdriver (Photo 2). Apply O-ring grease (usually included in the new kit) to the new rings, then replace the rings one at a time, matching each one to its replacement. Install the new bumpers, piston seals and piston stops and reinstall the cap. Then replace the trigger valve (Photo 3).

Prolong the life of your air nailer by using only nail gun oil (photo below).

The right oil for your gun

Lube your nail gun regularly with the right oil. NEVER use impact air tool oil, WD-40 or motor oil—they can destroy the O-rings in your gun. Also, use special winter grade oil when operating your gun in cold weather.

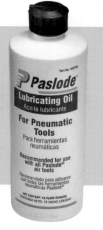

Rebuild your ratchet

Got a ratchet that's jammed, rusted or won't switch directions? Don't toss it, rebuild it. In most cases, you can slap yours back into shape with just a good cleaning and new grease. But if you've broken a spring or a pawl, you'll need to buy a rebuilding kit. A rebuild kit for most major brands costs about $10 to $30. To find one for yours, just search for the ratchet brand and model number or try ebay.com.

Before you buy a kit, disassemble the ratchet to assess its condition. Use combination snap ring pliers to remove the internal or external snap ring from the ratchet head (Photo 1). Or use a small flat-blade screwdriver to remove a spiral snap ring (Photo 2). If your ratchet doesn't use snap rings, it'll come apart with either a hex wrench or a screwdriver.

Throw a towel over the ratchet (to capture flying springs) and slide the entire ratchet assembly out of the head. Clean the parts with brake cleaner and an old toothbrush. Remove any rust with a rust removal chemical. If the spring ends are intact and the pawl teeth are sharp, you can reuse them. If not, buy a rebuild kit. Then apply a light coating of wheel bearing grease to all the parts. Don't use engine oil;

it'll just drip out. And don't pack the head with grease—that'll prevent the pawl from reversing. Then reassemble (Photo 3).

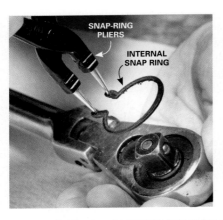

1 REMOVE AN INTERNAL/EXTERNAL SNAP RING
Jam the prongs of snap ring pliers into the holes on the snap ring. Then compress the internal snap ring and lift it out of the retaining slot. Change the pliers over to external mode to expand an external snap ring.

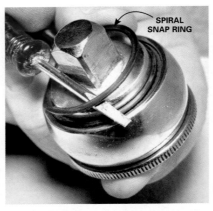

2 REMOVE A SPIRAL SNAP RING
Locate the clipped end of the spiral snap ring and twist it out and up with a small flat-blade screwdriver. Then "unwind" the snap ring in a counterclockwise direction. Reverse the procedure to reinstall.

3 GREASE AND REASSEMBLE
Compress the pawl assembly with your fingers and slide the entire ratchet into the head. Rotate it in both directions to check the pawl's operation and spread the grease. Then reinstall the snap ring or screws. Double-check the operation.

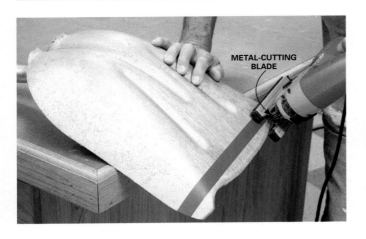

Restore your grain shovel

Aluminum grain shovels are perfect for snow shoveling, or as a substitute for a big dustpan in your shop. The only drawback is that the soft aluminum edge wears out and gets bent, making shoveling more difficult. Here's an easy fix. Make a straight line across the blade with a piece of masking tape. Then saw along the tape with a jigsaw and a metal-cutting blade to straighten the front edge of the shovel. If you want, you can polish and sharpen the edge slightly with a belt sander.

Rebelt your snow blower

If you haven't changed the belts on your two-stage snow blower since the day you bought it, do it now. Factory belts typically last about five to seven years, depending on how hard you work your snow blower each year. Don't even think about replacing them with V-belts from the auto parts store. Even though they're cheaper, you'll barely get one season out of them—they're just not heavy-duty enough. Get genuine factory belts from the dealer or online. You'll need your snow blower's make and model number and the engine brand and model number.

The belt removal/replacement procedures are different for each make and model, so refer to your owner's manual. If you don't have yours, try downloading a copy from the manufacturer's site. With the cover off, inspect the condition of the belts. If you see cracks or cuts anywhere on the belt, shiny glazing along the sides, or fraying, it's time to replace them.

Most two-stage machines have belt retainer bars and idler/tensioner rollers that have to be loosened before you can get the belts off (Photo 1). Then empty the gas tank and tip the entire machine up so you can remove the bottom access plate. Then slide each belt out, paying attention to which belt fits on which pulley. Reverse the procedure to install the new belts.

BELT GUARD

1 **GO RIGHT TO THE TOP**
Remove the upper belt guard so you can get to the top pulleys. Use a 12-in. extension bar, ratchet and socket.

2 **SLACK BEFORE YOU SLIP**
Slack off the belt tension by prying the tensioning rollers back, removing the tension spring or loosening the tension mechanism. Then slip the belts off the drive pulleys and wiggle them out.

3 **INSTALL NEW BELTS**
Clean the pulleys and slide on the new belts. Then thread the new belts into place.

Renew your garden tool handles

1 SAND THE HANDLES SMOOTH
A random orbital sander makes short work of the sanding job. Keep it moving so you don't create a flat spot.

RANDOM ORBITAL SANDER

READER PHOTO

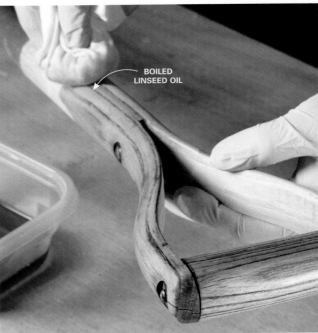

BOILED LINSEED OIL

2 RUB ON BOILED LINSEED OIL
Dip a rag into a container of boiled linseed oil and wipe it onto the sanded tool handle. Let the oil soak in for a few minutes. Then wipe off the excess with a dry rag.

H ere's a tip sent in by Ken Werner, one of our readers: "Each spring I sand our gardening tool handles with 120-grit sandpaper and then rub a coat of boiled linseed oil on them. The handles stay smooth throughout the gardening season. Then I do it again before putting the tools away in the fall." The tools look terrific, and the smooth oiled surface resists cracking and is much easier on the hands.

If you're more like Oscar than Felix and your tool handles have never been sanded, they're probably as rough and worn as ours were. In that case, use a random orbital sander (Photo 1). You'll still have to hand-sand the spots you can't reach with the sander, but it'll save you a lot of effort.

Fix a broken starter rope

You tug one last time to get the lawn mower started, and suddenly the rope breaks and the end goes spinning into the hole. Don't blow a gasket. If you have even a tinge of mechanical aptitude, replacing a starter rope is pretty easy. If the spring breaks—a rare event, according to our repair expert—the fix is a lot harder, and we recommend you take the mower to a repair center.

The first step is to remove the rewind assembly from the lawn mower, and how you do this varies. It's usually held on by three or more screws. Remove the screws and lift off the rewind (Photo 1). Some mowers have a shroud covering the top of the mower. On these you'll have to search for and remove the screws that hold the shroud in place. If your rewind unit is held on by rivets instead of screws, see "No Screws?" on p. 268.

After you remove the rewind unit, flip it over and look inside to find the knotted end of the broken rope. Grab it with needle-nose pliers and pull it out. You'll thread the new rope through this hole. You'll find replacement starter ropes at home centers, hardware stores and small-engine repair centers.

Before you install the new rope, you have to rewind the spring by twisting the rope pulley in the same direction it goes

1 **REMOVE THE REWIND UNIT**
Remove the screws that hold the rewind to the engine and lift it off. Use a nut driver to remove hex head screws.

2 **REPLACE THE ROPE**
First, remove the broken piece of rope by unwinding it, grabbing the knot and pulling it out. Then rewind the spring and hold it in place with a screwdriver.

3 **TIE A KNOT**
Tie a knot in the end of the rope. Let the pulley wind the rope back into the rewind. Reinstall the rewind unit and any other parts you've removed.

No screws?

Rivets hold this rewind unit to the metal shroud. To access the rewind unit, remove the bolts that hold the shroud to the engine. If the rivets are loose, drill them out and replace them with bolts and locknuts.

when you pull on the rope. You'll know when you're turning the pulley in the right direction because it will get harder to turn. Keep turning the pulley until you feel resistance and it won't turn easily. Then let it unwind about one-half to one revolution until the hole in the pulley lines up with the hole in the rewind housing. Wedge a screwdriver against the pulley to keep the spring from unwinding while you thread the rope through the holes (Photo 2). **Tip:** With leather gloves on, melt the end of the rope with a match. While the plastic is hot, give it a quick twist to create a pointed end so it's easier to thread in.

Push the end of the rope through both holes and tie a knot (Photo 3). Heat the knot a little bit with a match and pull it tight to keep it from coming undone. Remove the screwdriver while you keep pressure on the pulley with your finger, and gradually let the rope wind onto the wheel. You may have extra rope to cut

off after everything's back together. Mount the rewind unit and reinstall any shrouding or other parts you had to remove. Put the handle on the rope and tie a knot. Position the knot so that there's a little tension on the rope when you release the handle. If the rope on your lawn mower extends up the handle, make sure to place the rope handle in its final position before tensioning the rope slightly and tying the knot.

Loosen a stuck throttle cable

If your lawn mower's throttle cable is hard to move or stuck, here's a fix. Disconnect both ends of the cable from the mower. You'll probably have to remove a bolt and disassemble the lever assembly near the handle to get the cable out. Take a photo to help you put it back together when you're done.

At the engine end, loosen the clamp that holds the cable to the engine and unhook the cable from the carburetor. Pour penetrating oil into the cable (Photo 1). Grab the inner cable with pliers and work it up and down to loosen it. When the cable moves freely and all the penetrating oil has drained out, squirt silicone lubricant into the funnel to keep the cable sliding freely. Reinstall the cable (Photo 2).

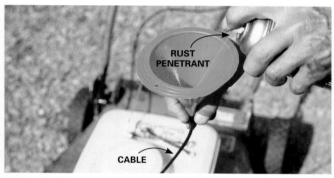

1 **SOAK WITH PENETRATING OIL**
Stick the end of the cable into a funnel and wrap electrical tape around it to create a seal. Spray or pour penetrating oil into the funnel. Position the opposite end of the cable over a small container to catch the penetrating oil as it drips out. Then lubricate the cable.

2 **REINSTALL THE CABLE AND ADJUST THE CHOKE**
Remove the air cleaner assembly so you can see the choke plate. With the throttle control lever in the "choke" position, pull on the outer jacket of the cable near the clamp until the choke plate opens. Tighten the clamp with the cable in this position. Reassemble the air cleaner.

Replace a vacuum cleaner belt

Replacing broken or stretched drive belts is one of the most frequent repairs for canister vacs. Inside the motorized carpet-cleaning head, a rubber drive belt connects a small motor to a spinning brush that beats the carpet pile and loosens dirt to be sucked up into the machine.

Jot down your vacuum's brand and model, and buy a replacement belt at either a fully stocked hardware store or a vacuum cleaner service center. Buy several belts so you have spares. Then, take about 30 minutes to repair it yourself.

Unplug the vacuum cleaner and follow the steps shown in Photos 1 and 2. Once the new belt is on, ensure that it's properly installed and centered on both drums by turning the motor shaft by hand. If the belt is properly sized and installed, it'll spin the brush.

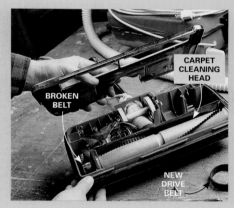

1 **Access** the inside of this model of carpet cleaner head by first unplugging the vacuum, then taking out the screws and lifting off the cover. Other heads may snap on and off. Cut off any tangled carpet threads wound around the brush's roller.

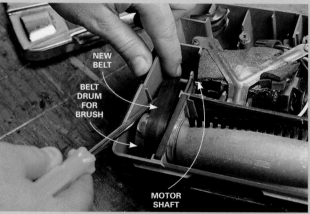

2 Remove the broken drive belt and study how the belt connects the motor shaft with the brush's drum. Some models require you to pull out the brush to attach a new belt (our model didn't). Install a new drive belt by first threading it around the drum. Using a large straight-slot screwdriver, pry the other end of the belt around the motor shaft's roller. Spin the drum by hand to check the tension, then reinstall the cover plate.

Change bagless vacuum

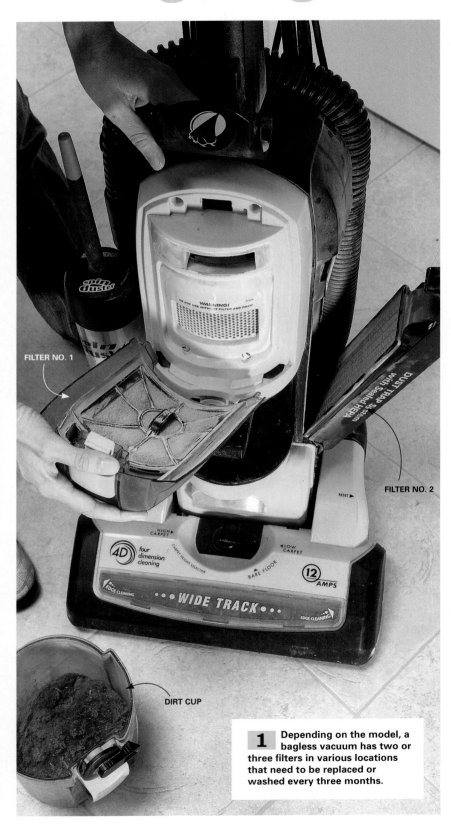

FILTER NO. 1

FILTER NO. 2

DIRT CUP

1 Depending on the model, a bagless vacuum has two or three filters in various locations that need to be replaced or washed every three months.

Our vacuum cleaner expert, Russ Battisto, has a repair shop that's brimming with bagless vacuums, and most of them are there for the same reason: filthy clogged air filters and air passages.

It's critical to replace the filters on bagless vacuums every three months. That's because instead of having a big paper bag filtering out the dust and hair, bagless units rely on relatively small filters, which get clogged fast. Clean air filters are critical for air movement on bagless models; even a modestly dirty filter can cut a vacuum cleaner's suction in half.

The tricky part is knowing exactly where the filters are located (Photo 1). Some bagless vacuums have two or more filters that need to be washed or replaced (depending on the model) every three months to keep the vacuum in tiptop condition. If you have a washable filter, you can use gentle water pressure from the kitchen sprayer or outside spray nozzle on your hose to clean both sides. To prevent mold or mildew, let the filter dry thoroughly before reusing it.

You can find replacement filters for most models at hardware stores, home centers and vacuum repair shops. For hard-to-find filters, go online to your vacuum cleaner's manufacturer's site to get a list of locations.

WASHABLE FILTER

2 Use gentle water pressure from a sprayer or faucet to clean both sides of the filter.

Get a clog out of any vacuum cleaner

1 Use a shop vacuum to suck clogs out of the suction port or hose.

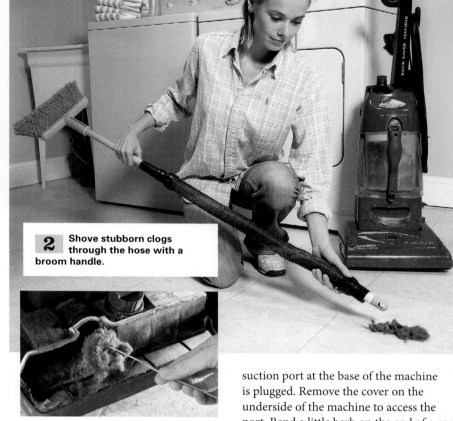

2 Shove stubborn clogs through the hose with a broom handle.

3 Pull clogs out of the suction port with a bent wire coat hanger or stiff electrical wire.

If your vacuum cleaner isn't picking up dirt, and cleaning or replacing the filter or the bag doesn't help, you probably have a clog.

If the attachment hose has no suction, either it or the hose suction port is clogged. Try sucking out the clog with a strong vacuum. If that doesn't work, use the bent hanger technique shown in Photo 3 to remove the clog. Stubborn clogs in hoses can be forced through with a broom handle (Photo 2).

If the machine isn't picking up dirt and the brushes are turning, most likely the suction port at the base of the machine is plugged. Remove the cover on the underside of the machine to access the port. Bend a little barb on the end of a coat hanger or electrical wire and use it to hook the clog to pull it free.

Fix clogged sprinklers

If you have a lot of iron or other minerals in your water, then you know the problem. Iron builds up on the working parts and in the holes of sprinklers. Impact sprinklers like the one here can quit working altogether. A simple soaking in a rust-removing solution followed by a spritz of silicone lubricant will rejuvenate your sprinkler. We used CLR Calcium, Lime and Rust Remover, but other rust-removing solutions will also work. Soak the sprinkler for about 30 minutes (Photo 1). Then remove the sprinkler and clean off any remaining mineral or rust buildup with a brass-bristle brush.

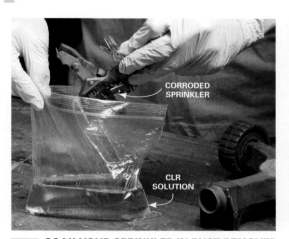

CORRODED SPRINKLER

CLR SOLUTION

1 SOAK YOUR SPRINKLER IN RUST REMOVER Fill a freezer bag half full of CLR or a similar rust remover and drop your sprinkler into the bag. Swish it around occasionally to distribute the solution. Remove the sprinkler after 30 minutes and rinse it in clear water.

2 SPRAY IT WITH SILICONE Spray silicone on the cleaned-up sprinkler to lubricate the parts and to prevent iron and mineral buildup.

Sharpen your lawn mower blade

You wouldn't take care of grass that's too long by tearing off the end of each blade, would you? But that's exactly what a dull lawn mower does, leaving the torn grass vulnerable to sun damage and disease. You could sharpen your mower blade with a file (it takes forever!), a rotary tool or a bench grinder, but we'll show you how to do the job with an angle grinder. It's fast and easy. If you don't own a grinder, you can buy one for less than $100 and use it for all kinds of other tasks too.

GAS CAP

PLASTIC BAG

SPARK PLUG WIRE

TORO
6.5 HP

1 Pull the wire from the spark plug. Remove the gas cap, put a piece of plastic over the opening and replace the cap. This will help prevent gas spills when you flip the mower to access the blade.

To sharpen your lawn mower blade, you'll need a socket or wrench to fit the blade nut. Tough nuts may call for a breaker bar and/or a penetrating lubricant. You'll also need two clamps, a block of wood and, of course, an angle grinder with a metal grinding blade.

Start by disconnecting the spark plug wire (Photo 1). Next, place a piece of plastic (a sandwich bag works well) under the gas cap to prevent gas from leaking out of the vent hole when you tip the mower. Tip the mower so the side with the carburetor faces up.

Clamp a 2x4 block to the side of the mower to keep the blade from turning while you loosen it. Mark the "grass side" of the blade so you don't reinstall it upside down. Use a socket wrench or a breaker bar to turn the nut counterclockwise to loosen it (Photo 2). If it's stubborn, soak it with penetrating oil for a half hour and try again.

Clamp the blade securely in a vise or to the edge of your workbench. Prepare for grinding by putting on your gloves, face shield, hearing protection and a long-sleeve shirt. Before you start grinding, hold the grinder against the blade and tip it up or down until the grinding disc is aligned with the angle on the blade. Try to maintain this angle as you grind. Keep the grinder moving and apply only light pressure so you don't overheat the blade or grind away too much (Photo 3). If you overheat the metal, it'll turn dark blue or black and become brittle. Then it won't hold an edge. Your goal is to remove the nicks and dents and create an edge that's about as sharp as a butter knife. A razor-sharp edge will dull quickly and chip more easily.

Make several passes across the blade with the grinder, checking your progress frequently. You don't want to grind off more than necessary. If your blade has a lot of nicks and gouges, try this. Start by holding the grinder at a right angle to the blade and grinding the edge of the blade flat to remove the nicks. Be careful to use light pressure and move quickly. It's easy to burn the thin edge. After you've removed the nicks, go back to grinding at the correct blade angle.

If your blade has deep nicks or is cracked, bent or worn thin, don't sharpen it; buy a new one. You'll find the best selection at stores that sell and service lawn equipment. Take the old blade with you to get an exact match.

If you don't grind away the same amount of metal from both sides, the blade can become unbalanced. You can buy a special blade-balancing cone or simply hang the blade on a nail (Photo 4). Correct an unbalanced blade by grinding a little metal from the blunt end of the heavy side of the blade until it balances on the nail. Make sure the marked side is toward you when you reinstall it and that you tighten the nut securely.

2 Clamp a block to the lawn mower skirt to stop the blade from spinning while you unscrew the nut. Use the longest wrench you can find to loosen the nut. It's likely to be very tight.

3 Grind the blade carefully with an angle grinder to remove nicks and dents and restore the edge. Make several light passes to avoid overheating the blade.

4 Balance the blade on a nail after you've sharpened both edges. If one side is heavy, it'll drop. Mark the heavy side so you'll know which end to grind. Grind a little off the heavy side and hang the blade on the nail again to recheck it. Repeat this process until the blade hangs level.

Rebuild a power tool battery pack

Fix your balky air compressor

When your power tool battery pack bites the dust, probably your first inclination is to buy a new one. But if the battery is out of production or the price of a new one is sky high, consider rebuilding it yourself instead of paying a professional rebuilder. You'll need new cells, a soldering iron and rosin-core solder, a glue gun, and some wire and tape. The whole process takes about an hour.

Most power tool battery packs use 1.7-in. x .9-in. "Sub C" size batteries. Remove the screws that hold the pack together and yank the top off. Then remove the cluster of batteries and measure one of the cells. Then get the milliamp hour (mAh) rating off the old batteries (or search online for the cell specs). If you're willing to spend more, upgrade to cells with a higher mAh rating—they hold more juice. Just make sure they have a discharge rating of 5C or higher. And always buy cells with the tabs already welded in place (all-battery.com is one online battery seller). Then get to work.

Using the old battery pack as a template, arrange the first row of new cells in the same configuration (Photo 1). Then solder the tabs (Photo 2). Duplicate the process with the additional rows of cells. Transfer the temperature sensor and insulators from the old battery and reinstall in the plastic case. Charge it up, test it out and start your next home improvement project.

1 **ARRANGE AND GLUE**
Lay out the new cells on a flat surface and arrange the polarity and solder tabs in the same direction as the old pack. Then glue them together with a hot-melt glue gun.

2 **SOLDER THE CELLS**
Protect the battery by clamping a heat sink onto the tabs before you apply heat. Then solder the tabs together with rosin-core solder.

If your compressor starts up fine on the first start of the day, but stalls and makes a loud humming sound on subsequent tries, you've got a bum "unloader" valve. The unloader valve is what makes the "psssssst" sound when the motor shuts off after reaching operating pressure. It's actually venting the residual pressure from the compressor head so the motor doesn't have to work as hard on the next startup.

The unloader valve is usually built into the pressure switch assembly. Contact the compressor manufacturer to buy a new assembly. Or, remove the cover from the switch (unplug the compressor first) and locate the pressure switch part number. Then search for that part. Here's how to replace it.

Start by unplugging the compressor. Then open the drain valve at the bottom of the tank to depressurize it. Next, remove the 1/4-in. line going to the unloader valve

UNLOADER VALVE

1 **DISCONNECT THE UNLOADER VALVE**
Slap two open end wrenches on the compression fitting and loosen the nut on the air line. Pull it out of the fitting.

(Photo 1). Then use slip-joint pliers or a small pipe wrench to remove the quick-connect fitting, pressure regulator and gauge from the pressure switch.

Disconnect the wires from the pressure switch (Photo 2). Then remove the old switch. Coat the pipe threads with pipe dope and install the new switch (Photo 3). Finally, apply pipe dope to all the plumbing parts and reassemble.

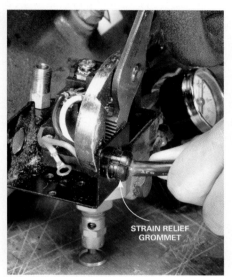

2 **REMOVE THE WIRING**
Disconnect the hot, neutral and ground wires from the old switch. Then squeeze the strain relief grommet with pliers and remove the cord.

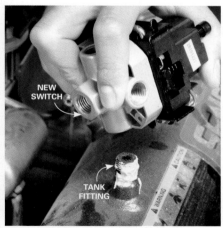

3 **INSTALL THE NEW SWITCH**
Spin on the new switch. Tighten the switch with a wrench and hold the stub pipe from the tank with pliers.

Repair a power tool cord

Got a nicked or cut power tool cord? Here's how to restore it to "almost new" condition. You'll need heat shrinkable tubing in both small and large diameters, a soldering gun and rosin-core solder, a utility knife, heat gun and wire strippers.

Start by removing a 6-in. section of the outer jacket (Photo 1). Save it for later use. Then cut all the wires and the reinforcement cord. Slide a piece of large-diameter heat shrinkable tubing onto the cord and push it out of the way for now.

Slide a small piece of heat shrinkable tubing onto each wire. Stagger the splices and solder (Photo 2). Let the solder cool, then slide the tubing over each splice and shrink it with a heat gun.

Finish the job by reinstalling the outer jacket. Then cover the entire patched area with the large tubing and shrink it (Photo 3).

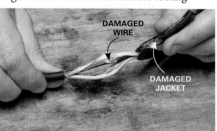

1 **SLIT AND PEEL THE JACKET**
Slice around the outer jacket about 3 in. on both sides of the damage. Then slit the jacket down the center and peel it off.

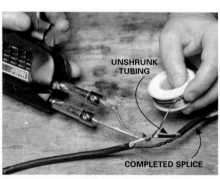

2 **STRIP, TWIST AND SOLDER**
Strip insulation off each wire. Then twist the strands together and solder. Solder each splice.

3 **COVER AND SHRINK**
Slide the shrinkable tubing over the splices and outer jacket. Shrink the tubing with a heat gun.

Make your gas grill look like new

If your gas grill is looking old and gray and the cart is starting to rust, you're probably thinking it's time for a new grill. Sure, it would be cool to own one of those shiny new stainless steel models—if you're willing to spend a fortune! But if the cart, base and cover of your current grill are still sound, you can whip it into like-new shape in less than a day.

You just need special paint, some new accessories and elbow grease. Buy the paint and supplies at home centers. And you can pick up new handles, knobs, emblems and a new thermometer from a local appliance parts store or online (grillparts.com is one source). You'll have to wait at least 24 hours for the paint to cure, but then you can get back to burger-flipping. Here's how to do the job.

Buy supplies

Stop at any home center and buy a bottle of heavy-duty degreaser, nitrile gloves, a respirator, a stiff-bristle scrub brush and a wire brush. Also pick up 80-grit and 120-grit sandpaper, brush-on or spray-on rust converter, primer for rusty metal and a few cans of heat-resistant paint (one choice is Krylon High Heat Max). You'll also need disposable plastic sheeting, a shop vacuum, a palm sander, a bucket and a garden hose.

Clean, sand and prime

Cleaning a greasy gas grill creates quite a mess. And the last thing you want is to move the grease from the grill to your driveway or garage floor. So do the project outdoors and tarp off the entire work area. Start the job by removing the burners, grates and grease cup. Use your shop vacuum to suck up all the loose crud from the bottom of the grill and any dirt and rust from the propane tank shelf. Next,

remove the knobs, emblems and thermometer (if equipped). Mix up a strong solution of degreaser using the dilution ratios listed on the label. Then grab your scrub brush and gloves and wash the entire grill (Photo 1). If you have a power washer,

soak the grill with degreaser and then blast off the grease and loose paint. Rinse it with water and let it dry in the sun.

Next, mask off the wheels, gas valves, warning labels, manufacturer's nameplate and any other parts that won't be painted.

1 **DEGREASE THE ENTIRE GRILL**
Spread degreaser inside the cover and burner area and over the entire exterior. Then scrub the entire grill with a brush. Make sure you remove grease from all the crevices.

2 **SAND AND WIRE BRUSH**
Sand pitted and corroded areas with 80-grit sandpaper. Use a wire brush in the crevices to remove surface rust and chipping paint. Then switch to 120-grit sandpaper and sand the entire grill and cart.

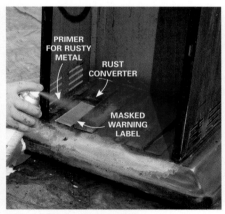

PRIMER FOR RUSTY METAL
RUST CONVERTER
MASKED WARNING LABEL

3 **SPRAY ON PRIMER**
Apply rust converter, then spray primer over the converted rust and bare metal areas. Let it "flash" for the recommended time. Then apply a second coat.

4 **APPLY THE FINISH COAT**
Paint the top of the grill lid first. Then spray down each side all the way to the bottom of the cart. Paint the front of the grill last. Apply a second coat after waiting the recommended time.

NEW EMBLEM
NEW KNOB

5 **INSTALL NEW PARTS**
Attach the new cover lift handle or knobs. Snap on the new emblems. Screw in the new thermometer.

Then grab your respirator and palm sander and sand the exterior (Photo 2). Pretreat the worst rust spots with a rust converter product. Once that dries, prime the rusty areas and bare metal with a primer for rusty metal (Photo 3). Let the primer dry.

Paint the grill and install the new parts

Wipe the entire grill with a tack cloth, then spray-paint it (Photo 4). Finish up by installing the new accessories (Photo 5). Remove the masking tape and let the paint dry for the recommended time. Then install the burners and grates and get grilling.

Winterize your grill

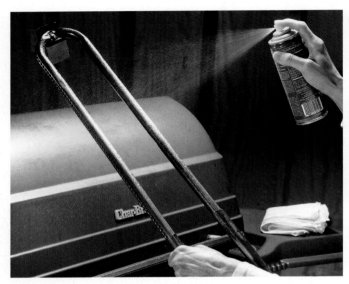

1 Spray the burners and other metal parts with cooking oil. Wrap the burner unit in a plastic bag.

2 Tape a plastic bag over the grill's gas line opening to keep out spiders and insects.

If you live in a cold climate and you're not a winter griller, it's best to pack away your grill before it's covered with a foot of snow. In addition to giving your grill a thorough cleaning to remove grease and food scraps, take these steps to help prevent any unpleasant surprises when you fire up your grill again next spring.

Shut off the gas at the LP tank and unfasten the burner and slip the gas tubes off the gas lines (check your owner's manual for how to do this on your model) and lift out the unit as a whole. Coat the burners and other metal parts with cooking oil to repel moisture that can build up over the winter and to prevent rust. Then wrap the burner unit in a plastic bag to keep spiders and insects from nesting in the gas tubes during the winter (Photo 1). This is a common problem that can make for balky starts, uneven flames or even a one-alarm fire the next time you light your grill.

If you're storing your grill outside during the winter, just keep the propane tank connected (but shut off) and put a protective cover over the entire grill when you're done cleaning it. If you're storing the grill indoors, don't bring the tank inside, even into the garage or a storage shed. A small gas leak can cause a huge explosion if the tank is stored in an enclosed space. Instead, disconnect the tank and store it outside in an upright position away from dryer and furnace vents and children's play areas. Tape a plastic bag over the grill's gas line opening (Photo 2) to prevent insects from nesting.

Great goofs

I've struck oil!

I recently moved to a rural area where power outages are common, so I bought a portable generator. When I woke up one morning to find my entire neighborhood without power, I started it up.

Having once ruined a lawn mower because it didn't have enough oil, I wanted to make sure my generator wouldn't suffer the same fate. The ingenious design engineers put the oil compartment at the very bottom of the machine—without a dipstick. The generator was humming along beautifully, but I couldn't stop thinking about the oil. I just had to check it. Here's what I learned the hard way—never, ever remove the oil cap while the machine is running. It's amazing how fast and how far oil can shoot out of an engine. I was covered from head to toe with dripping oil. I guess the generator was full of oil after all.

—Grace W. Glowacki

The right lube

Everything you need to know about the slippery stuff

Your local home center probably carries at least a dozen kinds of lubricant. Ever wonder why so many? We did. So we interrogated the guys in white lab coats and learned this: A lube formulated for a specific job usually provides far better results and wear protection than a general-purpose product or a product designed for a different job. And a specialty product usually lasts much longer. So by using the right lube, you'll lubricate less often, avoid frustrations, and save time and money.

We'll walk you through all the different specialty lubes and explain where to use each one. But don't worry about memorizing it all: There's a handy chart on p. 282. Refer to it any time you have a question about lubrication.

Dry PTFE lubricant

"Dry" lubricant actually goes on wet. But once the solvent dries, the product leaves a thin film of dry polytetra-fluoroethylene (PTFE)—the same product used to make nonstick frying pans. The main advantage of dry PTFE is that dust doesn't stick to it. That makes it a great lube for dirty environments like your garage or shop. PTFE bonds to metal, wood, rubber and plastic—so it stays put. It's a light-load lubricant, so it's not the best lube for equipment that carries a heavy load or transmits high torque. And it doesn't have any anticorrosive properties (although some manufacturers spike theirs with an antirust additive), so don't use it on outdoor metal.

Dry PTFE lube is available in both aerosols and squeeze bottles. Check the label to make sure the solvent won't harm the material you're lubricating. Note: Not all "dry" lubes are PTFE. Some are silicone, which is a different ball game.

Synthetic grease

Synthetic grease is the best choice for gears, axles and bearings that carry heavy loads, transmit high torque, operate at high temperatures or are subject to shear stress. Synthetic grease has less rolling friction than the petroleum-based grease you'll see next to it on store shelves. It resists thermal break-down and shear, too, so it lasts much longer than other types of grease.

Silicone lubricant

Silicone is the slip-periest of all lubricants, so it's a great choice for items that slide against one another. Silicone repels water, but not water vapor, so you can use it to dry out electrical connectors. But don't rely on it as a sealant in humid conditions. Use silicone to lubricate metal, wood, rubber and plastic. However, dust and dirt stick to silicone, so use it sparingly or use a "dry" version in dirty environments.

The biggest downside to silicone lubricant is that once you apply it to an object, you can never paint or stain it. And, since the spray drifts, it can contaminate nearby walls and floors. If you ever plan to paint anything in the surrounding area, mask off the spray zone before you spray.

Marine grease

Like lithium grease, marine grease is formulated to lubricate high-load items. But it's thicker and far more water resistant than lithium grease, so it does a fantastic job of inhibiting rust and preventing metal parts from "welding" themselves together with rust. Use marine grease to lubricate items that are directly immersed in water or constantly exposed to the elements. Like any grease, it's a tacky magnet for dust and dirt.

USE THE RIGHT LUBRICANT EVERY TIME

Rust penetrating oil

Other products will free up stubborn nuts and bolts—eventually. But they won't do it nearly as fast or as well as oil formulated just for that job. Rust-penetrating oil contains an aggressive solvent to penetrate the rust. And it contains a special low-viscosity, low-surface-tension lubricating oil that flows into micro-cracks in the rust to get lube deep into the threads. But don't use it for purposes other than stuck stuff; it does a poor job of keeping things slippery.

White lithium grease

Grease is the lube of choice for higher-load items like bearings and axles because it cushions parts. And unlike oil, which tends to seep away, grease stays in place and lasts much longer. White lithium is a great all-around grease for lubricating light- to medium-load items like tools and garden equipment. It comes in aerosol cans and in tubes. Aerosols are easier to use because the solvent helps the grease seep into tight spaces. That can save you the trouble of disassembling components to grease them.

Chain lube

Chain lube penetrates deep into roller chain links and doesn't fly off when the chain is in motion. To use it, clean off the old lube with spray solvent and a brush. Apply the chain lube and slowly rotate the chain to allow it to work into the links. Then leave it alone until the solvent evaporates. Chain lube resists water, dust and dirt better than ordinary oil. Use it for chains on bicycles, motorcycles, scooters, garage door openers and outdoor power equipment. But never use aerosol chain lube in place of a bar chain oil on chain saws.

Garage door lube

Garage door hardware operates in an environment that's often dirty and damp, sometimes hot and sometimes cold. That's why there's a special lube for it. Garage door lubes are formu-lated to penetrate deep into hinges, rollers and springs but dry to a fairly tack-free finish to resist dust and dirt buildup. Many brands also contain anticorro-sive additives to protect against rust.

Lubrication tips

Avoid the off-brands

Cheap brands cost less for a reason—they contain less of what matters. These two beakers show how much silicone was left after the solvents and propellants evaporated from a name-brand product and a cheaper "no-name" brand. The cheaper stuff cost 79¢ less—and contained far less lubricant.

Clean out the old lube

Adding fresh lube to old, degraded oil and grease is a prescription for equipment failure. To get the full advantage of fresh lube, always clean out the old lube with spray solvent and a rag (aerosol brake cleaner works well).

SOLVENT   PTFE LUBRICANT

Shake before using

All spray and squeeze bottle lubes contain solvents along with the actual lubricant. If you don't shake the product before application, you'll get a lot of solvent and very little lube.

Prevent seizing

Apply a thin coat of marine grease to a trailer hitch ball mount to prevent it from rusting and "welding" itself to the receiver.

Don't forget plain old motor oil

That leftover can of 30-weight motor oil isn't the very best lube for all jobs, but it's a handy and acceptable friction fighter for most. Heavyweight motor oil is thicker than most spray oils, so it provides a stronger film cushion. And motor oil has built-in anticorrosive additives to resist rust. Since it doesn't have any solvents, a full drop is really a full drop of lube. And it's cheap—a quart should last a lifetime.

Choose dry lube for dusty situations

Dusty and dirty conditions call for a lube that isn't tacky. Dry PTFE is a good choice for this vacuum cleaner. It dries tack-free and bonds well to surfaces, so the spinning parts won't throw off lubricant.

Lithium grease for garden equipment

Lubricate heavy garden equipment wheels with spray lithium grease. It'll stand up to the load better than oil, silicone or PTFE. Take the wheel off and spread grease on by hand or shoot it with aerosol white lithium grease. Spin the wheel to work the lube into the axle before the solvent evaporates.

Grease, not oil, for high loads

Reduce wear on gears and bearings with a heavy-duty synthetic grease. Spread it on all surfaces and rotate the parts by hand to distribute the grease. Never pack the gear case completely full unless directed by the manufacturer.

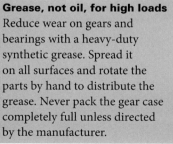

Lubricants

LUBE TYPE	BEST USES	ADVANTAGES	DISADVANTAGE
ALL-PURPOSE LUBE	Frees up lightly rusted tools and dissolves light rust. Lubricates light-duty mechanisms like drawer slides and hinges. Dissolves some adhesives and removes scuff marks from floors. Removes pressure-sensitive adhesive labels.	Safe for wood, metal and plastic. Works fast. Dissolves gummed-up old lube and relubricates. Flows quickly and penetrates deep into tight spaces. Protects against corrosion.	Lubrication and rust protection don't last long—you may have to reapply frequently. Not for use on rubber products. Not for heavy loads or high-torque applications. Attracts and retains dust and dirt. Works very slowly to free up nuts and bolts.
DRY PTFE LUBE	Light-load lubrication for drawer slides, rollers, hinges, hand tools, window tracks/mechanisms, latches and lock cylinders.	Won't gather dust or dirt. Once solvent evaporates, product stays in place (won't drip). Safe for wood, metal, most types of plastic and rubber.	No corrosion protection. Not for heavy loads or high-torque applications.
SPRAY SILICONE	Light-load lubrication for things that slide or roll—drawer slides, hinges, hand tools, window tracks/mechanisms, electrical connectors, weather stripping, etc. Prevents sticking on mower decks and snow blower chutes.	Slipperiest of all lubes. Repels liquid water (not water vapor). Stays wet and continues to spread with every sliding movement.	Remains tacky and holds dust and dirt. No corrosion protection. Once applied, the surface is unpaintable. Overspray makes floors dangerously slippery.
LITHIUM GREASE	Medium- to high-load applications like axles, rollers, bearings, spinning shafts on shop and garden equipment, and hinges that carry a heavy load. Any lubrication job where the lube must stay in place.	Lasts far longer than oil. Stays in place and doesn't drip. Aerosol versions allow grease to seep into tight places so you don't have to disassemble items to apply grease. Protects against corrosion.	Remains tacky and holds dust and dirt. Washes off in heavy rain.
MARINE GREASE	Trailer wheel bearings, shafts, rollers and gears immersed in water and continually exposed to the elements. Prevents rust and seizing of metal parts.	Handles high loads and torque. Stays in place. Most water-resistant of any grease.	Remains tacky and holds dust and dirt.
SYNTHETIC GREASE	High-load, high-torque lubricant for axles, bearings, gears or spinning shafts in power tools and equipment.	Lowest friction of all greases. Most resistant to breakdown under high heat. Stays in place. Dissipates heat well.	Remains tacky and holds dust and dirt. Most expensive of all consumer-type greases.
CHAIN LUBE	Bicycle, motorcycle and scooter drive chains. Garage door opener chain and outdoor power equipment chains.	Penetrates deep into roller links when first applied. Becomes tack-free and sling-free once dry, so it holds far less dust and dirt than other lubes.	Doesn't spread once dry. May harm plastic or rubber (check the label before spraying chains that contain nonmetal parts).
GARAGE DOOR LUBE	Garage door hinges, rollers, cables, reels and springs.	Penetrates, lubricates and protects against corrosion. Less tacky, so less likely to hold dirt.	May harm plastic or rubber parts.
PENETRATING OIL	Frees up rusty tools, tracks, slides, nuts and bolts.	Fastest option to break up rust and free fasteners. Dissolves grease and old, gummy lubricant.	Not a good permanent lubricant. Some formulas may dissolve paint or damage finishes.

Protect against electrical surges

2009FOTOFRIENDS/SHUTTERSTOCK

Here's how to extend the life of your electronics and appliances

Your home's electronic devices experience electrical surges all the time, both from outside and within the home. And every time there's a surge, it causes incremental damage to surge protection components built into your TVs, appliances, computers and every other device plugged into an outlet.

We contacted surge protection expert Karenann Brow, director of product marketing for Tripp Lite, a large manufacturer of surge protection equipment. She gave us some great tips on how to buy and implement whole-house and "point-of-use" surge protection.

No single surge protection device (SPD) can protect everything in your home. That's why Karenann recommends a two-layered approach that knocks down big surges from outside your home and absorbs surges generated inside your home.

Two ways to stop external power surges

Surge protectors that mount on your electrical panel are referred to as whole-house or Type 2 SPDs. They knock down the biggest surges before they can spread through your home's wiring and wipe out your electronics. Type 2 units and are available at home centers and electrical supply houses.

If you're comfortable working inside the electrical panel and have a vacant spot for another 20-amp 240-volt breaker, you can install a Type 2 SPD yourself. Otherwise hire an electrician. Most Type 2 SPDs can be professionally installed in less than an hour. If you don't have enough room for an additional breaker in your panel, the electrician can move a few existing breakers to a subpanel to make room or install a Type 1 SPD (where allowed by the utility) that fits between the meter and the meter box.

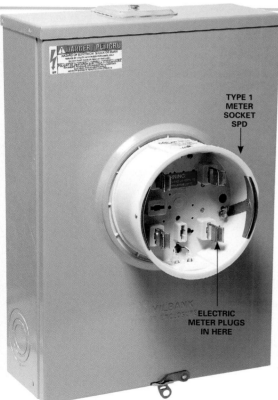

TYPE 1 METER SOCKET SPD

ELECTRIC METER PLUGS IN HERE

1 INSTALL AN SPD AT YOUR METER BOX
Hire an electrician to install a Type 1 meter socket SPD instead of a Type 2 SPD if you don't have enough room in your electrical panel for another 240-volt breaker. Some utilities won't allow meter socket SPDs, so check with your utility before hiring an electrician.

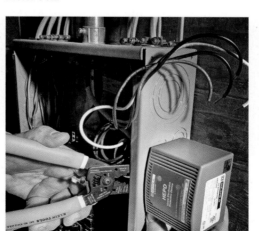

2 STOP SURGES AT THE PANEL
Install a Type 2 SPD at your main electrical panel to stop externally generated surges before they spread to the individual circuits in your house. Adding a Type 2 SPD requires the installation of a 20-amp 240-volt circuit breaker.

Two ways to stop internal power surges

Power strips and surge protection strips look alike but they're completely different animals. Power strips cost less than $10 and just allow you to plug in more devices—they don't provide any protection. Surge protection power strips and receptacles are available in many configurations and surge protection ratings, so it's important to buy based on specs, not price.

Install SPD receptacles behind your refrigerator, washer and dryer, wall-mounted TVs, built-in microwave and gas range—wherever you don't have enough room to accommodate a strip. Buy an SPD receptacle with an audible alarm for applications where you can't visually inspect the outlet's status.

Inexpensive SPD strips have short (3-ft.) cords, low surge ratings and weak warranties. A 3-ft. cord is rarely long enough, and daisy-chaining several surge protection strips or adding an extension cord are violations of the electrical code and reduce the effectiveness of the SPD. That's why Karenann recommends spending more to get an SPD strip with a cord that's long enough to reach between the outlet and your gear. If you have a newer home, chances are you'll need only a 6-ft. or 8-ft. cord. However, if you're buying an SPD for an older home or a dorm room, you'll most likely need a 12-ft. or 25-ft. cord.

Next, consider what you're protecting. For an entertainment center or office, you'll want a strip with eight or ten outlets, noise filtering to remove electromagnetic and radio interference (listed as EMI/RFI in the description) and surge protection for coaxial cable, Ethernet and telephone lines. Then choose a strip with the highest joule rating (the amount of energy the device can absorb before it fails). Karenann recommends at least 1,000 joules.

Generally speaking, the higher the joule rating, the better the surge protection, and three-mode protection (listed as L-N, L-G and N-G in the specs) is better than two-mode. Higher-priced units also include more convenience features like

rotatable outlets and outlets spaced for plugging in multiple AC adapters. Some higher-priced units even include internal USB charging ports to free up outlet space. Next, shop for an SPD that shuts down when it wears out instead of just turning on a red light. It's easy to miss the light and

think you're protected when you're not.

Finally, examine the company's warranty terms. The best ones offer lifetime protection against failure, while the weak ones expire in about a year.

Where do surges come from?

EXTERNAL SURGES
Lightning strikes create huge surges on nearby power lines, and those surges travel into all homes connected to those wires. External surges are also generated as power demands fluctuate and your electric utility operates switching gear to meet those demands.

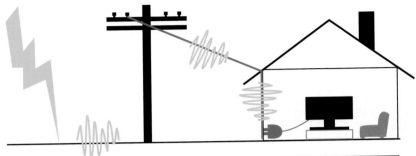

INTERNAL SURGES
All motor-driven appliances—air conditioners and refrigerators, even vacuum cleaners—generate surges and electrical interference when the motor shuts down.

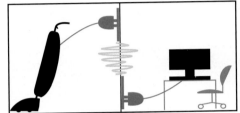

1 STOP SURGES WITH AN SPD STRIP
Connect your entertainment and office gear to an SPD strip with a surge protection rating of at least 1,000 joules. Buy an SPD strip with a long enough cord to reach between the outlet and your gear and with enough outlets to handle all your devices.

2 INSTALL AN SPD RECEPTACLE IN TIGHT SPACES
Replace unprotected receptacles behind your refrigerator, microwave, wall-mounted TV, range, etc. with SPD receptacles equipped with an audible alarm. The alarm alerts you when the surge protection is worn out and requires replacement.

Be Safe!

Tackling home improvement projects and repairs can be endlessly rewarding. But as most of us know, with the rewards come risks. DIYers use chain saws, climb ladders and tear into walls that can contain big and hazardous surprises.

The good news is, armed with the right knowledge, tools and procedures, homeowners can minimize risk. As you go about your home improvement projects and repairs, stay alert for these hazards:

Aluminum wiring

Aluminum wiring, installed in about 7 million homes between 1965 and 1973, requires special techniques and materials to make safe connections. This wiring is dull gray, not the dull orange characteristic of copper. Hire a licensed electrician certified to work with it. For more information go to cpsc.gov and search for "aluminum wiring."

Spontaneous combustion

Rags saturated with oil finishes like Danish oil and linseed oil, and oil-based paints and stains can spontaneously combust if left bunched up. Always dry them outdoors, spread out loosely. When the oil has thoroughly dried, you can safely throw them in the trash.

Vision and hearing protection

Safety glasses or goggles should be worn whenever you're working on DIY projects that involve chemicals, dust and anything that could shatter or chip off and hit your eye. Sounds louder than 80 decibels (dB) are considered potentially dangerous. Sound levels from a lawn mower can be 90 dB, and shop tools and chain saws can be 90 to 100 dB.

Lead paint

If your home was built before 1979, it may contain lead paint, which is a serious health hazard, especially for children six and under. Take precautions when you scrape or remove it. Contact your public health department for detailed safety information or visit epa.gov and search "lead paint."

Buried utilities

A few days before you dig in your yard, have your underground water, gas and electrical lines marked. Just dial 811 or go to call811.com.

Smoke and carbon monoxide (CO) alarms

Three out of every five home fire deaths resulted from fires in homes with no smoke alarms or no working smoke alarms. Test your smoke alarms every month, replace batteries as necessary and replace units that are more than 10 years old.

As you make your home more energy-efficient and airtight, existing ducts and chimneys can't always successfully vent combustion gases, including potentially deadly carbon monoxide (CO). Install a UL-listed CO detector, and test your CO and smoke alarms at the same time.

Five-gallon buckets and window covering cords

Since 1984, more than 75 children have drowned in 5-gallon buckets. Always store them upside down and store ones containing liquid with the covers securely snapped.

According to Parents for Window Blind Safety, hundreds of children have died in the United States in the past few decades after becoming entangled in looped window treatment cords. For more information, visit pfwbs.org or cpsc.gov.

Working up high

If you have to get up on your roof to do a repair or installation, always install roof brackets and wear a roof harness.

Asbestos

Texture sprayed on ceilings before 1978, adhesives and tiles for vinyl and asphalt floors before 1980, and vermiculite insulation (with gray granules) all may contain asbestos. Other building materials, made between 1940 and 1980, could also contain asbestos. If you suspect that materials you're removing or working around contain asbestos, contact your health department or visit epa.gov/asbestos for information.

For additional information about home safety, visit homesafetycouncil.org.
This site offers helpful information about dozens of home safety issues.

Index

Visit **familyhandyman.com** for hundreds of home improvement articles.